MONOLOGUES FOR LATINO/A ACTORS:

*A Resource Guide to Contemporary
Latino/a Playwrights for Actors and Teachers*

VFS Acting

MONOLOGUES FOR LATINO/A ACTORS:

A Resource Guide to Contemporary Latino/a Playwrights for Actors and Teachers

Edited by Micha Espinosa

Author Profiles by Jason Davids Scott

Smith and Kraus Publishers   2014

ISBN   1575258854
ISBN 9781575258850
Library of Congress Control Number: 2014932460

Typesetting and layout by Elizabeth E. Monteleone
Cover by Borderlands Press

A Smith and Kraus book
177 Lyme Road, Hanover, NH 03755
editorial 603.643.6431 To Order 1.800.558.2846
www.smithandkraus.com

Printed in the United States of America

ACKNOWLEDGMENTS

I am grateful to the writers who generously offered their work and enthusiasm to the project. I benefited greatly from their willingness to interact and provide suggestions to improve their individual chapters. I omitted several significant and emerging writers whose work I could not fit into the anthology or for whose work I could not obtain the rights—I'm sorry I could not include everyone. I look forward to new editions. I will also feature a new writer quarterly on the *Latinoactor* website.

Many thanks to the supremely talented José Rivera for his foreward. I first met José in 1992 when I was in the La Jolla Playhouse production of *Marisol*. I have been in love with his work ever since and am humbled and honored that he agreed to write the preface.

One of the best decisions I ever made was to bring on collaborator Jason Davids Scott who has mastered the biography. Capturing the essence of an entire career and its impact on the field in one paragraph is truly an art and I am forever grateful to Dr. Scott's commitment and dedication to the project.

I give my sincere gratitude to Smith and Kraus, who guided this nervous author painlessly through the publishing process. I am grateful to my colleagues in the School of Film, Dance, and Theatre at Arizona State University, who have always supported my vision. I want to give a special thank you to the Arizona State University students who inspired me, offered superb research support and unending encouragement, and quite a few lattes during the progress of this project: Marcelino Quiñonez, Léana Courtney, Adriano Cabral, Ashley Kerin Martinez, Freddie Lara, Alberto Ley, Julio César Sauceda, and Benilda Pachecho-Beretta. I am indebted to my mentor Catherine Fitzmaurice whose friendship, guidance, and teachings have shaped the person and teacher I am today. Thanks to Nan Elsasser of Working Classroom and Jack Reuler of Mixed

Blood Theatre, for their encouragement and support. Lastly, but not least, I want to thank my family—my mother for bragging on me, having meals ready when I come home, and Kai (my son) for staying in after-school care while Mommy finished her writing.

—Micha Espinosa

TABLE OF CONTENTS

ALPHABET OF LOVE: FOREWORD

"I shall seek an alphabet of love," says Lolo in Nilo Cruz's play *Capricho*. A Latino actor living in the United States, of any age, from any country, reading that line will immediately understand its meaning. To be a theatre artist *at all* is to seek love in all its forms: love of expression, love of community, love of self, love of creating, love of the divine in whatever form it takes. So what could be better than an entire *alphabet* of love? What could be more fun and meaningful than to constantly seek such a treasure?

> *I got the smell of peaches on my brain so I won't ever go hungry.*
>
> —Migdalia Cruz

The book you're holding (or scrolling through) will never claim to be anything as monumental as an alphabet of love. That alphabet will only be available to you after a lifetime's worth of journeying through the world and interrogating its mysteries. But this book is a small stop along that path. There's great love in these pages. Obsessive characters with exquisite passion. Characters able to articulate utter darkness and the yearning they feel for community and home—and a loved one to share both. Monologues written by new and veteran Latino writers driven by nothing greater or smaller than their love of the theatrical experience . . . the language, not just of love, but of solitude, of sex, of courage, of creativity and the imagination.

> *"Cuz when you dehydrate you can't form a single tear."*
> —Quiara Alegría Hudes

I am happily able to boast that many of the writers in this collection are friends of mine, new and old, fellow veterans of the culture wars, heroes whom I look up to, sources of pride and inspiration. Whether we were born in the U.S.A. or the many beautiful else-wheres of Latin America, whether we're Boomers or Millennials, many of us share the same life story: emotional immigration, difficult adaptation, falling in love with language, deciding to craft a life in theatre, first plays, first rejections, first openings, first bad reviews, first acceptance by our peers . . . then the slow, painful mastering of an artform as arcane and difficult as building harpsichords.

> " . . . *Carmen Miranda is the answer to one of the great mysteries of sexual identity.*"
> —Guillermo Reyes

To have one country but two souls. To hold secrets deep within ourselves, about our identities and the conflicts between them. To pass through life without a safety net. To ruthlessly love words. To adore community. To rage against injustice. To be an annoying de-tective of human motivation. To attempt to articulate what is often just the smoke of a shadow of a dream of a good idea. To craft little diamonds of insight, some rough and illogical, some so finely tuned to our subconscious yearnings and fears they sparkle and radiate with magic. These are my friends.

> " . . . *for what I seek is an angel's rest* . . . "
> —Caridad Svich

Poetry is often at the heart of many of the speeches represented in this anthology. A poetics of self-discovery, horror, and survival. What metaphors do you reach for when talking about your sense of belonging? How do you craft a language capable of describing the transcendent—or even your mother's rice and beans, or your father's rage, or your sister's eyes? How do you explore characters with an aching need to understand on what side of the hyphen (and there are many hyphens here, personal and political) to stand on? Is that hyphen even strong enough to hold so many contradictory dreams?

> "*I want to go to a place where everyone walked on clouds.*"
> —Rogelio Martinez

In these pages, you'll confront the myths and poetics of character. Many of the dreamers and lovers and seekers and condemned in this

10

book are larger than life. Characters staring into an abyss —whether it's self-made or imposed on them by a world they didn't make and don't control and barely understand. There are many speeches exploring the darkest aspects of human nature. And many others are about pure nasty joy. You'll meet characters who are beaten down by circumstances, by a husband, by a disease, by God's wrath, by their own stupid impulses and fears—and rise up again and again. Sexy wanderers and religious devotees and drag queens who will take you on journeys, who make the astonishing hard work of life look easy one minute and then look harder than the trials of Sisyphus the next.

> *" . . . soaring into the blueness of memory . . . "*
> —Octavio Solis

So much of the writing here is flat-out beautiful, many monologues are themselves poems, obsessive and uncanny. Some are filled with such personal pain and yearning, you'll want to look away but you absolutely can't. Others are filled with humor so dark, it's like no light escapes their core. In these pages you *won't* find writers who necessarily enter your world to describe it to you. Usually the opposite is true. Here, you will enter *their* worlds and come to understand the peculiar physics they've created, the deep and startling psychology of startling people. Their worlds may have clouds in them or they may have ghosts. Their worlds may have time as we understand it, or they may not.

> *" . . . how her heart would move from her chest to meet him there between her legs."*
> —Nilo Cruz

What's exciting to me about this book is knowing that these pieces are only one small part of larger, greater works, and that *those* plays are only one play in the wide-ranging body of work these writers have created over the years. Just glancing at some of the titles created by these authors tells you that Latino writers are exploring new wavelengths in our culture: curving lines of logic and aesthetics that float about the natural and pleasing realism of much of American playwriting. Take a tour with me for a moment, and feast on these titles . . .

> *. . . Lorca in a Green Dress. Jane Austen: Action Figure. Cigarettes and Moby Dick. The Fat Free Chicana and the*

Snow Cap Queen. The Faraway Nearby. How Else am I Supposed to Know I'm Alive? Dark Root of a Scream. From Dating to Death in Five Easy Steps. Generation Sex. The Labyrinth of Desire. The Happiest Song Plays Last. Barefoot Boy with Shoes On. Joy of the Desolate. Earthquake Chica. Mariachi Quixote. Ghost Dance Messiah. Orchids to Octopi: An Evolutionary Love Story. Two Things You Don't Want to Talk about at Dinner. What to do about Your Acute Case of Mexiphobia. In a Land Called I Don't Remember. That Douche Bag's Play. i wonder if its possible to have a love affair that lasts forever? (or things i found on craigslist).

" . . . arizona state police are itching to tattoo serial numbers on the forearms of every brown person they catch in a traffic stop."

—Teatro Luna

These are writers who write about what pisses them off. Writers who can't stop exploring the meaning of exile, political violence, domestic violence, rape, the AIDS crisis, NAFTA and the Dream Act, Monsanto, the Catholic Church, ritual, body image, war, vengeance, poverty, loss, betrayal, *latinidad*, unemployment, racism in all its forms, deportation, family loyalty, Jewish identity, queer politics, farm labor rights. So many questions: what is the cost of living in a free country? How do we honor what writer Carmen Rivera describes as "the magic and sacredness of nature?" Several writers represented here explore the U.S./Mexico border as myth, as geography, as scar tissue of the mind, as warning, and as challenge.

"When I was like, I don't know how old, old enough to feel like I was a full grown man, my father gave me one of those beatings that break off a bit of your soul."

— Tanya Saracho

These are writers with multiple personalities. Writers who are also painters, teachers, artistic directors, actors, mentors, journalists. Many are de facto political activists: artists with an acute sense of social justice, clear-eyed enough to see the contradictions in our hyphened country, strong enough to denounce the many wrongs inflicted on the poor and marginalized, impatient enough to write play after play seeking answers and speaking truth to power. They are witnesses to history and detectives of archetypes and of the heart. Explorers of the many ways that language affects relationships, affects love itself.

> *"When I kiss you, I can't feel my legs."*
> —Fernanda Coppel

There are monologues present for every type of actor, in every phase of their lives and careers. Coming-of-age stories when you first learn (or don't learn) how to articulate joy and pain. Midlife stories of discovery, of turning points fraught with peril and paradise. Stories of death told by characters "with music in their blood." Stories that take the living stage seriously, as a sacred place, a place to store and retrieve (and distort and amplify) our memories, an arena in which we're allowed to redefine and recover ourselves, a circle within which we place the most terrifying spectacles and then ask for the deepest redemption and hope.

> *"Why do they leave someone alone on their first night of dying?"*
> —Luis Alfaro

In closing I just want to make one personal observation. I think the state of Latino theatre in America has improved greatly over the past decades—though the day-to-day struggle of creating work and getting that work on the stages of this great country often seems harder than ever. When I first started writing plays in the 1980s, I was often forced to cast non-Latino actors because there was simply not enough good, trained, motivated talent out there. Today it's very different. It seems that each day I see more and more young, hungry, accomplished, articulate, driven, trained, knowledgeable, and talented young theatre artists with hyphens in their identities. Artists for the future. Artists who are put here to make a real difference. Artists who will take the sweat of our words and turn them into gold.

That would be you.

> —José Rivera
> *Brooklyn, NY*

13

INTRODUCTION

Every actor must have audition material. Auditions provide you the opportunity to join a company, obtain a callback, land your first big role, and/or sign with an agent. Finding appropriate material is one of the most daunting tasks for a young actor.

As a Chicana professor of voice and acting, I have spent countless hours searching for monologues for myself and for my students. I have mentored actors from diverse ethnic, racial, and national backgrounds, but Latino/a actors either naturally gravitate toward me or were sent my way via recommendation because of our shared cultural experience. My research giving voice to non-dominant students who study theatre and my mentorship of Latino/a actors are what made me aware of the unmet need for material that reflects and portrays the history, culture, and aesthetic of the Latino experience.

I have found that the Latino/a actor's search for monologue material opens the door to a much broader and more profound self-reflection/questioning: *What do I have to offer? How am I perceived? How does my body type and voice affect my casting and my future career? Am I Latino/a enough? Am I too Latino/a? Why does everyone think I speak Spanish? What do I want to share with others about who I am?* I came to realize that finding just the right piece for an early career artist became an important milestone for identity development and artistic growth.

I was initially shocked at my own lack of knowledge about plays and playwrights that focus on the Latino/a experience. I scoured my reading lists and found only one or two Latino/a playwrights. Almost everything I had been taught or referred to was from the Eurocentric canon. This book is my response to a pivotal moment that occurred during departmental auditions as I watched a young immigrant Mexican actor performing a monologue that had nothing to do with his lived experience. When I questioned him about his choice, he simply stated, "I don't know any Latino playwrights."

Why would he? The majority of his experience is in watching, reading, learning and performing in the Eurocentric tradition. This student had never seen himself "portrayed." The actor explained that he had looked but could not readily find a guide, nor had he read, studied, or seen a play with a Latino in it.

This led me to a search for resources: there are materials for actors of color and multi-cultural actors but I did not find resources specifically for the Latino/a actor. Because monologues for Latino/a performers are only included in these "multicultural" collections, finding the material is difficult, and also further stigmatizes the student as "other." While researching monologue books, I found one massive collection (over 1000 monologues) where there were only three Hispanic/Latino plays referenced.

The Latino population in the US is expected to triple in the next 40 years. Yet most theatre departments across the country have been ignoring these demographics and only offer environments where Latino students still feel like "outsiders"; these institutions do so because they do not consistently teach or produce work from the rich Latino/a canon.

When Latino/a students enter the dominant world of theatre and film, they immediately experience the pervasive invisibility or stereotyping of Latino life and culture, particularly a genre of stories focused on sadness. Unfortunately, few teachers realize the emotional duress their bi-cultural/bi-national/bilingual students experience when continually expected/asked to perform material from the dominant "mainstream" culture.

I discovered that by providing audition material specifically for these students/actors, they naturally develop their sense of *latinidad*. So, I wrote the book I wanted to read. I want my students to take pride in their *cultura* and advocate for the work to be done. I want them to know that they belong and that they will create the theatre of the future. I want my students to see themselves as culturally, economically, artistically, and politically viable.

I actively sought to find material and writers whose work would reflect/exemplify the complex and varied histories and cultures of Latinos/as in North America. I wanted to provide monologues providing students with opportunities to explore identities that were hybrid, bi/tri-cultural, bi/tri-lingual, political, and socially specific.

The 42 authors featured here generously donated monologues for inclusion in this book, even though a few of them may not self-identify as Latino/a playwrights.

The one thing all of the authors and myself agree on is that there is no such thing as a generic Latino/a. *Latinidad* is complicated. It can be multiracial, multicultural, multilingual, and it is self-declared.

It is a tapestry of cultural identification that includes heritages of Native, African, and Spanish-speaking cultures and nations. It is male and female, queer and straight, and includes multiple phenotypes and voices.

Throughout the book, I use the umbrella of "Latino/a" and not "Hispanic" because for many, the latter carries the weight of Spanish colonialism and imperialism. The use of the label "Latino/a" is a political act that contributes to the identity formation of a growing number of North Americans. It is an ongoing process of local, national, and trans-national food, language, music, literature, dance, film, television, and theatre. Latinos/as are the new mainstream. Our numbers are too large and the amount of theatre available too rich. Our numbers demand our own collections and resource guides.[1]

ABOUT THIS COLLECTION

The structure for this book was inspired by *Speak the Speech* (by Rhona Silverbrush and Sami Plotkin, Faber and Farber Inc., 2002), which illuminates well-known Shakespeare monologues. It is the authors' commentaries that make their resource superior and which made me realize the importance of additional explanatory information to readers. This book, together with Cicely Berry's *The Actor and his Text* (Applause, 2000), and other similar Shakespeare resource guides supported my own efforts to develop a cultural competence with the Bard.

From those student days, I clearly remember how overwhelmed I felt when offered a collection of plays, often asking myself: *Is there anything in these plays for me? Where do I begin? Whose work am I reading?*

Everyone needs a starting point. Although, ideally, we would like our students to study the canon before performance, in reality many students have limited time to prepare monologues and research authors. Consequently, in auditions, few actors "own" the playwright's name, mainly because they know little or nothing about him/her.

Since I believe this knowledge and understanding is the most important part of the process, I arrange the chapters in this resource guide with a focus on playwrights, an underutilized, and undervalued

---

1   For more a more complex discussion on the ingrained ideologies surrounding *latinidad*, I highly recommend the research of scholars Alberto Sandoval–Sánchez, Marta Caminero-Santangelo, and Luz Angelica Kirschner. A complete list of my publications linking ethics and pedagogy and the politics of actor training for Latino/a actors can be found on my website, michaespinosa.com.

approach in published monologue collections. My goal is to inspire actors to read plays and, when they audition, to say the name of the play and the play's author with pride and to actually KNOW whom they are talking about. The biographies and "performing the monologue" sections are not exhaustive but offer a cogent glimpse into each author's work and the work of others. The chapters are meant to tease, to whet the appetite for the author's body of work. I like to think of each chapter as *tapas* introducing students and teachers to a wide variety of authors with enough *sazon* to motivate them to engage with the work and research the author and his/her style more fully.

In the "performing the monologue" section, I use my 20 years of experience as a voice coach to highlight my belief that, above all, live theatre is a verbal and physical art form. I invite the actor to research, experiment, look for rhetorical devices, and consider the logic as they enter the world of the play.

The authors are listed alphabetically. The Spanglish sprinkled liberally throughout the book honors my own hybridity. It is how I speak and how I hear the world, and more often than not how my Latino/a students speak and hear the world. We are the new Americans and in using Spanglish, we shamelessly display our cultural voice.

Because working in native tongue can unlock an actor who is new to English, five of the monologues are offered in Spanish. Providing practice material in both languages is an effective teaching and practice methodology that encourages a fluid relationship to language development. It aids in identity development and expands job opportunities as more companies offer bilingual productions as well as Spanish-only theater, film and television. A few of the monologues in the book are best suited to monolingual and/or bi-lingual actors with accents, while others require actors whose Spanish is free of any hint of a gringo accent (noted in the "performing the monologue" sections).

I suggest that students re-read the "performing the monologues" section after selecting a monologue and reading the play in its entirety. I also highly recommend that actors first look more closely at the playwright whose subject matter or writing style inspires them —taking the time to engage in the playwright's body of work before finding a monologue. This is the approach I take with my students, and it has provided an abundance of material.

There are a number of growing advocacy groups and resources available to the Latino/a theatre community. I would especially like to bring your attention to two that I feel are moving the profession forward:

◊ The Association for Theatre in Higher Education—
Latino Focus Group maintains a list of Latino/a
playwrights and Latino/a theatre companies
(https://sites.google.com/site/latinofocusgroup/).

◊ The HowlAround Theatre Commons/Café Onda
(http://howround.com/latina/o-theatre-commons)
is an on-line platform, think tank, and networking
community that seeks to promote the breadth of
Latino/a Theatre across the United States.

Bringing the Monologues to Life

There are a number of excellent resources on the art of audition-
ing and performing monologues for the stage. These include, but
are not limited to, *Audition* by Michael Shurtleff (Bantam, 1979),
Auditioning: An Actor Friendly Guide by Joanna Merlin (Vintage
Books 2001) and *The Monologue Audition: A Practical Guide for
Actors* by Karen Kohlhaas (Limelight, 2004).

Although mainly associated with auditioning, monologues are
also for use in classroom and solo performance. I offer three practical
thoughts on the art of performing a monologue, no matter what the
purpose of your rehearsal. First, read the play, read the play, read
the play. It is impossible to know one's given circumstances (*Who
are you? To whom are you talking? What do you want? What is
preventing you from getting what you want?),* one's initial reactions
to the material, and one's moment before and after without this first
step. I would also recommend reading the play more than once.
Nothing is more humiliating for actors than being asked a question
about their monologue and having to admit they have not read the
play. Even when using the monologue out of its original context,
understanding the playwright's intention and one's initial reactions
and impulses to the play feeds artistry.

Second, monologues can be viewed as a play with a clear beginning, middle, and end. I suggest that the actor look for this structure
and seek to orchestrate or shape his or her choices to honor this
form. Another way to think about monologue structure is to think
about how the character transforms, makes up his or her mind, or
illuminates some aspect of his/her humanity. I suggest dividing up
the monologue into measurable, digestible units, using punctuation
as a clue to the author's intention. The character might resolve his

19

or her thinking on the final line or may set out in one direction and then abruptly shift and return to the original idea. Every monologue has its own unique structure. The journey of the text is the journey of the character's thinking, which will heighten as actors expand or contract their choices.

Lastly, one of the biggest challenges to acting alone on stage is the ability to penetrate one's imagined environment and create the imagined presence of another person, image, or connection. I recommend the actor practice and play with *focus line* and *focal points*. The focus line, introduced to me by my mentor, Catherine Fitzmaurice, is one of the foundational principles of Fitzmaurice Voicework. It is a technique of using the whole body to translate through the eyes to the image or imagined person/s. Using the focus line gives directionality to the voice and is crucial to the ability to master the art of the monologue. The connection to the image is that which inspires the actor to speak.

The use of *focal points* is a tool to help clarify meaning and provide shape. A monologue might have one or any number of imagined partners, but without clearly imagined images, actors appear to be wandering or confused. By clarifying focal points, the body will have more physical energy and natural breath support. Just as I recommend dividing monologues into digestible thinking units, I also suggest that one find places in the space to focus the eyes. It is best not to make an auditor one of the focal points. It is theatre etiquette not to allow the gaze to linger with an auditor, as this distracts from their experience of watching the performance.

Some monologues demand direct address to the audience, a device often used in Shakespeare's plays, and they can be problematic because young actors tend to scan a space without making a specific connection. These connections can be as simple as center, left, balcony right, but to be successful, I suggest practicing the focal point connections. The emphasis on the first and last focal points cannot be overstated. This process is commonly known as "the moment before" and "the moment after." For an excellent explanation of orchestrating focal points look to Scott Kaiser's *Mastering Shakespeare: An Acting Class in Seven Scenes* (Allworth Press, 2003).

For audition purposes, you may feel compelled to choose gender- and age-specific pieces. However, there are plenty of selections that lend themselves to experimentation. I invite you to be curious about monologues that move beyond preconceived limitations. There are trans and gender-neutral selections and a wide array of ages.

Immersing myself into the writing of these playwrights, listening to the music of their prose, and hearing the rhythm of their heritages has been thrilling. I'm delighted to share their work, and I hope that the advice and tools I offer will help create more confident, creative, and culturally competent actors. First coined by Delores Huerta to the United Farm workers, I offer you the oft-repeated ever-significant guiding principle to inspire, "¡Si, Se Puede!"

—Micha Espinosa
Phoenix, AZ

How To Use This Book

Jason Davids Scott

You will notice that this book is arranged a little differently than most published collections of monologues. We have chosen to present monologues in the context of a short chapter about the playwright(s) who created the work.

There are two reasons for this. First, as Professor Espinosa emphasizes in her introduction, it is important for an actor (and their teachers, directors, and acting coaches) to connect the work on the page to the writer and the writer's career. The more than fifty artists showcased in these pages each represent a theatrical success story, and each has a unique path and personal history. Their written work is only part of that story, and the words they write can often find new resonance and meaning when they are seen as part of each playwright's overall journey.

Second, this allowed us to work carefully with each writer to ensure that the information in this book is factually correct. Every chapter has been developed with the aid of the playwright or playwright's representative. Since almost all of the writers here are still producing new work in theatre, film, television, new media, and performance art, the information in these chapters should not be considered definitive. We encourage readers to follow up with their own research on their favorite playwrights and theatre companies as new work is produced.

Each chapter is arranged in several sections:

About the Playwright: More extensive and traditional "biographies" of many of these playwrights are easily accessible elsewhere. Rather than simply repeating the basic information and "facts" about the writer's life, these brief profiles will inform you of the playwright's cultural background, and often include quotes from the writers about their work or comments from critics and scholars to help put the entirety of their careers so far in context. We also hope that these profiles offer a glimpse of theatre professionals whose work is not only limited to playwriting: there are poets, novelists, screenwriters, directors, devisers, actors, activists, teachers, cultural critics, musicians, songwriters, and visual artists featured here. The totality of what they have accomplished individually and collectively is astonishing and inspiring.

List of Plays: These lists have been approved by the playwrights, but each playwright approaches their "resume" a little bit differently. Some have included shorter plays or works-in-progress; others have restricted titles only to plays that have been professionally produced or published. Where requested, we have included publication information. However, just because publication information is *not* included here does not mean the play is not available. A simple web search of the author's name should provide the reader with the latest in terms of available publications: you also might do a search on the websites of theatrical publishers such as Samuel French or Dramatists Play Service.

The most comprehensive digital resource (as of the publication of this collection) is the Latino Literature database, which is operated by Alexander Street Press. This is a subscription-only resource usually made available to libraries. If your high school or local public library is not a subscriber, check with your local college or university library: even if you are not a student, most institutions will allow you guest access if you visit in person, and any librarian should be able to help you find this treasure trove of Latino art and culture. Most of the more established playwrights in our collection have several plays accessible through Latino Literature. (Librarians and teachers: alexanderstreet.com contains information on how to subscribe to their databases.)

Playwright Information: Again, each playwright has asked us to include slightly different information in this section. Many authors have personal websites or blogs that are listed; others have asked us to include theatre companies they are closely affiliated with. Some have asked us to simply list their faculty or professional web pages or e-mail addresses, while others have designated representatives to handle inquiries regarding publication or production. A reminder that information that is accurate upon this volume's publication may change.

Performing the Monologues: This section is discussed in more detail in Professor Espinosa's introduction. As always, we remind students who plan on using this material for audition, class work, or performance that it is crucial to read the entire play whenever possible to best understand the context of the monologue.

The Monologues: Each monologue features a description of the character and a brief italicized note giving some context for the situation. The text of some monologues has been excerpted, edited, or reformatted with the original writer's permission so that there is a consistency between all of the works selected and presented here. As a result, the monologues might not look exactly like another published version for a number of reasons, but that has been merely in the service of crafting these pieces as effective and useful for a solo actor. Stage directions, pauses, and beats indicated here are from the original text of the play; at times, paragraph breaks or spacing have been reformatted from the original. We have also left the original punctuation, spelling/misspelling, or other non-standard elements as the writers intended. Each monologue as presented here has been reviewed and approved by the writers themselves or a designated representative.

The Playwrights And Monologues

Note: In some cases, the monologues as presented here may have been edited or reformatted so that they are slightly different from other published versions. In many examples, lines from other characters have been eliminated. Each of these edited and reformatted versions are presented here with the permission and approval of the original author or their representative. Those monologues that have been most heavily edited are introduced as "Excerpted from" the plays in question.

CARMEN AGUIRRE

About the Playwright

Born in Chile and currently based in Vancouver, Canada, Carmen Aguirre's intensely passionate and self-reflective work is drawn from her own experiences across the Americas as an activist, artist, performer, and survivor. Her family initially lived in Canada in exile, but in 1979, when Aguirre was eleven, they moved to Peru in order to actively work against the tyrannical Pinochet government in neighboring Chile. "The people that I refer to as uncles and aunts were people coming directly from concentration camps," Aguirre recalls. "Not a lot of people at my school would have that experience, and I already knew I was leading a double life."[2] The tension of holding secrets that both literally and figuratively cross borders is at the root of Aguirre's theatre.

In Aguirre's work, characters are often forced to keep deep, probing questions to themselves, or else risk a future full of emotional isolation and/or physical torture. "When I was young I thought that if you were not screaming and running around pulling your hair out you weren't terrified," says Aguirre. "But so often terror is more about disassociation, about leaving your body and becoming numb."[3] While her plays often rely on the darkest aspects of human experience, they also reflect the joy and honesty of survival and remaining true to one's self, no matter how complex or damaged that self might be. Aguirre's *Something Fierce: Memoirs of a Revolutionary Daughter* will be republished by Random House in 2014.

List of Plays

Anywhere But Here
The Trial of Tina Modotti
Blue Box
Ana (co-written with Michael Scholar, Jr.)
Canadian Tango 09
The Refugee Hotel
The Trigger
End of the Game (adapted from the story by Julio Cortazar)
Spics 'n Span
Doña Flor and Her Two Husbands (co-written with the Electric Company, based on the novel by Jorge Amado)

2   Carmen Aguirre, Interview with George Strombouloplous, George Stromboulopolous *Tonight*, CBC, May 2, 2012.
3   Patrick Barkham, "A childhood on the run," *The Guardian* (UK), 11 November 2011.

RubyCab2000 (co-written with RubyCab ensemble)
The Body Says I am a Fiesta (co-written with James Fagen Tait, based on Walking Words by Eduardo Galeano)
¿QUE PASA with LA RAZA, eh? (co-written with Latino Theatre Group)
Chile Con Carne
Dreams of Reality (co-written with Sonia Norris and James Fagan Tait, based on *The Book of Embraces* by Eduardo Galeano)
1-900-Tell Me That You Love Me (co-written with Marcus Yousself)
Women & Fear (co-written with Mercedes Baines)
In a Land Called I Don't Remember
Of Roots and Racism (co-written with Puente Theatre Collective)
Maqui and the Southern Cross

PLAYWRIGHT INFORMATION

Playwright's agent: Sally Harding, The Cooke Agency
sharding@cookeagency.ca

PERFORMING THE MONOLOGUES

Carmen Aguirre's plays are courageous, raw, and often autobiographical. Her plays demand actors who understand rhythm, can hold presence, and maintain constant focus. They are full of humor and life, and the character of Zap would be a wonderful piece for someone with dance skills —Aguirre wants her characters to skillfully move. Zap's name is illustrative of his emotional life; he is ready to move and sexually frustrated. Aguirre suggests in *¿QUE PASA with LA RAZA, eh?* that her characters are larger than life. It is my suggestion that the actor manifest that direction into bringing a strong physical energy, which will then unlock the humor in the writing.

Trigger recounts Aguirre's personal experience with rape and her family's immigration to Canada. The actor who tackles this piece must understand the psychological depth of how a young girl struggles with adult horror. The actor would be wise to clearly understand the history of Chile and the refugees that fled from Pinochet, so that the deep truth that ultimately forms the foundation of this text is not forgotten. Aguirre writes descriptively; and at times poetically, the actor should bite into the language and find the humor of the piece. Carmen's monologue has a clear build. The actor must keep the energy going to the end. It is my suggestion to find a strong physical button for the end of the selection.

EXCERPTED FROM:

¿QUE PASA WITH LA RAZA, EH?

Carmen Aguirre and Eduardo Villasenor of the
Latino Theatre Group.

Character: Zap (male), early twenties.

*Zap, a biracial Mexican/Canadian, talks to his buddies
about his sense of belonging and not belonging. Zap
is confused about whom he should date and is looking
to a higher power, whether that be religion or a dating
service, to solve his identity crisis. In the second section, Zap pleads to the Virgin Guadalupe to solve his
dating dilemma. The monologue can be separated if
necessary; I suggest performing the entire piece and
making full use of the stage in order to penetrate the
environment.*

Zap: Yeah, right. Clear as fuckin' mud. I'm twenty years old and I
still look at myself in the mirror every morning wondering who
the hell I am. Am I Mexican? Am I just plain Latino? Am I
Mexican-Canadian? Am I Latino-Canadian? Do I wanna—I
don't know who I want to marry 'cause I don't know who I am.
I'm so mixed up I don't know if I wanna be with a white girl or
a Latina girl—yeah every time I'm with a chick all I can do is
compare her to a Latina or a white girl. It's making me crazy.
You guys don't get it 'cause you're only with Latinas. Let me
give you this analogy. It's like white girls are like a bottle of
chilled white wine. Goes down smooth. But they're cold. Latin
girls are like red wine. Goes down hard and rough. But they're
warm. Hot-blooded. Passionate—fuck. Forget about the girls.
I'm so confused in myself—Maybe I should go to some cross-
cultural support group or something—
I mean, like pray—
Hi, Virgin. It's me. Zap. Just came from another date. I had
nowhere else to go. This time it was Becky. You know, your
typical suburban "Brady Bunch"-meets- "Melrose Place" white
girl, you know. Run-of–the mill. Pretty. Cute. She was cute, she
was polite. We met in Poli-Sci class. She was really nice, but all
she wanted the whole night was for me to speak in Spanish, or
at least, you know, do my best Spanish accent in English. Run
her hands through my sparsely balding chest. You know, all she

wanted was to talk about Che Guevara and the revolution.

I don't know about white girls, Virgin. I mean, in a way it's good. You don't have to call them for weeks on end. You call up and they're at it, hey, yeah, let's go. With a Latin girl, you have to call her everyday thrice a day or it's over. You know, it's over. And when it comes to stuff like sex, with white girls all I have to do is clean the sheets afterwards and it's okay. She's happy. A little pillow talk and she's happy. Latin girls? Let's just say sex is basically the signing of the prenups. But white women exude this unintentional coldness. I'm not sure if you can understand what I'm talking about. I mean you have sex and stuff and afterwards it's just like, hi, yeah how's it going. Latin girls? They're like leeches. But they have this intangible, indescribable warmth that you can't feel with white girls.

Forget about the girls, Virgin. What am I? Who am I? This is a nightmare.

EXCERPTED FROM :

THE TRIGGER

Carmen Aguirre

Character: Carmen (female), teens.

At this point in the play, Carmen recalls her first experiences with love, coming of age, romantic ideas about being a revolutionary Chilean, and, ultimately, her schoolgirl crush on "Happy Days" actor Scott Baio.

Carmen: I was raised to be a revolutionary. When I was born there was an unspoken vow: I would have choices and opportunities none of my elders had had. I would be the one that didn't have to marry, and if I did, it would be to man that was my equal, who treated me right, who was not sexist, abusive, cheating pig. And who had no vices. The question of virginity, according to my parents, uncles and aunts, was not a question at all. I could start shagging any time I wanted to. But there had to be love. And I started fantasizing at a very young age about who I would give my virginity to. The one I would give my virginity to would be a revolutionary. Preferably wearing fatigues stolen from the military, and definitely smoking a cigar, balancing a glass of rum in one hand and a Communist Manifesto in the other. My revolutionary comrade in struggle and in bed would always have an M-16 nonchalantly slung across his right shoulder, left fist perpetually raised in the air. He'd have a great body, mischief in his eyes and a perfect, dimpled smile. Black hair, black eyes, bronze skin, smelling like a cappuccino with a little bit of tobacco rolled in. My comrade in the struggle and in love would always be fighting revolutions—no, LEADING, revolutions—all over Latin America and yet he would drop everything at the mere mention of my name and cross mountains, rivers, and roadblocks to meet me in clandestine place, where I would be waiting in a white peasant dress, M-16 slung over my back, wearing lapis lazuli earrings and beads around my ankles. We would both be sixteen and in love. And I would give my virginity to him. Once the revolution was won all over Latin America, and Latin America was one big honking nation like Bolivar envisioned, we'd hold our M-16s high above our heads as we took Santiago and my comrade in the struggle and future husband would meet on the balcony of La Moneda Palace where we would declare Latin America a liberated continent and then we we'd kiss passionately. A diamond ring, stolen from one of the aristocratic mansions as part of the redistribution of wealth incentives, would appear as if by magic in my comrade in the struggle's future father of my children's hand, and we would be engaged and married simultaneously as hundreds of thousands of comrades cheered us on and declared me President of the Revolutionary nations of Latin America and him Minister of Defense. Just so he could keep the M-16 slung sexily around his manly, tanned shoulder. This is the man who I would give my virginity to and no one else would do. Unless he was a hunky, working-class Italian North American in white overalls and no shirt underneath and was Fonzie's cousin, Chachi, of course.

LUIS ALFARO

About the Playwright

"We're in a transformational business. All we do is go from change to change."[4] Luis Alfaro has crafted a career writing about the people of the Chicano barrios that surround his native Los Angeles, where decades of culture and tradition have inspired him to become one of his generation's most acclaimed playwrights. With biting humor, Alfaro's work often delves into the complicated relationship between LGBT/queer activism and Latino identity, particularly his early plays which look at the AIDS crisis from a Latino perspective.

More recently, Alfaro has turned to the classics for inspiration, resetting ancient Greek myths in contemporary Los Angeles. *Electricidad* tells the story of an emotionally drained, modern-day Electra who refuses to leave the side of her dead father; *Oedipus el Rey* imagines the doomed Greek hero as a Latino gang member recently out of prison; and *Bruja* renders a Medea taken from her native country and abandoned as an unwanted immigrant. "We all come from a street corner somewhere, but we join the world," says Alfaro. "I am fully American. I was born and raised in this country, yet your soul is always Mexican. That's the thing, right? You're raised in the language. You're raised in the rituals. It's really about culture. It's not about those borders. It's about how you live. I am fascinated by how hard it is to change that."[5]

List of Plays

Aesop's Fables
Alleluia, the Road
Black Butterfly, Jaguar Girl, Piñata Woman and Other Superhero
    Girls, Like Me
Breakfast, Lunch & Dinner
Bruja
Downtown
Electricidad
Ladybird
Mojada
No Holds Barrio
Oedipus El Rey

---

4   Emily Wilson, "Interview: Bruja Playwright Luis Alfaro on Assimilation, Teen Felons, and Witchery," *SF Weekly*, 8 June 2012.
5   Wilson, "Interview."

St. Jude
Straight as a Line
The Gardens of Aztlan (An *Acto Hecho a Mano*)

PLAYWRIGHT INFORMATION

Faculty Website: http://dramaticarts.usc.edu/faculty-administration/faculty/luis-alfaro.aspx
Any and all inquiries concerning the Author and related plays should be sent to:

Leah Hamos, Abrams Artists Agency
275 Seventh Avenue, 26th Floor
New York, NY 10001
(646) 486-4600
Leah.Hamos@abramsartny.com

PERFORMING THE MONOLOGUES

Alfaro's plays deal with big themes: redemption, religion, ritual, vengeance, societal roles and expectations. Whether writing a comedy that reflects on pop culture or a fresh adaptation of the Greeks using gang culture, Alfaro dives into the human condition with passion. He is a poet and his use of Spanglish (a mixture of English and Spanish) is fresh and unforced and requires vocal specificity and physical articulation. Spanglish is typical of areas of the west and southwest.

Both monologues from *Electricidad* would be best suited for an actor who could authentically speak the Spanish language without a *gringo* accent. Clemencia, inspired by Clytemnestra, the troubled Queen of Argos from Ancient Greek theatre, is a complex character who in this monologue openly reveals her motivations. She is materialistic, a feminist, and she will use every tool in her power to get what she wants. Research into both the Ancient Greek era and gang culture is imperative to understanding the world in *Electricidad*. Clemencia and Electricidad (the present-day Electra) are both obsessed with resolving the past, and they believe in the power of their rituals and curses. The actors playing these roles must have access to clear unfettered emotion.

Breakfast, Lunch, and Dinner is a surreal comedy about body image, sex, sisters, and intimacy. The characters in some way are all starving and seeking to satisfy their hunger. Al's love for his wife is genuine and constant. Even though this is a comedy, the actor should not seek theatricality, but a realistic affecting performance: his monologue is not a well-worn series of jokes, but an in-the-moment series of observations that ultimately lead to a spontaneous and hilarious realization.

EXCERPTED FROM:

ELECTRICIDAD

Luis Alfaro

Character: Clemencia (female), early forties.

A Chicano take on the tragedy of Electra by Sophocles, the play is set in "the City of Los, the East Side, by the river, that house by the end of the street over by the freeway." Clemencia, the matriarch of the family, is trying to get her daughter Electricidad to stop defending her father's corpse and to come inside and join forces to run the family business.

Clemencia: You know how I met your sweet papa. On the boulevard. I was thirteen. He smelled good, like VO5, and I flirted. What's wrong with that, huh? I was an innocent. But he took my girlhood from me. In the back of a car. And he brought me here. My father looked at me and called me a tramp. My mother hid in a back room to save herself a black eye. And he sold me to him. Because he thought I was dirty. This is what they do.

Did I get to *escoger*? No my stubborn daughter, I didn't get to choose. And neither will you. History just keeps repeating itself. *Cholos* don't move forward. They just keep going farther into the past. Oldies, oldies, oldies . . .

And I want to change it. I want to take back every bruise your father gave me and turn it into a dollar. I want the memory of every one of his punches to be a kiss that could make me believe in myself. I am going to make a business. In his name, if you want. I could give you a cut. Then you could have a piece of him that's worth something. The piece that makes *dinero*.

You and I are cut from the same cloth, Electricidad. Imagine us working together. These *hombres* wouldn't know how to deal with the both of us. They wouldn't be able to ignore us, I'll tell you *eso*. Think about it. Then you could honor his *nombre*, if that's what you want to do. We could even make a statue and put it out here where his stinky body sits. Come on. Come back inside the casa.

ıED FROM:

ELECTRICIDAD

Luis Alfaro

Character: Electricidad (female), early twenties.

> *Electricidad is the eldest daughter in the family. In this monologue, she is grieving and protecting the corpse of her father, which she has stolen from the mortuary. She has placed him in the front yard as if he were an altar. She speaks to him and vows that she will keep the chola ways.*

Electricidad: Oh you should have seen it Papa.
>They had you lying there in the mortuary
>On display.
>Like a dummy in a store window.
>I couldn't have it, Papa.
>Laying there all night by yourself.
>Why do they do that?
>Why do they leave someone alone on their first night of dying?
>It isn't right, Papa.
>You are not dead to me.
>You are the rey of this neighborhood.
>Everybody waits for you to give your orders.
>No one stopped me from bringing you here.
>Thought that I had gone crazy.
>They don't know what I'm capable of when it comes to my love and loyalty to you, mi rey.
>You are the old ways, Papa.
>You are the history and the reason we know how to live.
>I want to live the old cholo ways, Papa.
>Simple and to the point.
>You mess with me. I mess with you back.
>You want to party, party in your own backyard.
>You shoot, I shoot back.
>It's simple.
>Why can't we live the old ways?
>She says I act like a man.
>Good.
>I'm not a girl.
>I'm a chola!
>DE LOS EAST SIDE LOCOS!

EXCERPTED FROM:

BREAKFAST, LUNCH AND DINNER
Luis Alfaro

Character: Al (male), twenty-five to forty-five.

*Al confides in his maybe soon-to-be brother-in-law,
Officer Fernandez. Al is slowly losing his high school
sweetheart to a bizarre weight issue which is causing
her to balloon. In this monologue, Al realizes his days
of drinking, watching sports, and hanging with the guys
is over, as he has traded roles with his wife.*

Al: I gotta go.
   I have to pick up the kids.
   Microwave things.
   Go to the market.
   Pay bills.
   Clean the bathroom.
   Do the small talk with the other parents.
   Feed the dog.
   Wash the dishes.
   Clean the oven.
   Wake them up.
   Get them dressed.
   Drive them to friend's houses.
   Do the wash.
   Wait for them while they try on clothes at Target.
   Do the dry.
   Watch Nickelodeon.
   Fold things.
   Get the mail.
   Help them with algebra.
   Talk to my mother.
   Discipline them.
   Clean the yard.
   High School Musical.
   Put gas in the car.
   Take them to their practices.
   Cook something other than pizza.
   Lemon Pledge.
   Make sure they brush their teeth.

Make the bank deposits.
Pay the mortgage.
Go to the mall.
Make their beds.
Unclog the toilet.
Wash the car.
Fix the bicycles.
Make it a Blockbuster Night.
Doctor appointments.
Yell at the neighbors.
Make little cookies with raisin faces.
And look for her—up there.
   (Beat)
Oh my God. I'm a mother!

MANDO ALVARADO

ABOUT THE PLAYWRIGHT

Mando Alvarado describes the kind of theatre that excites him: "Honest, risky, take(s) me on a journey, emotionally challenges me, makes me forget about the day, makes me feel like a kid sitting on the mat ready for story time, other worldly, dangerous, raw, unconventional, nontraditional . . . NON-ALL AMERICAN THEATER in the traditional uninviting sense."[6] A playwright with extensive experience as a professional film and television actor, Alvarado's plays reflect a world of influences that extend far beyond his native South Texas, driven by nuanced characters who speak with distinctive, everyday voices. His credits include imaginative adaptations such as *Sangre* (based on Lorca's *Blood Wedding*), *A King of Infinite Space* (which melds the story of *Hamlet* with the music of Pearl Jam), and *The Yellow Brick Road* (a bilingual adaptation of *The Wizard of Oz*).

Alvarado's plays also evoke specific spaces that also manage to resonate on a universal level. The *New York Times* notes how *Basilica* reflects "the ways a small town both defines and destroys its inhabitants. The play, though set in the present, also exists out of time."[7] *On the 5:31* takes place in one location—a bar—but travels back and forth in time and alternate realities in order to penetrate the sense of loss and grief that define the three characters.

LIST OF PLAYS

Throat
Post No Bills
Basilica
(o)n the 5:31
Splitting Mama
Parachute Men
Sangre (adaptation of Blood Wedding)
A King of Infinite Space (adaptation of *Hamlet* set to the music of Pearl Jam)
Diablo Love (Musical)
A Yellow Brick Road (Musical)
Mambo Love (One-Act)
Rear Exit (One-Act)

---

6   Mando Alvarado, Interview with Adam Szymkowicz, "I Interview Playwrights, Part 274: Mando Alvarado," 29 October 2010. http://aszym.blogspot.com/2010/10/i-interview-playwrights-part274-mando.html

7   Claudia La Rocco, "Its Streets Are Paved with Drama: *Basilica*, by Mando Alvarado, at the Cherry Lane Theater," *New York Times*, 23 May 2013.

Eugene's got to eat (One-Act)
Elemental (Ten Minute)
4 (Ten Minute)

SCREENPLAYS:

Cruzando (Co-writer)
After You
Basilica (Based on the play)

PLAYWRIGHT INFORMATION

For all rights, including amateur and stock perfmances:
Those Guys and That Girl Films
PO BOX 480826
Los Angeles CA 90048.
General inquiries: mandate.alvarado@gmail.com

PERFORMING THE MONOLOGUES

Mando Alvarado is an actor and became a playwright by writing his own pieces. He understands the actor's process and his writing reflects it. In *Basilica* we find Ray, a young man ready for a new life and trapped by his environment. Don't hold back: really "own" the character's reality and make truthful choices. A high level of personalization is applicable to this rich, realistic text using emotional and sense memory. Questions to illustrate the point might include: have you ever wanted to go away to somewhere different? Has an authority figure ever wanted you to do something differently than the way you wanted to do it? Can you remember what being stuck feels like? There is plenty for the actor to relate to when preparing this selection.

In *(o)n the 5:31,* time shifts between present, memory, and somewhere in between. Gina is working in a bar. She is unafraid of love, but alone. In fact, the man she is speaking to is like an everyman in her life, just another in a long series of wrong guys. She is brutally honest and risky. The actor who plays Gina must be able to shift from speaking to self to speaking to other clearly. The monologue will lose its effect if it is not clear that Gina is speaking to one person, calling him by the wrong name because he is interchangeable with previous lovers. My suggestion is that the performer pay special attention to the comic timing as Gina makes mistakes with the name, as there is a rhythm/tempo shift that, if honored, will make this monologue pop.

EXCERPTED FROM

BASILICA

Mando Alvarado

Character: Ray (male), early twenties.

*San Juan, Texas, a town near the border with Mexico,
the present. Ray seeks answers. A good Catholic boy,
he confides in Father Gill, recently returned to town,
with whom he has found a special connection.*

Ray: Well. I just got accepted to Lake Forest College in Chicago.
Do you know it?
I don't think my parents are going to let me go.
They're going to want me to go to Pan Am. *(Beat.)* Man, I really hate it here.
Not the Basilica. San Juan. I hate it here in San Juan. I bet you
were glad when you got out.
It's like we're stuck in this time warp. Everyone's in your
business and they pretend to care but they don't. They're just
looking to find something to bring you down with. Bunch of
crabs in a bucket.
I don't want to be a part of that anymore. People just want
to sit at home and drink and bitch about how their life sucks.
But no one wants to do anything about it. I can't handle that
bullshit—sorry.
I don't know. I don't want to tick them off. You know what the
Bible says, "He who brings trouble on his family will inherit
only wind, and the fool will be servant to the wise. " But I can't
stay here. I'll end up killing myself.
Relax, I was just being metaphorical to prove a point.
They're not going to listen. No one around here wants to listen.
The counselors, the teachers, there's not a single person in this
place that has a clue about anything. And I can't take it anymore.
That's why I came here, that's why I'm talking with you. You
left, got out. There's got to be more than this, right? Right?
Father? Tell me my life isn't over. Tell me that I should go.

(O)N THE *5:31*

Mando Alvarado

Character: Gina (female), twenties.

Gina recalls her memories. The "he" takes on the shape of all her ex-boyfriends. She lets him know that she will no longer put up with his bullshit.

Gina: Don't you think I have bad days? Don't you think that I don't want to wake up? Just lie in bed and not work. Don't you think I wish my arms didn't hurt? Because they're not wrapped around someone that really loves me.

Stop it. I'm not buying what you're selling Frank.

John. I've been down this road to many times, making the same mistakes. I'm not doing it again.

You wanna know the last time I felt really happy with you?

I came across this short story. About a lady who lived in the country or some farm or something. And every morning, her husband would take the train into the city for work. One of those mornings, she was watching the news and she saw that there had been a train wreck. No survivors. The train was the 5:31 . . . her husband's train. A flood of relief came over her. Not sadness, relief! And she started dancing around her living room, dreaming of all the things she would do—now her life would really begin! Then the doorbell rings. She opens it. And standing there is her husband. Sadness washes over her and she begins to sob. He assumed it was for him, for being lucky he didn't get on the 5:31. But it was for herself. For the death of her soul. And I think about that. About her. And then I think about you Juan—

Jim. I think about you. And what you're doing to me. Killing my soul. And I imagine that you were on that train. And that thought. Your body smashed to pieces. Limbs ripped apart. Face mangled, unrecognizable. That brings a small smile to my face. Because I have my soul back. Just for a moment. Do you understand what I'm saying to you?

I need you to get on the 5 fucking 31.

49

ELAINE AVILA

ABOUT THE PLAYWRIGHT

"Elaine Avila makes the astonishing seem easy," writes theatre artist Erik Ehn. "The fluid and novel associations, the radical re-contextualizations, the graceful aplomb of her inventions. Although her plays are immediately pleasing (to read, to rehearse, to watch), there is more going on in terms of rhythm and dissent than may at first appear."[8] A Canadian of Portuguese descent, Avila's plays have been produced all over the Americas and Europe. Her ability to evoke dramatic material from shared spaces and cultures give each of her plays a unique shape and tone. Each character's traditions and identities are both constructed and deconstructed through the examination of the relationship of exterior objects and ideas to internal desires and frustrations.

Witness the way Avila balances 43 different characters in seemingly disconnected scenes in the hilarious and powerful *Jane Austen, Action Figure*; her bitingly incisive insights into women's working relationships in *Quality, the Shoe Play*; or her delicate and deliberate construction of a couple's unraveling as they build their dream house in *At Water's Edge*. "Smart without being a smarty-pants, compassionate without being maudlin, activist for the sake of action over ideology, Avila is a writer to cleave to as a sister, as a force in the family we're all on a mission to cohere."[9]

LIST OF PLAYS

Quality, the Shoe Play
Lieutenant Nun
Good Fooling
At Water's Edge
Burn Gloom
Jane Austen, Action Figure
Strike
Social Media
Made in China
Santisima

PLAYWRIGHT INFORMATION

Website: www.elaineavila.com

---

8   Erik Ehn, introduction to *Jane Austen, Action Figure and Other Plays* by Elaine Avila (New York: NoPassport Press, 2012).

9   Ehn, introduction.

PUBLICATIONS:

> *Jane Austen, Action Figure . . . and Other Plays*, No Passpor-Press, 2012.
> "Change." From *24 Gun Control Plays*, No Passport Press, 2013

PERFORMING THE MONOLOGUES

Avila's selection from *Quality, the Shoe Play* introduces us to Roxanne, an uncompromising woman who will sacrifice—indeed has sacrificed already—to follow her truth. Her boutique provides the wealthiest women more than just shoes, but extreme works of 'art' that cost as much as shoes can cost. She has no time to sit and think—she is in work mode. Thus, this selection provides a fun and active monologue that allows the actor to role-play. First, with her physical relationship to Pippa; and later as she allows herself to transform into the businesswoman. A different vocal quality or tone and a shift in physicality are suggested.

In *At Water's Edge*, we meet Paolo, who is forced to examine his core values and his lack of shared cultural values with his wife when he builds her a dream house with a nightmare budget. As he speaks, a contemplative Paulo discovers the moment when their life began to unravel; this is a realization, not a memory. Paolo is fighting to save his marriage, which has been tested on every level, but he may have just had enough. Avila's smart and heartfelt writing provides the actor with a rich, complex character who had been denying his past but has now chosen to speak his truth and fight for his future. This selection has a clear beginning and end, and it would be best that the actor honor the writing and find those acting moments with clarity. Visual research into the landscapes of the Tofino and the islands around Vancouver, and the architecture of Frank Lloyd Wright and his contemporaries, would help tremendously with the imagery in this selection.

EXCERPTED FROM

QUALITY: THE SHOE PLAY

Elaine Avila

Character: Roxanne (female), thirties.

Roxanne manages the chic, up-scale, and exclusive shoe boutique, Tremendulo, located in the heart of the city. She is a lioness on her plot of land and she is testing her new and gifted protégé/cub on her first day of work.

Roxanne: Your hair. An updo would be better. Mr. Tremendulo likes to think of our boutique as a cross between a hair salon, a lingerie store, and an art gallery.
Mr. Tremendulo hates marriage—you aren't married, are you? Ever been married? This is strictly out of curiosity, you understand, not a job requirement. Of course, that would be illegal. Are you serious about anyone?
Excellent. We are like brides of shoes to him, a kind of nunnery of fashion. Handmaidens. Don't gain a pound. Not one pound. We get an occasional tourist. Smile at them directly. It will intimidate them if they don't have the money to spend on the shoes. If they are too pushy, call our security guard, Ricky. Oh, there he is.
  (She waves hello, she goes weak in the knees, he is a devastatingly sexy 'hunk.')
Hello Ricky.
  (She recovers from the sight of Rick.)
People who aren't here to buy must not waste our time . . . which is spent fostering relationships. Then you can get on the phones and sell twenty at a time.
You have a certain something. You know hidden things. About the shoes? How?
Natural gifts aside. You've got to focus on the client. The women. Everyone thinks it's the shoes. But it's the women that matter. We use intimacy in the service of selling. Let's practice. I am a rich business woman with a case of dissipated ennui. I want a promotion. I'm shopping. Go.
  (Roxanne pretends to be this businesswoman, examining shoes.)

"Hmmm."

Too assertive. Try again.

No. No. Women of certain age hate to be called ma'am. Too spinsterish.

Oh God, no. Think foreign.

Yes. Perfect. Signorina in a pinch. Try again. I'm shopping. I desperately need shoes that intimidate my subordinates and impress my superiors.

(as business woman)

"They see me as a function, not as a master. I need shoes to change all that." Go.

EXCERPTED FROM

AT WATER'S EDGE

Elaine Avila

Character: Paulo Flores (male), thirties.

A well-to-do, ambitious, and traditional Portuguese-American man, Paolo has poured more than just his assets into this dream home and now has second thoughts. The house is now done, but he cannot live in it, and he asks his Japanese-Canadian wife, Alice, to make a different choice and a different future.

Paulo: Alice, what did you think I'd have to do? To afford our life, I have to work. Hard. My grandparents were peasants, fisherman. Just like yours. We gotta work.

    (pause)

Have you ever agreed to something, made decisions . . . It's like water is all over me, above me. I can't break through. I thought I could live out here. It means so much to you. But it's too remote—all this water—what about storms? Getting cut off. What if my parents get sick? What if we change our minds and want kids? Alice. I can't live here. It's too . . . isolated. I wanted to be strong. To give you the house like a magical present. I thought I could take it. You not wanting to have kids, or take care of my parents, but it feels like you're rejecting a part of me. The part of me that moves into the future. IT'S EVERYTHING THAT STANDS BETWEEN US. Alice, we were so close, those late nights in Tofino, sheltered from the wind and the rain, huddled, whispering secrets, interested in every thought, inside each other, it didn't get any closer. Now, we have this fucking glass wall.

My grandmother's tablecloth brought her closer to her sister. That's art. Not this house.

This isn't art. It's a tomb. A monument. We were going to make a new future, remember?

Fuck the past.

I think it all began with my dusty old toy Mr. Wiggles. At the dumpster. We threw him out because he wasn't part of our perfect new life. That's when we started hiding who we are. I wish we could go back six months, a year, replay everything and see if it would come out differently. Alice, it's our last chance. Come with me. Forget about this place. Let's leave. Right now. Come with me now.

FERNANDA COPPEL

ABOUT THE PLAYWRIGHT

Born in Mexico and raised in San Diego, Fernanda Coppel's writing features "sharp and bold humor," but also "a poetic sparseness that is very much her own."[10] Coppel had every intention of becoming a lawyer, until experiencing the theatre community at University of California Santa Cruz changed her major and her career. As a graduate student at New York University, Coppel developed an instinct for creating hilarious characters embroiled in painfully real relationships.

Not many playwrights lay claim to a New York debut with the prestigious Atlantic Theatre Company before the age of 30, let alone a gay Latina who has been supporting herself since the age of 16 and didn't discover her passion for theatre until college. Playwright Marsha Norman, one of Coppel's mentors at NYU, explains that Coppel writes "about young Latin American women facing all the challenges of life in America, made more difficult by gender, sexual identity, and cultural origin."[11] Coppel has also expanded her career to television, writing for the acclaimed drama *The Bridge*, where she is the only Latina on the writing staff. She has not been intimidated by the traditions of conquering a new medium, and her passion for authentic characters has survived the transition. "As a Latina I'm hyper aware of all the Latino/a stereotypes on TV and in film, so I was constantly trying to pitch story lines that went against the popular narrative."[12]

LIST OF PLAYS

La Soñadora
Chimichangas and Zoloft
That Douche Bag's Play (10-minute play)
PUSSY
The Leak
Sinaloa Cowboy

10   Cusi Cram, "Chimichangas and Zoloft with Fernanda Coppel," *The Brooklyn Rail*, 2 April 2012. http://www.brooklynrail.org/2012/04/theater/chimichangas-and-zoloft-with-fernanda-coppel

11   Peggy Townsend, ""Alumna Fernanda Coppel is taking New York theatre world by storm," UC Santa Cruz Newscenter, 25 April 2012. http://news.ucsc.edu/2012/04/review-fernanda-coppel.html

12   Vanessa Erazo, "FX's 'The Bridge' Writer Fernanda Coppel Talks Depicting Mexico Authentically and Watching Demian Bichir Barf," *Remezcla*, 20 September 2013. http://www.remezcla.com/2013/latin/fernanda-coppel-playwright-the bridge-fx/

PLAYWRIGHT INFORMATION

Website: http://fernandacoppel.wix.com/website

PERFORMING THE MONOLOGUES

Snappy dialogue and quick pacing make for fantastic audition pieces. Fenanda Coppel generously offered three selections from her cleverly written play *Chimichangas and Zoloft*. What makes Coppel's characters compelling is that underneath their sarcasm and wit are messy lives and genuine emotion. In a middle-class, Mexican-American neighborhood in Los Angeles, housewife and mother Sonia struggles with depression and responsibility. Neighbor Alejandro is tortured by his own lies, and his self-described "soul excavating" sex with the father of his daughter's best friend—Sonia's husband Ricardo. Finally, world-weary 15 year-old Jackie is already taking on the role of parent to Sonia and Ricardo. Note the heightened, almost lyrical dialogue in the first monologue. That heightened language equates to the heightened moment. Sonia has a decision to make—or has she already made it?

In the second selection, it is important that Ricardo be a presence. Alejandro speaks in response to him, his looks, and his reaction to Alejandro's confession. In the third selection, how does Jackie change? The actor approaching this text might identify with revealing a secret, and/or revealing an aspect of themselves in which they are afraid they might be judged. In other words, what journey has been taken during the length of the monologue?

EXCERPTED FROM

CHIMICHANGAS AND ZOLOFT

Fernanda Coppel

Character: Alejandro Lopez (male), thirty-eight, Mexican, very handsome, a bartender.

Alejandro confronts Ricardo, a family friend, neighbor, and his secret lover.

Alejandro: *(He points to a large bruise/cut on his arm.)*
You see this? You know how I got this?
I tripped on the stairs outside.
You had just kissed me goodbye
and I got out of the car turned around
and fell on my walk up to the door.
Can you believe that? I fell walking UP the steps.
Look, I do feel things, deeper things than usual.
When I kiss you, I can't feel my legs,
I have no grounding,
No balance, except for your eyes.
And, when you're not looking I don't know
what to think of it.
It feels like nothing, like a silly idea.
Like those impulsive voices that tell you to leave your kid
and buy a convertible and drive as fast as you can,
and as far away from your life as you can.
But then the night comes and it's easier to love you
in the dark . . . where no one can SEE us.
We have children.
We have obligations.
We can't LIVE in the fucking dark, Ricardo.
I mean, have you even REALLY thought about it.
Feelings aside, just like sorted out the FACTS.
Do you think that we're magically gonna just move to West Hollywood together
With our two daughters
(that fight like cat and dog as friends)
and be the gay power couple neighbors
with an amazing lawn
cuz the one that acts like the "girl"

has a green thumb.
And bleach our fucking teeth
and wear those stupid rainbow bracelets,
and then adopt some baby from China
and march it up and down the street during
the *PINCHE* gay pride parade de *MIERDA* . . . and, and just
live happily ever after??
Without any fucking consequence?? HUH???

Excerpted From

CHIMICHANGAS AND ZOLOFT

Fernanda Coppel

Character: Jackie Martinez (female), fifteen; Mexican-American, a tomboy, an old soul.

Struggling to keep her family intact, Jackie opens up to her father and explains to him the moment she knew she was gay.

Jackie: Janet Jackson.
    I just know cuz of her.
    I just . . . I love her music . . . and . . . um
    Have you ever seen "Poetic Justice?"
    Ya know that movie where Janet is this emo poet lady
    who falls in love with Tupac, who's a mailman
    That was the first time,
    I . . . just . . . saw her . . . and . . . well . . . I drenched my underwear.
    Not like your average wet feeling,
    it was like a water balloon had popped in my fuckin vag
    and, I HAD to leave the room.
    I was sooooo embarrassed,
    I told Mom I just had to pee really bad and ran into the bathroom.
    But in actuality I was hot . . . I was hot, for Janet.
    I didn't want Mom to worry
    so I quickly changed and ran back in to watch the movie.
    But then that "Again" song came on
    and she was all like "I'll never fall in love with you again",
    and talking about her soul and shit,
    and crying out *(sings)* "Hold ME, HOLD ME".
    I melted like some grilled cheese!
    I just, melted and
    I knew that the tingling in my chest was something that wouldn't
    go away.
    No matter how much I pretended like it was nothing.
    This was who I am, and this is what makes me tingle
    (shrugs) That's the way love goes.

EXCERPTED FROM

CHIMICHANGAS AND ZOLOFT

Fernanda Coppel

Character: Sonia Martinez (female), forty years old, Mexican-American, tired, doesn't know why she is hurting.

In this direct address to the audience which starts the play, Sonia talks about how she has just turned forty. She is not happy about it, and packs a bag as she speaks.

Sonia: *(The sound of a fart.)*
What? *(to audience)* That wasn't me OKAY. *(beat)*
What? You think I'm gassy cuz I ate a chimichanga?
Huh? Maybe it's because, lately,
vodka tastes like tap water
AND my eyes look like a third world country.
OH and smiling, just seems obsolete
My heart feels like a metal weight in my chest
Affecting the gravitational pull of my insides
AND voices of people that died
seem to ring in my ears.
Like an old teacher of mine, who once told me
"Sonia, youth is walking down a hallway
with hundreds of open doors, and as you get older
and time passes doors close and close..."
AND fast forward to this morning,
I woke up BLOATED after my 40th birthday dinner
cuz I went a little loco and had four chimi-fucking-changas.
I looked past my panza to see a pair of breasts
that USED to look ambitious on my chest
AND rolled over to a man
that has these gross grey HAIRS growing out of his ears,
AND fumbled into my closet to find that my daughter
gave me a pair of *PANTUFLAS* for my birthday!
FUCKING *PANTUFLAS*, I'm 40 not 65 damn it.
This can't really be how my life turned out, right?
If met the 20 year old version of myself
NOW I think she would kick me in the *Cho Cho*,
so that I could feel SOMETHING, ANYTHING again.

65

I mean, I'm 40 years old, damn it.
I want to say that with an excited inflection in my voice,
not the pouty tone that mimics my breasts.
　　(She violently zips the overstuffed duffle.)
AND, I FUCKING hate being bloated. None of my pants fit!

JORGE IGNACIO CORTIÑAS

ABOUT THE PLAYWRIGHT

"In this country, discussion of race stresses people out," writes Jorge Ignacio Cortiñas. "And when people are stressed they retreat into reductive thinking. . . . Too often, artists of color are complicit in this one-dimensional thinking. We want to retreat into an identity marker that will protect us from the homogenizing influence of dominant culture. We should be careful what we wish for."[13]

A political activist who studied playwriting with Octavio Solís, María Irene Fornés, and Cherríe Moraga, Cortiñas' plays are not explicitly political, but bear cultural resonance that would be identifiable to viewers on either side of a border. Sometimes the border is one marked by ethnicity and national identity; at other times by sexual orientation; at other times still, simply by the basic markers of gender, class, and age that characters use to define and separate themselves from each other.

Cortiñas is also a dedicated teacher who is mentoring a new generation of playwrights, while continuing to create work that is both sensitive to his audience's preconceived notions about identity politics as well as challenging and provocative, often in hilarious and unexpected ways. His plays are filled with dynamic characters who seem both all-too-familiar in their weaknesses and all the more remarkable in their uniqueness.

LIST OF PLAYS

Bird in the Hand
Blind Mouth Singing
Our Dad is in Atlantis
Look! A Latino
Sleepwalkers
Tight Embrace
The Charm of Preparedness

PLAYWRIGHT INFORMATION

For all rights, including amateur and stock performances:
ICM Partners (aday@icmpartners.com)
730 5th Ave. New York, NY 10019
Attn: Val Day

---

13   Jorge Ignacio Cortiñas, "Are We Dancing to Our Own Beat?", *American Theatre*, May-June 2004.

PERFORMING THE MONOLOGUES

The New York Times admired *Bird in the Hand* as "perceptive and original, no small feat for this ancient and angsty genre."[14] Jorge Cortiñas' Felix is the smart, sassy, witty hero of this memory play, but all of his ironic persona is a veneer for his feelings of dislocation, entrapment, self-exile, and pressure/expectations from his parents. The actor who tackles Felix must remember that Felix is speaking from a vulnerable place even though he has a comic tone. The character's identity crisis and subsequent development draw attention to the struggles that gay and bicultural youth face.

In The *Charm of Preparedness*, Cortiñas explores growing up with a focus on college life. In this selection, Ginger is facing her first major heartache. Cortiñas provides a wonderful comic heroine: neurotic, obsessive compulsive, a little anal retentive, meticulous and extremely analytical, she has a plan for every scenario, and follows her own rulebook.[15]

---

14   Catherine Rampell, "Birds of a Feather: A Boy and Flamingos," *New York Times*, 13 September 2012.

15   For suggestions on how to approach the "Neurotic" character, look to Scott Sedita's *The Eight Characters of Comedy: A Guide to Sitcom Acting and Writing* (Atides Publishing, 2005).

EXCERPTED FROM

BIRD IN THE HAND

Jorge Ignacio Cortiñas

Character: Felix (male), twenty-seven.

Felix is a Cuban-American living in Florida, smart, a prankster; he begins to recount events that transpired when he was eighteen years old.

Felix: I look back at my story the way a tourist studies a cheap map. I'm trying to remember how I got from Point A to the point called The-Man-I-Am-Today. You would think there would be a line I could draw. You would think I'd be able to re-trace my steps. Let me rewind.

Point A was the place I grew up: Florida. Maybe you don't care, but just so you know, people actually have to grow up in Florida.

So back at Point A, my father was this immigrant. Now thing about immigrants is they're prone to clichéd behavior. So it's like my father was compelled by evolution, you know, to set up a "small business." But instead of setting up something normal like a corner store or a shop that sold religious statues, I mean even a medical supply outlet would have been acceptable. But my father went and opened a theme park. For the tourists. Bird Land Family Theme Park. He even did these commercials which everyone in my high school made fun of, where he'd use his thick accent and say, come and see my birds of the tropics.

I was so traumatized by this that I developed a mild case of Stockholm syndrome and so I ended up getting a job there. The tourists would waddle in with their lobster sunburns and their unflattering shorts and I'd tell them the story of how—better yet, let me show you.

The flamingos were the main attraction, i.e. they were over here.

(A flamingo squawks.)

And I'd walk in and I'd go, so welcome to the flamingo exhibit I guess. And yes, that is a bad attitude you hear in my voice because I resent being guilt tripped into having to work here and I resent being your tour guide.

We've started now. That was me back at Point A. That was back when I was a bit of a smartass.

So, first thing: The flamingos you see here today are so not native to Florida. They were brought here, just like everyone else was. Total fact. The dude who first brought these flamingos to Florida was this, you know, real estate developer. This was way back. Before there were shopping malls or tollbooths.

(A flamingo squawks.)

See, this city used to be swamp. The real estate developer dude, came and saw that this land was lonely and overgrown, so he sails to Cuba and buys a flock of flamingos. When he lets them out of their shipping crates, the flamingos start to squawk. I'm talking major honking. Then they take off, circle once in the sky—and fly themselves right back to Cuba.

Real estate developer goes back to Cuba. Buys another flock. But this time he clips their wings. Every six weeks he clipped their wings. When the flamingos laid eggs, he took the chicks away, raised them separately. Told them this was paradise.

That real estate developer is dead now, but the flamingos are still here. The animal rights petition people say we should send the birds back. And it makes you think: if bringing these birds to Miami was a mistake, then so is this job. If building a city on this swampland was a mistake, then so are our lives.

Any questions?

EXCERPTED FROM

THE CHARM OF PREPAREDNESS

Jorge Ignacio Cortiñas

Character: Ginger (female), early twenties.

Ginger is a sorority girl who has begun to suspect that her boyfriend, Tariq, is staging an elaborate "disaster drill" in order to get close to another girl.

Ginger: Why would we be breaking up? Hypothetically. And in this scenario, would the other woman hypothetically love you back? And like, how would any news of this kind make me feel? Should this theoretical scenario ever occur? If you ever said something like that to me Tariq, I swear, I would, I don't even know. Would I have feelings about it? Yeah. It would be like, OK, you know how in between the police station and the liquor store there's that empty lot with the weeds and —? It would make me feel like that. No. It would be like I was a kite and I trusted you to keep hold of the rope, but you got bored and cut the line, like my soul is—oh—that's too corny. You know what it would be like? It would be like I came out as a lesbian – obviously I'm not a lesbian, but in a way I understand them now, because I took a chance and came out, kind of, came out to this relationship, and now people are so not being supportive. No, that sounds weird. It would be like I was old and—It would make me feel like Sylvia Plath. Well maybe that's a little pretentious. What would it feel like? I dunno. WORSE THAN A PARKING TICKET. OK, for sure. You know how I always talked about having four kids so we could turn them into a string quartet? So they could play classical music when we entertained? Well Tariq I guess you've killed the music. There is silence in the dining room of my heart. No, there is. You can hear the forks rattle against the china plates because there is no string quartet and no one is talking. If you ever told me something like that, it would make me feel—(. . .) you know what? —just FUCK YOU Tariq because I would lose sleep. It would affect my G.P.A. What am I suppose to tell my parents when they ask me how you are? This would affect a lot of areas of my life.

Migdalia Cruz

ABOUT THE PLAYWRIGHT

Migdalia Cruz mastered the art of dramatic writing while studying at the International Artist Relations (INTAR) Hispanic Playwright's Lab. Like her mentor at INTAR, María Irene Fornés, much of Cruz' work features fractured narrative structures influenced by both cinematic and avant-garde techniques. Her characters, however, are often very familiar types, drawn from Cruz' observations and experience as a Puerto Rican living in the Bronx. That juxtaposition sometimes proves uncomfortable for artists and audiences approaching Cruz' work, as she explains in an interview:

> *I was doing a play at INTAR and a Puerto Rican woman working in the office said what a wonderful writer she thought I was but . . . she asked, "Why are you always writing about junkies and pregnant teens? Our community has moved beyond that." I said, "Well, there are lawyers and doctors, but I don't know any lawyers or doctors. If that's where I came from I would write about that. These are the people I find interesting and poetic and these are the people I love." I was taken aback by her understanding that what I should be writing about as a Puerto Rican would be so exclusive.[16]*

Cruz' work features characters equally capable of displaying boredom, desperation, and the sublime. Though they might seem as if they are rendered through a constantly shifting and dizzying array of theatrical devices, these figures are, at their core, determined to assert themselves as powerful and deserving of respect. Cruz' advice? *"Respect your history, listen to your ancestors, tell the truth, and write your own story—or someone else will write it and get it all wrong."[17]*

LIST OF PLAYS

Satyricoño (Work In Progress)
Two Roberts: A Pirate Blues Project
El Grito Del Bronx
Fur

---

16 Tiffany Ana Lopez, "Violent Inscriptions: Writing the Body and Making Community in Four Plays by Migdalia Cruz," *Theatre Journal* (52:1), 2000: 51-66.

17 Diana Pando, "Interview with Migalia Cruz, Playwright," *Collaboracion*, July 2009. http://collaboraction.typepad.com/collaboraction/2009/07/interview-with-migdalia-cruz-playwright.html

Another Part of The House
Telling Tales
Song For NY: What Women Do While Men Sit Knitting
X & Y Stories
The Have-Little
Yellow Eyes
Primer Contacto
Miriam's Flowers
Hamlet: Asalto A La Inocencia
Featherless Angels
Mariluz's Thanksgiving
Danger
Salt
¡Che-Che-Che!
Dylan & The Flash
So . . .
Cigarettes and Moby Dick
Dreams of Home
Lolita de Lares
Winnie-in-the-Citie
Frida: The Story of Frida Kahlo
Rushing Waters
Lucy Loves Me
Running For Blood: No. 3
Whistle
Street Sense
Occasional Grace
The Touch of An Angel
Welcome Back to Salamanca
When Galaxy Six & the Bronx Collide
Loose Lips
Coconuts
She Was Something . . .
Sensible Shoes
Not Time's Fool
Latins in La-La Land
Broccoli
Grace Falls
Safe
This Is Just a Test
Dripping Down
Pillar of Salt

Translations

Three Sisters (Work In Progress)
Alaska (with Author Gibran Portela)
Las Meninas (with Author Ernesto Anaya)
Van Gogh in New York (with Author Jorge Celaya)

Playwright Information

Website: www.migdaliacruz.com

Publications:

El Grito del Bronx & Other Plays by Migdalia Cruz. No Passport Press, *Dreaming the Americas Series*, ed. Randy Gener, Jorge Huerta, Otis Ramsey-Zoe, Stephen Squibb, Caridad Svich, 2010.

Many of Migdalia Cruz' plays and monologues have been published and excerpted in other collections; for a complete list, visit her website.

No part of this work may be re-printed, re-produced or performed without the permission of the author or author's agent:

Ms. Peregrine Whittlesey
279 Central Park West
New York, NY 1002
pwwagy@aol.com

Performing the Monologues

Migdalia Cruz' elevated lyricism on psychic despair, the body, memory, desire, and the possibility of redemption is clearly evident in the opening selection from *Cigarettes* and *Moby Dick*. Lush, poetic dialogue, as in, "It's red feeling" is a clear gift to the actor who can embody and verbalize the image. The monologue can be performed without the cigarettes and book, but reading Herman Melville's *Moby Dick* is imperative to understanding the imagery. Melville and Cruz both employ stylized language, symbolism, and metaphor to explore their themes. They both explore obsession. Jump into her language, find the structure in her stream of consciousness, and physicalize Miranda's street-tough human needs. After all, she's "a pirate too." In the second monologue, we find Miranda in her most vulnerable state and wounded by love. An alternative ending can be found at "slip in and be home." The cigarette does not need to be lit in order to be an effective prop.

Cruz' *Lucy Loves Me* introduces us to cross-dressing Milton Ayala. The playscript describes him as a "Cuban man who sells dresses, shy with women in person—stuttering in their presence, but an animal on the phone." Milton seeks someone to share his penchant for violent fantasies and devotion to Lucille Ball. In this beautifully written monologue, the actor is given the rare gift of performing a character's deepest darkest inner dialogue. Don't let the language sweep you away, keep rooted in truth of his world. An alternate ending is suggested at the line "They want to move to a place with trees."

Cruz' work is not realism and the actor tackling her material must enter her world. Explore her monologues without a preconceived notion of stylistic convention. I suggest breaking down the ideas and making them crystal clear. A strong commitment to language, imagination, and physicality is required.

EXCERPTED FROM

CIGARETTES AND MOBY DICK

Migdalia Cruz

Character: Miranda (female), twenties.

Miranda is an assimilated, downtown Puerto Rican. Sexy and self-destructive, she stands alone on a pier in Manhattan. In this opening monologue, Miranda shares how she sees the world and her perspective suitors.

Miranda: People don't look out for the details like I do. I got all the ammunition in myself to fight most anything. I got the smell of peaches on my brain so I won't ever go hungry. I got the feeling of a telephone in my hand so I can call anybody I want to—so I'm never lonely. I got the taste of uncooked meat in my mouth so I know when I'm bleeding.

It's red feeling. Deeper than I thought there was room to go. I feel long now. I can touch the top of anything.

I almost finished reading this book, but it made me sad. Men almost always make me sad, when it's just them alone—without women. They always do crazy things when they're all together like that. Like pirates. I bet they did weird shit on the ocean. In the middle of the great big like that . . . they probably ate too much fish. I bet that did something bad to them. I bet they started to smell like fish and I bet a lot of fights broke out. Who stinks more than who and shit like that. I bet most of the fights were about smells . . . I bet there was one guy who smelled like a woman . . . he was a really busy guy. He drove all the other men nuts for his smell. They rubbed up against him, trying to steal his sweat, cop his smell. They put out long pieces of fabric for him to roll up in, naked. And leave his body stains there for them to raise like a flag. That was no ordinary Jolly Rogers on this pirate ship—this ship floated on the fluids of a man who smelled like woman. It was a slow ship. Languid. It liked to take naps in the afternoon and make love for many hours at a time . . . I'm a pirate too.

Excerpted From

Cigarettes and Moby Dick

Migdalia Cruz

Character: Miranda (female), twenties.

Miranda holds a ring from her lover, Lila.

Miranda: Women know how to hurt you the best. They've got fingernails on the veins to your brain and they're shaped like tongues. Those tongues are sharp, like razors, like sticking knives used to puncture the jugulars of fine young cattle. That's good eating. Prime beef. When you bleed it just right, its flesh stays moist . . . but maybe it's just organs, protrusions, that are different. Maybe men and women are exactly the same . . . "Dainty shapes equal hairy apes." I think I read that on a bathroom wall. The bathroom in Phebe's, where we had our first date. She's my first lover—without a dick. She says her name is Lila, but I saw her passport. It's some weird thing I can't even pronounce. Lookiechoona or something. She has a scar from her neck to her right nipple. Her father wanted to be able to find her in the dark. She's very easy to find. You can always smell her first—even through a Camel Straights cloud I could pick up her scent. She's very tough. She hates children. Especially crying ones. When one starts to cry in the street or in a restaurant, she turns to the mother and says, "Shut that fucking kid up or I'll kill it." She's so sexy when she does that. So powerful. I took her to the movies and with the sound of "Gentlemen Prefer Blondes" in the background, I lay her on the red velvet couch— the one with the camelback and the mahogany arms. There's one spot near the left arm that's completely worn away. "Lila lay here," it tells me. I lay Lila here. I sit on that spot sometimes . . . Sometimes when I'm lonely, and her smell comes up through the springs of the cushion and embraces me. Embraces me. Velvet is like flesh to me. Warm mother's flesh. A mother who loves you. A mother who lets you come home—no matter what. And no matter how long you been away she keeps your nightgown on the bed, so you can just slip in anytime, slip in and be home.

(She takes a deep drag on the cigarette.)

I'd like to faint and wake up with a cigarette inside. I want to give birth to cigarettes. Maybe I could. Maybe there's things people don't think can happen that happen all the time, but we just don't know. I don't think she'd want to be the father of a cigarette, but that's okay. I don't feel anything for her anyway. She's not going near any of my little filters. No smoke in her eyes.

(She takes a drag on her cigarette and begins to cry.)

She goes off without telling me where she's going. Lila doesn't understand danger like I do. Comes home smelling like sweet perfume—like she's been with somebody who spends many hours in the bath. Someone who's not me. Stupid fucking ring.

Excerpted From

Lucy Loves Me

Migdalia Cruz

Character: Milton (male), twenties.

It is Halloween night and Milton is alone. He is taking his nightly bath in his tiny studio in Manhattan. He bathes in blood from a dead rooster and scrubs away his sin. He is singing the Béla Bartók song "Only Tell Me."

Milton: *(Singing)* "Only tell me, dear one, by which road you lead me. Tell me and I'll plough it with a golden plough share. I will hoe it also with my golden plough share. I will plough it, I will sow it. And that road I'll harrow with my golden plough share . . ."
(Speaking)
The bathtub's my favorite place. It's the only place where I feel alive. The warm water tinted green by the bubble bath does things to me. I'm a horse in this tub. A racer. My thick hair mats down over my tight muscles and invades those secret places where I hide things. Big things. Trucks, steamboats. Masculine things. Warplanes, tanks . . . Little red sleds, pictures of my father. There are many folds on my body and in each fold there's a pocket. In the pocket is a timepiece. Ancient, worn—rocks with shadows measuring the passage of every second, every minute. The minutes go to hours—on to days—then to weeks—and weeks add up. The flaked skin loosened by the heat floats to the surface and I eat it. It contains all my memories. It is the tasteless wafer of confession. Some days it doesn't smell so bad, but today it's bad. I can smell my mother bending down to kill a roach with her thumb. She loved the crunch of it. Roaches were her breakfast cereals. She snapped them and cracked them, but couldn't figure how to pop them. My father popped them and wouldn't show her how. They were collectors. Each had more than one of everything. Except children. Just one of those. But he had ten toes and ten fingers and two elbows. Just one nose. They were disappointed with the nose. Although it was a big nose and could hold more than its own weight in mucus and bacteria. And milk. And lo mein. Once, I went to a Chinese

81

restaurant and was seized by a fit of laughter while swallowing
. . . some lo mein. Out of my nose it came, but which way to
go. To pull or to snort. I was wondering how much damage I
was doing to my throat. All this food going down and coming
out and returning to that secret inner cavity where I kept my
collection. I was afraid they would take away my things so I
swallowed them. I didn't know I was losing them from the other
end. I never checked that part. I didn't know I could lose things
I loved so much. When I found out, I waited and held it for the
bath so I could leaf through it, my body a sieve for my treasures.
In the water, all was clean—And I was careful about my soap.
Some soap really dried me out. My skin went raw and red like
I'd been bitten by a bug. Popped and cracked. Sometimes I
squeeze the space between my thumb and forefinger and white
juice spurts out. Sometimes it just oozes. If I look at my hand
palm side up, I could follow the ooze through the distance of
my life. It ran its course and flowed over love and Mars . . . No
wonder people still live in San Francisco. They all know they're
going to die—so why not on a crack. And mud slides are from
people thinking too much and too hard about everything. That's
why I'm safe in the tub. No room to think. It cleans my soul. My
soul is tinted green. If I use a different bubble bath, if it's not
green—the green inside makes the water red and I'm scared of
red water. I cut my finger on a razor and held it in the water and
it ran red until I thought I would die. I won't shower because
I'm afraid the water will hit my face. Afraid I'll like it too much
and it'll pull me down until I can see the color inside of me. So
when I close my eyes, I look in. So when I stop breathing, I'm
happy. But it only lasts for ten seconds because my toes and
fingers cry out for me. They want to keep moving. They want
to move to a place with trees.

(Long pause)

What will I do tonight? Hello. Hello. I'm only doing this for
you. I don't always do this. It's my favorite day. My day of all
days. It's Goosey Night. Mischief night. Guess what I'm wearing. Yes? Yes? Yes, of course. Of course, the white gold. Not
the gold gold. Who would wear that? Who'd be caught dead in
such a get-up? I got back early from the store. To have enough
time. To have the time to get everything. I stay younger with
the blood from a cock in my bath. But it takes time. So much
ritual. Everyone names everything. There is a formula. You
take out the gizzards after it's sliced through the neck. But the

gizzards are at the other end. Why not go in that way? Why not go in through the back door and cut up? Rules. There are rules for everything. Jack the Ripper broke the rules—had consented sex before he killed his women. Better to rape I think. First. Give them a little psychological preparation as it were. A bit of warning. I always wanted to rape a woman, but I never could. I wanted to have that God-like power. Did God love Mary? I wonder. He invaded her. I'm sure of that.

NILO CRUZ

ABOUT THE PLAYWRIGHT

"It's important to document our stories," says Nilo Cruz. "Writing is always personal, but characters don't have to be the exact carbon copy of who you are. Writing about your life indirectly may liberate you as writer."[18] A Pulitzer Prize winner for his play *Anna in the Tropics*, Cuban-born Nilo Cruz was a protégé of María Irene Fornés and found that playwriting helped give voice to his own experience as a Cuban in exile (he moved to Florida with his parents at the age of ten). "I just thought what she was doing was amazing," he says of Fornés. "And also because she's Cuban; here was a Cuban woman who was really writing for the American theater. And I thought, if she can do it, I can certainly try and do the same."[19]

Like Fornés (and another mentor, Paula Vogel), Cruz writes plays that combine lyrical passion and guttural frustration, with characters who yearn for a better life but often find themselves equally confined by both their own internal ambiguity as well as external forces beyond their control. Sensual and breathtakingly vibrant on the surface, these same characters are ultimately portrayed with intelligence and sensitivity that make Cruz' plays simultaneously joyous, riveting, and heartbreaking. As one of the Latino playwrights who has successfully "crossed" into the mainstream of American theatre, his work not only represents the craftsmanship of a master playwright, but is also a testament to how theatrical stories about Latino and Cuban history, culture, and identity can both entertain and provoke audiences from all walks of life.

LIST OF PLAYS

Dancing on Her Knees
Night Train to Bolina
A Park in Our House
Two Sisters and a Piano
A Bicycle Country
Hortensia and the Museum of Dreams
Anna in the Tropics
Lorca in a Green Dress
Capricho
Beauty of the Father

---

18   "Pulitzer Prize Winner Nilo Cruz," *PBS Online NewsHour,* July 2003. http://www.pbs.org/newshour/forum/may03/cruz2.html
19   Jody McAuiffe, "Interview with Nilo Cruz," *South Atlantic Quarterly* 99.2/3 (2000): 461-470.

The Color of Desire
Hurricane

Playwright Information

From *Capricho* by Nilo Cruz. Published in *Two Sisters and a Piano and Other Plays*, Copyright ©2007 by Nilo Cruz. Published by Theatre Communications Group. Used by permission of Theatre Communications Group.

From The *Color of Desire* by Nilo Cruz. Published in *The Color of Desire / Hurricane*, Copyright ©2011 by Nilo Cruz. Published by Theatre Communications Group. Used by permission of Theatre Communications Group.

Performing the Monologues

Capricho is a Spanish word which means "whim" or "folly." Nilo Cruz no doubt drew inspiration from Francisco Goya's 1799 aqua prints, which Goya called *Los Caprichos*. Goya described his series as "the innumerable foibles and follies to be found in any civilized society, and from the common prejudices and deceitful practices which custom, ignorance or self-interest have made usual."[20] This selection offers the actor rich language and endless opportunity for fun. When Lolo discovers the line "an alphabet of love," he should relish in it. The actor focuses his energy into the text and finds the verbal muscularity and delights in word play. This piece also demands that the actor brings the offstage presence alive.

In The Color of Desire, Belén transforms from a young innocent to a carnal lover to a ruined woman. This transformational journey should be embodied into the actor's physicality. Cruz' artfully crafted dialogue is poetic in nature—notice the repetition and the contrasting images. The structure of this monologue allows the actor to plot the emotional state of the character. Pay attention to how the thoughts are broken up. There are short thoughts, then much longer thoughts, and thoughts that build clearly one upon the other.

---

20   Linda Simon, "The Sleep of Reason," *The World & I Online*, 2003. http://www.worldandi.com/newhome/public/2004/february/bkpub1.asp

EXCERPTED FROM

CAPRICHO

Nilo Cruz

Character: Lolo (male), eighteen to thirty.

Lolo is a young soulful actor lost in time. He waits somewhere underneath the stage in Madrid, Spain. The year is 1936 and he is the understudy. He has been waiting to perform. He speaks to the skeleton Manolita, also an understudy, who died waiting to perform. In a moment of delusion and grandeur he thinks that he is the leading actor and that any minute the stage manager is going to knock on his door and call places.

Lolo: They're coming, Manolita. They're coming! Any minute now! Any minute!

Oh lord! Oh lord! The potty! Do you have to go to? The potty! Do you have to go?

I know you're feeling it too, Manolita. The excitement. The nerves. This is why we do theatre! And not going on every night keeps us on our toes! The . . . . The . . . The euphoria . . . The . . . the thrill . . .

Ah, you should've seen me the night I got to go on! The night I got to perform with Maria Banda. That was the beginning. Bah! I know you don't like for me to talk about Maria. But I say, "The beginning," as one says . . . . As one says, "The beginning . . . ." I say, "The Beginning," because there's always a beginning: a clear point of departure when you take your hat and place it on your head to go. And when it's time to go, you go. No one can stop a hat from going, at least not this hat.

(grabs hat and puts it on)

Oh Lord! What's my first line? What's my first line, Manolita? It's something like . . . . If . . . If I . . . If I . . . . What's my first line? Ah yes, "If I should . . . if I should . . . if I should find . . . find . . . Shall . . . shall . . . If I shall ever have . . . have . . . If I shall have the likeness of your love, then I shall seek an alphabet of love . . . "

(savors the lines)

"An Alphabet of love!" Ah yes! Love!

Yes. Love. A new alphabet in my mouth. Yes. In every word I'd find her name. In every syllable her hands. Me in love, as if pushed off by God. No longer myself. Threaded to her . . . to her face . . . only her face . . . Ah love!

I'm sorry, Manolita. I wandered off. That was Turin's line. My first line is,"I, my lady . . . I, my lady, dare not . . . " That's my first line. And I say that line to you now, Manolita. I won't dare talk about love in front of you. I know you don't like it when I talk about my past. And before you start pulling your handkerchief, I promise that I won't talk about Maria Baranda.

Manolita, they're calling the actors! They didn't call us, but they're calling the actors.

EXCERPTED FROM

THE COLOR OF DESIRE

Nilo Cruz

Character: Belén (female), mid-twenties

Belén's aunt hopes that her niece's prince from America will offer her a better life than Castro's Cuba. It is a work morning in the costume shop and Belén confronts her tía. She makes it very clear that the older woman's dream is really a nightmare.

Belén: I don't care what you feel!
I don't care for your sympathy!
She's still set on the American taking me up North . . .
Do you know what I do when I go see him? Do you know what your niece does?
Well, you should! I use another name that is not my own when I enter his house. That's right, your niece . . . I meet him to fulfill an agreement, to play a fantasy, to play another woman who's not me, except there's no stage where he lives. What we do takes place here, in the mind, in our imagination . . . the same as when you drink a magical potion in a play to dream up another reality. Then we enter his room. And he places me on his bed, in the exact place she used to occupy. And he whispers in my ear what her body used to do—how her heart would move from her chest to meet him there between her legs.
No, you hear me out! Then he opens my dress . . .
He opens my dress and caresses my breasts.
Then he enters me and stays there unmoving at first, so I can let him spread inside me, so I get used to him. You get the picture. I lie to him and I lie to myself. I disguise myself and conceal who I am so I can be part of a world that's different than mine. And it's a dark world . . . but also magnificent, because I can dance and forget the smell of gunpowder that still lingers in the air from the death squads. And all these nights you know what I think to myself, Tía Nanda? That maybe one day something new is going to emerge from all this. That maybe one day he's going to see me for who I am . . . But that's never going to happen, because from the beginning it was always too late . . . always too late . . .

I don't want you to hate me. I don't want you to be ashamed of me. I don't want to live in shame.
And I don't want you to pity me either. You mustn't feel sorry for me.

KRISTOFFER DIAZ

ABOUT THE PLAYWRIGHT

When his Pulitzer Prize-nominated play *The Elaborate Entrance of Chad Deity* debuted off-Broadway, the *New York Times* noted that "Mr. Diaz knows that it requires a well-armed cartoonist to take on a world populated by human cartoons."[21] A Brooklyn resident who earned degrees at NYU and Brooklyn College, Diaz is a playwright finely attuned to popular culture and its relationship to personal identity. Whether looking for the intersections between pro wrestling and global politics, or the surprising correlation between the history of hip-hop and one family's grief, Diaz' plays are dazzling excursions into contemporary theatricality, in all of its forms.

Diaz' penchant for spectacle does not overshadow the raw humanity of his characters, who are defined by their desperation for a kind of success they don't quite believe in. Ultimately, redemption is found—or at least sought for— in the basic human desire to connect to a community through a sensual, theatrical experience. "So many of us get into theater because we were nerds who didn't quite fit in anywhere else in high school," says Diaz. "We find our community in the theater, and we blossom into real live adults. So I think it just makes sense to stay a part of that community as you get older."[22]

LIST OF WORKS

The Elaborate Entrance of Chad Deity
Welcome to Arroyo's
The Unfortunates (with Jon Beavers, Ramiz Monsef, Ian Merrigan, and Casey Hart)
The Upstairs Concierge
#therevolution
Swag (or Fucking Vigwan)
Brink (co-creator, Humana Festival 2009)
The Trophy Thieves: A High School Love Story (one-act)
Fly Girls and Other Poems (poetry)

21 Ben Brantley, "Bodyslam to the American Dream," *New York Times*, 21 May 2010.

22 Amy Marsh, "Focus on a Playwright: Kristoffer Diaz," *Breaking Character*, 16 April 2012. http://www.breaking-character.com/post/2012/04/16/Focus-on-a-Playwright-Kris-Diaz.aspx

PLAYWRIGHT INFORMATION

Website and blog: http://kristofferdiaz.wordpress.com

PERFORMING THE MONOLOGUES

Mace's monologue from *The Elaborate Entrance of Chad Deity* is full of charging rhythms and evocative, sometimes lengthy, images. Note the change from urban prose to urban poetry. There is verbal adrenaline throughout, but when Mace speaks of his dream, his language clearly becomes heightened and there is a shift in his emotional journey. Let the clear structure of this selection feed your imagination. The actor working on this part has to think of many things: his status, the status he wants, the need to get the facts across, that he is living this life (his physical pain is immediate), and the dream that he holds dear and has been shattered.

The charm in *Welcome to Arroyo's* is that Lelly is crazy about this guy, but has a difficult time telling him. She uses her intellect and metaphysical thinking to protect her from just saying that she really that digs him. There is real humor and delight in this piece that comes from finding the balance between revealing her true feelings and honoring the swift movements in the language. This is a heightened moment in Lelly's life, and the language is equally heightened to match the moment. This requires accurate memorization and clarity in thought. I recommend emphasizing the moment at the end, as she becomes cognizant that she has revealed a bit too much.

Excerpted From

The Fabulous Entrance of Chad Deity

Kristoffer Diaz

Character: Mace (male), late twenties.

Macedonio "Mace" Guerra is an undersized Puerto Rican wrestler who works for THE Wrestling. EKO (the owner of THE) has just made it very clear that that Mace has nothing to complain about. Mace is left alone with the audience to ponder his status. He has achieved his Saturday morning American dream and is proud of it. He is smart enough to know his role as the fall guy in this national ritual.

Mace: I am one of THE Wrestlers. I'm one of the really fucking good THE Wrestlers, and that means, unlike other jobs where when you get really good, you become a boss or a star or you get paid more, in wrestling being really fucking good—like really fucking better than like how good you think I'm gonna be from me telling you that I'm really fucking good—when you get really good at the wrestling part of the wrestling business, you're not rewarded. You're unrewarded. De-rewarded. De-warded?
Point is, being really skilled in the ring is a disadvantage, because being skilled in the ring means you make the other guy in the ring with you look better than he is, so you get in the ring with some guy who sucks, and he looks like he's kicking your ass, and the audience wants to see guys who can kick guys' assess, so that guy gets the applause, and then that guy gets the credit, and then the bosses love the job you did making that guy look like he didn't suck, because the more guys who don't suck the better for THE Wrestling because guys who don't suck sell t-shirts, but the problem with that is that while you're getting your ass kicked by guys who only look like they don't suck because you're making them look like they don't suck, the audience starts to think—guess what? You're the one who sucks. So— and let's drop the metaphor because I'm not really talking about you, but thank you for playing along—so then I go to the bottom in the minds of the boss because I'm losing so much, and as bad as I want to walk into his corporate nightmare office and remind him that wrestling is not a legitimate sporting event and I am

losing because he is writing scripts that tell me to lose, as bad as I want to tell my boss that, I don't tell him nothing.
Because it's actually a good job.
A dream job.
An Underoos-and-bootleg-Frosted-Flakes-on-the-floor day-dream job.
And I'm happy to lose.
And I'm happy for the audience to tell me that I suck.
Because when I wake up in the morning, I don't even need an alarm clock.
And I don't mind that my knees hurt.
My hands hurt.
My everything's hurt.
I don't mind.
Because I'm one of THE Wrestlers.
And I'm in love with who I am.
Now I don't have no illusions about who I am though.
I am one of THE Wrestlers.
I am A THE Wrestler.
I am not THE THE Wrestler.

EXCERPTED FROM

WELCOME TO ARROYO'S

Kristoffer Diaz

Character: Lelly (female), twenty-four.

Lelly is a suburban Puerto Rican college student who lives, sleeps, and breathes Manhattan's Lower East Side. Her research is focused on the finding the originators of the hip-hop movement. While tracking down the infamous and elusive Latina DJ Reina Rey, she meets Alejandro and it is evident that her research has become more than scholarly.

Lelly: No, but what do you think about sushi?

I think about sushi, I think about Japan. It's an archipelago—I mean, it's a bunch of islands, so they fish. Fine, that makes sense. Then I think about the fact that they don't cook it. Then I think about crab roe. And seaweed. And wasabi and ginger. And yes, I know, I'm just exoticizing the other, I've read Edward Said, I'm familiar with orientalism. But wasabi and ginger? Where did that genius come from? I think about how what they eat affects their body types, and their body types affect the amount of energy they have, and their energy affects the way they live, and the way they live affects what they produce, and that affects what we produce, and that affects what I eat, whether I turn around and eat sushi or not.

And you're probably wondering what this has to do with you, and it really doesn't have anything to do with you, except that . . . well, lately I've been thinking about you the same way I think about sushi.

(Silence.)

I mean, you're a bartender.

Bartenders do important work. You help teachers burn off the stress of mandatory testing and escalating violence with a beer and some good company. Big business gets done over rounds of shots. Babies get made in your bar—I mean, not made, but planned—I mean, not planned, but the process gets started and you start it.

Those drinks—and by extension, this bar—and by extension, you—make up a central concentric circle of this neighborhood, which happens to be one of the central concentric circles of New York City, which, as everyone knows, is the center of the universe, which makes you one of the central concentric circles of the center of the universe in a way, and oh my god why am I saying concentric so much like an arrogant neophyte college student and oh my god, neophyte?—I'm doing it again. I'll shut up now.

EVELINA FERNÁNDEZ

About the Playwright

A native of East Los Angeles, Evelina Fernández has been writing since grade school and made her professional debut as an actress starring in the first production of Luis Valdez' *Zoot Suit*. Choosing to remain in California to raise her family (she is married to director José Luis Valenzuela), Fernández worked with the pioneering Latino/a theatre companies of the 1980s such as El Teatro de Esperanza in Santa Barbara, and later the Latino Theatre lab at the Los Angeles Theatre Center, before writing her first play (*How Else Am I Supposed to Know I am Still Alive?*).

Her professional experience as an actress and her lifelong friendships with Latina performers guides Fernández' writing, which showcases a wide variety of Latina lifestyles and personality types. "All my life I have been inspired by passionate women," she says in an interview.

> The women that I know as Latinas have always been strong and passionate and smart. But the roles that I auditioned for as a Latina actress was the maid, the undocumented worker. It was frustrating for me because that is not who we are. It is a small part of who we are but there is so much more! We were always seen as victims and that is not who we are as Latinas. We run our communities! The reality is that *la mujer latina* is at the forefront of whatever happens in our community. We are not followers, we are not victims, we are leaders.[23]

Fernández' impact on Latinos in the industry is significant, particularly with *Luminarias*, originally written as a screenplay, adapted for the stage, and then revised once again for a film production in 2000. In an era when Hollywood still routinely cast non-Latino actors as major Latino characters, *Luminarias* was one of the first films to mark a shift towards employing Latinos and Latinas both in front of and behind the camera, and is considered groundbreaking by both film professionals and audiences.

List of Plays

A Mexican Trilogy: Faith: Part I; Hope: Part II; Charity: Part III
(Published by Samuel French)

---

23 "Evelina Fernandez – In Her Own Words," Latinopia.com, 15 June 2010. http://latinopia.com/latino-theater/evelina-fernandez-in-her-own-words/

Solitude
Dementia (Published by Samuel French)
Liz Estrada in the City of Angels (An adaptation of Aristophanes'
    Lysistrata)
La Virgen de Guadalupe, Dios Inanztin
Luminarias
Premeditation
How Else Am I Supposed to Know I'm Still Alive?

PLAYWRIGHT INFORMATION

Playwright's Agent: Maggie Roiphe Agency,
Los Angeles, CA

PERFORMING THE MONOLOGUES

How Else Am I Supposed to Know I'm Still Alive? is a comedy
of loss and friendship written for Fernández' friends, iconic Chicana
actresses Lupe Ontiveros and Angela Moya. Both actresses were
considered extremely gifted, but were rarely given the opportunity
to play leading roles. The selection below is the climax of the play
for Nellie, a widow who's not afraid to strut her stuff, flirt, bend the
truth if needed, and who speaks directly to God. As was *Luminarias*,
an equally important play about middle class Chicanas. This was one
of the first works that expanded and explored the complex issues of
latinidad, feminism, and chauvinism. The selection below introduces
us to Jesus, speaking to his nephew Joey. Joey's mother Andrea, a
divorce lawyer herself going through a divorce, has just introduced
her family to her new boyfriend, a Jewish lawyer who is opposing
her in a case. Jesus—not your típico Latino male—paves the way to
understanding the complexity of relationships for his nephew. His
action may be to comfort his nephew, but his obstacle comes from
speaking the truth about *machismo*. Allow the cultural challenge of
facing this subject with a teenager to be palpable.

A short but poignant exchange is offered for the last selection.
Take your time when performing this selection. The beauty of this
one minute monologue is that it need not be rushed, and the gift is
really in seeing Joey's reactions to his mother's words.

HOW ELSE AM I SUPPOSED TO KNOW I'M STILL ALIVE?

Evelina Fernandez

Character: Nellie (female), forties.

Nellie remembers her husband and mourns her loss.

Nellie: *(smiling through her tears)* But, we sure had fun trying. And boy did we try. We'd make love in the morning, when he'd come home for lunch and at night before we went to sleep. Boy, I loved that man. And he loved me. If he didn't he would've left me as soon as he found out I couldn't give him any babies. He wanted children so bad. We both did. We wanted them right away, too. One right after the other. We wanted a house full of kids running in and out, yelling and screaming and fighting and laughing and crying. I pictured myself with one hanging onto my apron, one at my *chichi* and one on the way. So, as soon as we got married we got to work at making them. When it didn't happen at first we didn't really worry cuz we were having so much fun trying. Then, a year went by. Then, another. Then, we just stopped talking about it. After five years I remember I brought it up. I said "*Viejo*, maybe I can't have babies." Louie laughed and said "You never know honey, maybe I'm the one who's shooting blanks." It wasn't his *huevitos*, it was mine. They just weren't going where Louie's could get to them.

Back then there wasn't any of this artificial test tube *chingadera*. There just wasn't anything to do about it. The day we found out we drove home from the doctor's and didn't say a word. Louie just held my hand and looked straight ahead. it was like we lost all the babies we never had. *El travieso del* Little Louie *y la preciosa de la* Little Nellie and all the rest of them we'd dreamed of. I never cried about it. But, Louie did. That night he cried like a baby. I held him in my arms like the mother I would never be. I rocked him and I sang to him until we both fell asleep. Then, we never talked about it for a long time. Like we were in mourning. 'Till one day, Louie came home from work in a real good mood. He sat down at the table and said "Come here, baby." I walked over to him. He hugged my waist, put his head on my *panza* and kissed it. "You know, Nellie," he said,

"God didn't give us babies cuz we love each other too Nellie but you . . . and how could you love anybody but me? But, hey, that's okay with me. As long as I got you, Nellie, I'm a happy man. You're all I want. You're all I need."

Yeah. But, now he's dead and here I am . . . If we at least would've had one or maybe adopted one . . . It's funny, huh? I've wanted a baby all these years and you have one inside of you and you don't want it.

(To God)

You sure can be shitty sometimes.

EXCERPTED FROM

LUMINARIAS

Evelina Fernandez

Character: Jesus (male), twenties.

*Jesus offers up advice to his nephew, Joey, about Joey's
mother's new white, Jewish boyfriend.*

Jesus: What's wrong, *mijo*? Don't like your Mom's friend?
  (Joey shrugs.)
Hey, I understand how you feel.
No, I've never been through it. But, I watch you, my man. I'm
your *Nino*, remember?
You don't wanna share your Mom? Hey, I can understand that.
Look, your Mom loved your Dad. Man, she loved him more
than you'll ever know. Your Mom's a beautiful woman. But,
she wasn't enough for your Dad. And let me tell you something.
We men . . .
  (He looks around to make sure nobody's listening.)
Sometimes we can be real *pendejos* you know that? Don't get
me wrong. I like your Dad. He's my homey from way back.
My *compadre*. But, if he loses your Mom, he'll lose a good
thing. Your Mom's still young, full of life and full of love and
as hard as it is, *mijo*. You have to know that we all need to be
loved. Your Mom needs to be loved. It's what *Dios* put us on
this earth for. *Entiendes*?
Mijo, there're some things that just can't be explained. But, believe me, in a couple of years you're gonna understand. You're
gonna see a fine-looking young lady and sas! It's gonna hit you.
You're gonna know the difference between loving a woman and
loving your Mom. Mark my words.
  (Joey nods.)
And as far as your Mom's friend is concerned. Well, I'm not
telling you to love the guy. Just give him a chance. Don't make
up your mind about him in such a hurry.
Now, let's check out the damage to homeboy's BMW.

EXCERPTED FROM

LUMINARIAS

Evelina Fernandez

Character: Andrea (female), thirties.

Andrea light-heartedly comforts her teenage son Joey. She is about to meet his first girlfriend, who is not a Latina.

Andrea: Nervous?

Why? Because I'm gonna meet her?

Mijo, please, don't let my hang-ups get in the way of your happiness, okay?

You know, *mijo*. We have a lot of stuff going on inside of us, we . . . Latinos. We've got these great feelings of love. We love who we are. We love being who we are. And . . . we have this rage inside of us. This rage that comes from all the hurt, all the stuff we've been through and our ancestors have been through. And it comes from way back. It's like it's part of our genetic memory. And that's good, too. Because it keeps us strong, it keeps us fighting.

Because we know things aren't fair. But, *mijo* . . . don't ever let that rage take over. Don't let the rage get in the way of love.

And don't worry. Your Mom can hang with a white girl.

María Irene Fornés

About the Playwright

"Fornés' work has always been intelligent, often funny, never vulgar or cynical; both delicate and visceral . . . the plays have always been about wisdom: what it means to be wise."[24] A true giant of the theatre, María Irene Fornés' impact on the American avant-garde and the establishment of "Off-Off-Broadway" cannot be underestimated. Influenced as much by cinema and the visual arts as she is by traditional drama, Fornés has been forging new ground on the stage for almost six decades. A nine-time winner of the OBIE Award (for both writing and directing), Fornés also founded the INTAR Hispanic Playwrights in Residence Laboratory in 1981, a program which has now supported and nurtured generations of major Latino/a theatre artists.

Born in Cuba, Fornés came to America during World War II and later lived in Paris. She initially studied art, but turned to theatre and moved back to New York, where she found herself at the nexus of new artistic and cultural movements—political theatre, feminism, and critical theory—that would shape her work. Although it is difficult to generalize Fornés' work, one can recognize her plays by the disjointed narrative structure which emphasizes character over plot, and her remarkable ability to create vivid figures who, despite seemingly unconquerable physical, cultural, or political obstacles, struggle to better themselves. "She is unmistakably a writer of bicultural inspiration," wrote Susan Sontag, who was Fornés' partner for many years. "One very American way of being a writer."[25]

List of Plays

A Matter of Faith
A Vietnamese Wedding
A Visit
Abingdon Square
And What of the Night? (Four one-act plays: *Hunger, Springtime, Lust and Nadine*)
Aurora
Blood Wedding (adapted from *Bodas de Sangre* by Federico Garcia Lorca)
Cap-a-Pie (music by José Raúl Bernardo)

---

24 Susan Sontag, preface to *María Irene Fornés: Plays* (New York: PAJ Publications, 1985): 9
25 Sontag, preface, 7.

Cold Air (adapted and translated from a play by Virginio Piñera)
Dr. Kheal
Evelyn Brown (A Diary)
Fefu and Her Friends
Hunger
Letters from Cuba
Life is a Dream (adapted from *La vida es sueño* by Pedro Calderón de
　la Barca)
Lolita in the Garden
Lovers and Keepers (music by Tito Puente and Fernando Rivas)
Manual for a Desperate Crossing
Molly's Dream
Mud
Nadine
No Time
Oscar and Bertha
Promenade
Sarita
Summer in Gossensass
Tango Palace
Terra Incognita
The Annunciation
The Conduct of Life
The Curse of the Langston House
The Danube
The Mothers
The Office
The Red Burning Light
The Successful Life of 3
The Widow

PLAYWRIGHT INFORMATION

　　Any and all inquiries concerning the Author and related plays
should be sent to:

Leah Hamos, Abrams Artists Agency
275 Seventh Avenue, 26th Floor
New York, NY 10001
(646) 486-4600
Leah.Hamos@abramsartny.com

PERFORMING THE MONOLOGUES

Fornés' plays are very complex and have a unique style and tone, and any actor approaching her work must keep in mind that the characters, although believable and lifelike, are not intended to be presented in the mode of traditional realism. *Conduct of Life* forces the audience to consider the cost of military action: how war affects family, how one lives their life, and the personal and political choices one makes. Orlando, who is ruthless and ambitious for power, is a sociopath who has found his profession (as a torturer for a totalitarian regime). In this selection, the actor must convey his very human side, almost child-like in his delusion and narcissism—note how the text emerges in short, rhythmic bursts, suggesting a strong, overpowering physicality.

In *Mud*, we meet Mae, a young woman whose attempt to make a better life for herself and find a new existence is doomed. We see the limits of her compassion when she is forced to take care of her physically challenged companion, Lloyd, in terrible poverty. The actress playing Mae should study the language in the text closely. In the beginning, her language is sparse, almost animal-like, reflecting the key metaphor of the play—that the characters are like pigs caged in a muddy pen. But when even the slightest glimmer of hope appears, we see how the language, although still economical, blossoms to reveal her humanity and pure ambition.

EXCERPTED FROM

CONDUCT OF LIFE

María Irene Fornés

Character: Orlando (male), late twenties to early thirties.

Orlando has strong allegiance to his profession as a soldier. He has the job of retrieving information. Some might view him as a torturer for a totalitarian regime, ambitious for power, but in his heart and mind he is following his call of duty.

Orlando: Let me see that.

O. K. so it's a trap. So what side are you on?

So what do they want?

Who's going to question me? That's funny. That's very funny. They want to question me. They want to punch my eyes out? I knew something was wrong because they were getting nervous. Antonio was getting nervous. I went to him and I asked him if something was wrong. He said, no, nothing was wrong. But I could tell something was wrong. He looked at Velez and Velez looked back at him. They are stupid. They want to conceal something from me and they look at each other right in front of me, as if I'm blind, as if I can't tell that they are worried about something. As if there's something happening right in front of my nose but I'm blind and I can't see it.

(He grabs the paper from Alejo's hand.)

You understand?

What kind of way is this to treat me?—After what I've done for them?—Is this a way to treat me?—I'll come up . . . as soon as I can—I haven't been well.—O. K. I'll come up. I get depressed because things are bad and they are not going to improve. There's something malignant in the world. Destructiveness, aggressiveness.—Greed. People take what is not theirs. There is greed. I am depressed, disillusioned . . . with life . . . with work . . . family. I don't see hope.

(He sits. He speaks more to himself than to Alejo.)

Some people get a cut in a finger and die. Because their veins are right next to their skin. There are people who, if you punch them in their stomach the skin around the stomach bursts and the

113

bowels fall out. Other people, you cut them open and you don't see any veins. You can't find their intestines. There are people who don't even bleed. There are people who bleed like pigs. There are people who have the nerves right on their skins. You touch them and they scream. They have their vital organs close to the surface. You hit them and they burst an organ. I didn't even touch this one and he died. He died of fear.

EXCERPTED FROM

MUD

María Irene Fornés

Character: Mae (female), mid twenties.

Fornés describes Mae as "a spirited young woman, she is single-minded and determined, a believer." Henry, an older man, has just moved in and become Mae's lover. In this selection, Mae explains to Henry her relationship with Lloyd, a surrogate brother with whom she has a disturbingly close bond.

Mae: What can I do, Henry, I don't want you to be offended. There's nothing I can do and there's nothing you can do and there is nothing Lloyd can do. He's always been here, since he was little. My dad brought him in. He said that Lloyd was a good boy and that he could keep me company. He said he was old and tired and he didn't understand what a young person like me was like. That he had no patience left and he was weary of life and he had no more desire to make things work. He didn't want to listen to me talk and he felt sorry to see me sad and lonely. He didn't want to be mean to me, but he didn't have the patience. He was sick. My dad was good but he was sad and hopeless and when my mom died he went to hell with himself. He got sick and died and he left Lloyd here and Lloyd and I took care of each other. I don't know what we are. We are related but I don't know what to call it. We are not brother and sister. We are like animals who grow up together and mate. We were mates till you came here, but not since then. I could not be his mate again, not while you are here. I am not an animal. I care about things, Henry, I do. I know some things that I never learned. It's just that I don't know what they are. I cannot grasp them.

(She goes on her knees as her left shoulder leans on the corner of the table.)

I don't want to live like a dog.

(Pause.)

Lloyd is good, Henry. And this is his home.

(Pause. She looks up.)

When you came here I thought heaven had come to this place, and I still feel so. How can there be offense here for you?

JAMES E. GARCIA

ABOUT THE PLAYWRIGHT

"Writing plays is the perfect combination of letting your imagination run wild and having an editorial opinion about the climate," says Garcia. "Pretty much everything I've created onstage is also a commentary on the world I'm living in."[26]   The founder of the New Carpa Theatre Company in Phoenix, a company dedicated to producing Latino and multicultural works, Garcia is one of the nation's most vocal advocates for the DREAM Act and other immigration reforms that are based on basic human rights and civil liberties.

With a background in journalism, Garcia draws from the stories of family, colleagues, and students. Framing these stories with artful language, he powerfully communicates the real-life struggles of characters determined to assert their individuality in a contentious political environment. Whether his subject is an undocumented college student, a veteran of World War II, or a powerful Latino politician, Garcia's characters vibrate with a determination to be heard that allows audiences from all backgrounds to connect.

"Becoming American, truly American, is less about serendipity and more a product of intellectual maturation," writes Garcia. "The 14th Amendment to the Constitution granted me citizenship at the moment of my birth on U.S. soil (though my mother also was a citizen), but I did not earn and probably did not deserve that designation until I finally came to understand that liberty cannot exist without human dignity."[27]

LIST OF WORKS

The Mighty Vandals
Judgment Day
Everything You Always Wanted to Know About the Culture Wars (But Were Afraid to Ask)*
Deconstructing 1070
American Dreamer: The Life and Times of Raul H. Castro
She Knows from Nothing / De nada sabe (with Ruth Vichules)
Amexica: Tales of the Fourth World (with Alberto Rios)
American Pastorela:
   Mission to Mars
   Everything You Ever Wanted to Know About Ethnic Studies (But

26   "Best Dream Act Phoenix 2009 – James Garcia," *Phoenix New Times*, 2009. http://www.phoenixnewtimes.com/bestof/2009/award/best-dream-act-1454121/
27   James Garcia, "DREAMers Driving Freedom," *azcentral.com*, n.d. http://azcvoices.com/politics/author/jgarcia/. Retrieved December 30, 2013.

Were Afraid to Ask)
Show Us Your Papers
The Saga of Sheriff Joe
The Road to the White House
The Shepherds' Odyssey
The Eagle and the Serpent: A History of Mexico Abridged
The Manic Hispanic (with James Rivas)
The Tears of Lives
Dream Act
The Mighty Vandals
A Boy Named Cesar (with Julie Amparano)
Los Repatriados
Por Amor/For Love, an Operachi in One Act
Ghost Dance Messiah
Chuy
Voices of Valor
Don Juan: Love After Death
Freedom Fighter
Vermin of the Sky
American Latino Redux
The Crossing
Borderlines
Jesus Had the Eye
Behold, A Pale Horse
Ray
Casablanca Ballroom, Lady in Mourning, Don Pedrito de Jaramillo
The Vagrant
Testimony
El Dia de Los Muertos
Silent War

Playwright Information

New Carpa Theater Company: http://www.newcarpa.org/

Performing the Monologues

Arizona activist, journalist, and playwright James Garcia's 2009 one-act play *Dream Act* chronicles the struggle, the fear, and the perseverance of young people who are undocumented. During a 2012 interview, Garcia stated, "Dreamers are the best of our democracy, they are not the ACLU, they are not constitutional attorneys, they are a youth-led organization that has the spirit of every great civil rights movement."[28] Garcia's activism with Dreamers makes his writing palpable. His text resonates with truth because Garcia, a writing professor at Arizona State University, knows and bears witness to Arizona's tough anti-immigration stance for minors and young adults.

There are thousands of people in Arizona with stories like the protagonist Victoria Nava. Victoria is an undocumented immigrant and university student who dreams of becoming a doctor. However, she cannot get a driver's license, she cannot work legally, she has to pay out-of-state tuition, and yet she continues paying for her education and living in the library. Her parents, fearful for their freedom, have returned to Mexico. She is homeless, alone, and struggling to work and stay invisible. While students her age are usually worrying about grades and dating, she is fighting to survive.

Ignacio, a college student and Dreamer advocate with a local radio show, testifies to Dreamer issues. Sensing Victoria is in trouble, he reaches out to help. Pay attention to the structure of the monologues. By the time both characters have finished their thoughts they have changed. Victoria softens as she remembers her family and their good times. Ignacio becomes impassioned as his ideas come together with a final emotional plea to get people involved and caring.

---

28   Unpublished interview with Micha Espinosa, Phoenix AZ, 2012.

EXCERPTED FROM

DREAM ACT

James Garcia
Spanish translation by Léana Courtney

Character: Victoria (female), eighteen to twenty-one.

A college student and undocumented immigrant, Victoria has all the talent, but her dream of being a doctor is slipping away. Homeless and afraid of being deported in the face of an immigration crackdown, Victoria responds to a radio show.

Victoria: No . . . no offense, but you have no idea. I know you care . . . but you have no idea what it's like to be shunned by your own government. You see it really is my government. My Constitution. My Declaration of Independence. My mayor. My police department. It's what I grew up with. It's the government I was taught to respect. I have a little brother, you know. And when he turns 18, they could sign him up and send him to Iraq or Afghanistan . . . or wherever . . . to fight for my government, my country, the one I was taught to love and respect. My brother, my blood, could die for my country, but they won't let me stay. My government won't let me dream. *(a long beat)* When I was a little girl. I guess I was about five or six years old, I was just learning to read and write. One day after school my dad was helping me make a birthday card for my mom at the kitchen table . . . And he . . . uh . . . He said to me: *"Eres mi Victoria. Do you know what that means?"* And I said, "It means I'm your Victoria. I'm your Vicky." And he, "No, your name, Victoria . . . it means Victory. I picked that name for you so whatever you try to do in life will end in victory." I believe that. I still believe that.
I did quit once. Last spring. I couldn't take it anymore. I was so tired. My brain was exhausted, from fighting, I guess. You go to sleep saying, "Tomorrow I'm going to fight." You wake up and say it again. But if you don't, you go crazy worrying about who's going to stop you in the street. Or if your classmate's a closet bigot and he decides he's going to call the Sheriff and snitch you out. I decided not to shrivel up and blow away. Ever since I heard

there was a thing called college, I've never stopped thinking about it. When I earned my undergrad, my mom and dad came to the Hispanic convocation with like 40 people. Some of them weren't even related to me. I'm mean, sure, he brought my *tios* and *tias* and cousins, but there were all these other people I didn't even know. I found out later that some of them were just dad's co-workers, and one women who came he'd just met at the supermarket. He was just so proud that he invited everyone he knew to come and see me graduate. The graduation party after cost him a fortune. *(long beat)* It was the greatest day of my life.

Victoria *(Spanish)*: Yo sé que te preocupas y no te quiero ofender . . . pero ni tienes idea cómo se siente cuando tu propio gobierno te ignora. Este es mi gobierno, así crecí yo con mi constitución, mi declaración de independencia, mi alcalde y mi departamento de policía. ¿Ya ves? Por eso respetaba a mi gobierno.

¿Sabes qué? Yo tengo un hermanito y cuando él cumpla 18 años ellos tienen el derecho de mandarlo a Irak o Afganistán o a donde les da la gana a defender a mi gobierno, mi país. Y mi hermano, mi sangre, puede perder su vida por este país, este país que me enseñó a amar y a respetarlo, el mismo ni me deja quedarme aquí. Mi gobierno no me deja tener sueños. *(pausa larga)* Cuando yo era chiquita . . . debia haber tenido 5 o 6 años, apenas estaba aprendiendo a leer y a escribir. Y un día después de la escuela mi papá y yo estábamos sentados en la mesa de la cocina haciéndole una tarjeta de cumpleaños a mi mamá . . . y me . . . em . . . me dijo, "Tu eres mi Victoria. ¿Sabes qué significa eso?" le respondí "Sí, significa que soy tu Victoria. Soy tu Vicky." Me dijo, "No, tu nombre, Victoria . . . significa salir adelante. Yo te escogí ese nombre porque hagas lo que hagas siempre saldrías adelante, saldrías victoriosa." Me recuerdo de vez en cuando de esa conversación, a veces tanto que hasta me tiene harta de mi nombre *(ríe)*. Pero yo le creí. Todavía lo creo.

Había una vez, el año pasado, ya no lo pude soportar y me rendí. Estaba tan cansada y mi mente estaba a punto de agotarse, era por tanto luchar. Tu te vas a dormir diciendo, "Mañana voy a luchar." Y mañana te despiertas repitiéndolo. Pero si no, te volverás loca preocupándote por si te paran en la calle, o si algún conocido racista decide entregarte al Sheriff Joe.

Decidí que no podía dejarme por vencida. Desde que escuché

la palabra 'universidad', la idea ha vivido en mi mente, siempre luchando por seguir mi educación. Cuando agarré mi licenciatura mi mamá y papá vinieron a la graduación con 40 personas, algunos ni los conocí. Bueno, obviamente vinieron mis tíos y todos los primos pero también habían todas estas otras personas que nunca había visto en mi vida. Después me di cuenta que algunos trabajaban con mi papá. Una señora que vino la había conocido en el supermercado. *(ríe)* Mi papá estaba tan orgulloso de mí que quiso invitar a todo el mundo a mi graduación. La fiesta le costo una fortuna y *(pausa larga)* fue el mejor día de mi vida.

EXCERPTED FROM

DREAM ACT

James Garcia
Spanish translation by Léana Courtney

Character: Ignacio (male), eighteen to twenty three.

Ignacio is a college student with a campus radio show called PADUS and is not afraid to speak the truth and fight for his fellow classmates. He tries to calm a caller who is ready to start a revolution because of the news that the state will be cutting off funding for undocumented students going to college.

Ignacio: Hold on . . . take it easy, Manolo. Things aren't that crazy, yet. What we do need to do is change the laws. That's why PADUS is on the air. The time has come my friends to turn this thing around. Education, Manolo, and anyone else out there who's listening, is a human right. If you have a brain and you want to learn, you have a right to be educated. Don't let anyone tell you otherwise. I don't know about you, but I'm willing to fight for that right. And if we've got classmates out there who are undocumented, it's our job to fight on their behalf. Denying someone the right to learn is like saying, "Hey, everyone . . . This person right here gets to learn. This person gets to cultivate her mind and her imagination. But that person over there, he's out. He's going to remain ignorant." It's that simple. So let's call it what it is. Discrimination. *Discriminación.*

You see, it doesn't matter if it's about your skin color, or your race, or your gender, or if you just happened to be born on that side of the border. Listen up, *gente*, it's our job, you, me, everybody listening, to speak out now. Why? Because we can. So it's our job to speak for the ones who can't. Remember that girl who got shipped off to Chihuahua last year, three days before she was going to start at ASU. What did she do wrong. She went to pick up her car after the cops towed it. And they deported her? That's just wrong, man. It's our job to fight for that girl, to protect her right to learn. Why? Because we can. To ignore that duty is to deny our humanity. We've all heard it said. Silence is complicity. Silence, my friends, is denial. Silence is surrender. Read your history. Google your history. Whatever you gotta do. When people with power are silent in the face of injustice . . . That, my friends, is when the powerless in our midst suffer the most. It happened to the Native Americans. It happened to our African brothers and sisters. It happened to the Irish, to the Jews. It's happening in Darfur. Stay silent and the suffering continues. Stay silent and it'll only get worse. I hear some of you say, "Nacho, man, you're exaggerating, brother. How bad can it get? This is a democracy, right?" How bad? Open your eyes? Drive to the border and pick up the local newspaper. Read about the people who die in the desert every year, more than 200 last year, another record. Why? Because they had the guts and courage to chase their dreams. Go to Tucson. Go to Yuma. Check out the news reports that say "three illegal immigrants were found dead in the desert on Monday." And then on the day after, see if that newspaper printed the names of the people whose rotting corpses were found. You know what? Chances are you'll never hear about those people again. The powerless don't have names. It's up to us, *gente*. It's up to us to make the world remember their names. *(a long beat)* Sorry, I get a little wound up sometimes. *(a beat)* Manolo? You still out there?

Ignacio: *(Spanish)* Woa . . . cálmate Manolo. Las cosas no están taaan locas todavía. Lo que tenemos que hacer es cambiar las leyes. Por eso está PADUS en el radio, para decirles a ustedes, mis amigos que ahora es tiempo para una revolución. La educación—Manolo, y todo el mundo que tiene sus orejas prendidas—es un derecho del ser humano. Si tienen un cerebro que funciona y tienen el deseo de aprender, tienen el derecho de educarse. No dejen que nadie les convenca de lo opuesto, ¿entienden? No sé si ustedes están dispuestos a luchar por ese derecho pero yo sí, porque si tenemos compañeros de clase indocumentados, es nuestra obligación de hacer esa lucha por ellos. Negándole a una persona el derecho de educación es cómo decir, "Oye amigos . . . ésta persona aquí puede educarse. Ésta persona puede cultivar su mente y su imaginación todo lo que quiera. Pero ésa persona allá, él no. Él va a vivir su vida completamente ignorante." Así es, tan simple. Así que es hora de dejar de ser ciegos, amigos, y llamarlo por su nombre verdadero, Discriminación. *Discrimination.*

Sabes, no importa el color de tu piel, tu raza o tu sexo, ni importa de que lado de la frontera entraste a este mundo. Escúchenme, amigos, es una oportunidad, tuya, mía y de todos ahora es tiempo, es nuestra oportunidad para hacer una diferencia. ¿Por qué? Porque podemos. Tenemos que ser fuertes y dar esperanza a los que no se pueden defender. ¿Se acuerden de la muchachíta que fue deportada a Chihuahua el año pasado? Tres días antes de empezar sus estudios en la universidad estatal de Arizona. Y ¿qué mal cosa hizo ella? Fíjate, solo fue a recoger a su carro que se llevó la grúa ¿y la deportaron? N'ombre eso no está bien. Es nuestra responsabilidad de luchar por chicas como ella, de proteger su derecho de educarse. Y ¿por qué? Porque podemos. Si ignoras está responsabilidad estás fallando nuestra humanidad. Todos lo hemos escuchado, silencio es el peor enemigo. Amigos, silencio es el peor castigo que te pueden dar. Lean libros de historia, búsquenlo en Google, hagan todo lo que se pueda para educarse sobre su historia y verán, cuando la gente está callada frente las injusticias el silencio mata. Es la historia de los indígenas y la historia de nuestros hermanos en África. Es la historia de los irlandeses y de los judíos y está pasando ahora en Darfur. Si nos quedamos callados alimentamos al sufrimiento y nunca podemos cambiar la historia. Ya los puedo oír, "Nacho, no manches guey, el futuro no puede ser tan mal. Vivimos en un mundo de democracia." ¡Abran sus ojos! Vayan a la frontera, compren un periódico y lean sobre las cienes de personas que mueren en el desierto cada año, siempre rompiendo records y ¿por qué? Porque ellos tuvieron ánimo, tuvieron sueños de una nueva vida y tuvieron el coraje para seguirlos. Vete a Tucson o a Yuma y escucha los reportes que dicen "el lunes, tres inmigrantes ilegales fueron encontrados muertos en el desierto." Y luego revisa el periódico el próximo día y dime si identificaron los nombres de los cuerpos de los tres muertos perdidos en el desierto porque ¿sabes qué? Es seguro que nunca volverás a saber más de ellos porque los impotentes no tienen nombres. Nos toca a todos nosotros, a nosotros como individuales a recordar cada persona, cada hombre o mujer, irlandés o africano, cada voz muda para que el mundo los recuerde también. *(pausa larga)* Perdóname, a veces me emociono mucho. *(pausa)* ¿Manolo, todavía estás allí?

AMPARO GARCÍA-CROW

ABOUT THE PLAYWRIGHT

Writes Octavio Solis: "Amparo García-Crow, like myself, suffered from Texas on the brain. She writes with a sense of its oppressive mythologies, both past and present, and with the added prescience of the changes to come for that way of life."[29] García-Crow's Texas is a devastatingly unusual place, with time shifts, ghosts, hallucinations—powerfully magical elements that are firmly rooted in each character's skewed perception of their emotional world.

A veteran performer and director who consistently works both on-and-off-screen (as well as on- and off-stage), García-Crow's playwriting has drawn comparisons to Sam Shephard and Eugene O'Neill, and is heavily influenced by the visual, dreamlike possibilities of cinema as scenes blend into each other and characters reveal more and more layers of themselves, alternatingly devastating, horrifying, and intimate. "Experimental and innovative techniques for dialogue and monologue, poetic stage directions, unusual props and scenery, shifting actors and roles, are all effectively brought to bear in the vivid and compelling creation of the world," writes José Limon. "But above all is her use of unanticipated, sometimes jarring historical and cultural juxtapositions to philosophically and culturally de-center her mostly Texas world so as to persuade us of the deep and enlarged seriousness of her people."[30]

LIST OF PLAYS

Cocks Have Claws and Wings to Fly
Under a Western Sky
The Faraway Nearby
Esmeralda Blue: La Mujer Moderna—A Play with Music
THE UNKNOWN SOLDIER: The New American Musical of Mexican Descent
STRIP: a burlesque musical
The Bonobos
57 Varieties
Ocean Song from a Desert Place
Commodius Vicus
Cool Still Waters

---

29 Octavio Solis, preface to *The South Texas Plays* by Amparo García-Crow (New York: No Passport Press, 2009): 6.
30 Solis, preface, 15.

Falling for Superman
A Roomful of Men: one woman show
In Light of Oprah
Losses in Translation
Nuestro Barrio
In the West (contributor)
La Seniora Georgia O'Keefe
The Secret Order
El Taconazo, Texas: A Radio Play with music

PLAYWRIGHT INFORMATION

Website: www.amparogarciacrow.com

PERFORMING THE MONOLOGUES

Don't be fooled by the naturalistic language in both of these selections by Amparo García-Crow. The language in these must not only be intelligible but filled with purpose. This is obvious in heightened text but not as apparent with this life-like dialogue. Look for the build in Dolores' monologue. The actor who approaches this selection will have to be able to encompass the long thought and so illuminate the humor and irony of her attitude towards men.

In *Cocks Have Claws and Wings to Fly*, we meet Guero, a boy coddled by his mother and haunted by his future and past. This selection is full of action even though Guero is sitting at the kitchen table. He is reaching out to his sister, grappling with his fate, his state of being, and what he knows he must do. I recommend exploring how Guero's breath is affected by his changing objective. A good place to begin this exploration is with the first line, "something happened to me." Allow yourself be specific. Where is he feeling the breath in his body in that moment? Is it in his gut? His head? His heart? Is it a constricted feeling or more relaxed? The possibilities within his journey are numerous.

EXCERPTED FROM

ESMERALDA BLUE: LA MUJER MODERNA

Amparo García-Crow

Character: Dolores (female), late thirties.

A longtime resident of New York City, Dolores, has just inherited a fortune from a family she has never met in San Diego, Texas. Her longtime relationship with psychotherapist boyfriend Jairo is also in flux, and he continually analyzes her. Now, she is going in for something different, and reveals one of her new adventures in a private moment.

Dolores: I found him in the variations section of the Village Voice. His simple ad read: "A single WM, 40 male seeking height/weight proportionate female with all or some of these ingredients: adventurous, sexy, erotic, exhibitionist, Bi, petite, fun. No drugs/smoke. Age/race unimportant. Short/long term. And no talking, ever."
It was the no talking ever . . . that caught my eye.
I have to say, that appealed to me . . . very much.
Jairo, my ex-boyfriend . . . was a shrink. He would talk this way at the grocery store. We could be standing in line at the movies. Even dining at the finest restaurant, he would ruin a perfectly expensive dinner. I didn't know how to break up with Jairo exactly. He was the father I never had. So I answered Daniel's personal ad instead.
And I met Daniel the following Thursday at 2:00 in the afternoon.
And every week Daniel would reserve a room at this place in the upper west side. Kind of a youth hostel but more private. I didn't know Daniel's real name for at least six months. I only knew him by his e-mail address: "Dear tall dark and lonesome69: Won't it be great to never have to say to the other 'I think you should,'" I wrote him on the first day. "I can't even imagine a relationship without the punishing 'how come you didn't?' Or the narcissistic—'That's nothing, wait'll till you hear what happened to me!'" Or the know it all: "this could turn into a very positive experience if you just couldn't, wouldn't, shouldn't!" I

definitely won't miss the kiss ass "But it wasn't your fault, you did the best you could!" Or the self-referential, "this reminds me of the time. . . !" And definitely . . . not the platitudes: "Cheer up, don't feel so bad," or better still, the ridiculous pitying "oh, you poor thing!" Or—the diagnostic: when did this begin?" Can you imagine if we never have to offer each other the excuses: "I would have called but . . . ." And of course, my personal favorite: "that's not how it happened my love!"

EXCERPTED FROM

COCKS HAVE CLAWS AND WINGS TO FLY

Amparo García-Crow

Character: Guero (male), eighteen.

Guero, a high school student and a new father, lives with his mama in south Texas. He is an acid-head, used to having narcotic and spiritual hallucinations. Guero witnessed the murder of his father; wracked with guilt and having just been introduced to Shakespeare's Hamlet in English class, he is having a lucid moment. He risks opening up to his sister Sophia.

Guero: Something happened to me. I'm not talking about the drugs. I saw daddy. He was talking to me, it didn't sound like him, exactly, but I knew it was him. Did Miss Pena ever play those Shakespeare records for you, when you took her English class?

Well that's what she's doing in class right now, playing those records, everyday . . . so like they're in my ear . . . those voices . . . but every time I see the old man, he's as real as you are okay . . . he's wearing this black tux with a red band . . .

(Gestures to his waist.)

. . . right around here . . . right where he was stabbed! Whoa . . . I hadn't even made that connection, till right now, man! Wow.

But he was more real than that . . . he looks real concerned but he doesn't say nothing, but then like in a movie I start to hear that Shakespeare shit, some guy with an English accent, in my ear telling what I already know to be true.

When I'm in class, yeah and it stays with me . . . but it's the coincidences, man, there's no way to ignore it.

Mom, she doesn't even wait for the corpse to rot, man. Too many coincidences.

It doesn't look right. No respect. I got nothing against Tio, he's a damn good man, but she's running off with the uncle and shit. . . . something is definitely stinking in Denmark, Sofia . . .

I hate it when you condescend to me, I ought to slap you. I know the man who did it, I was there. I know exactly who killed him and how and the fucker is going to be out in six months. I'm supposed to avenge his death. Father's ghost is asking me to, okay? . . . .

The way my hairs stand up when I hear those voices, you just can't know what I'm trying to say. It's like seeing very clearly. Knowing. I don't know how to explain it better than that.

See, I knew I shouldn't have said anything. You only listen to me when I'm fucked up.

ANNE GARCIA-ROMERO

ABOUT THE PLAYWRIGHT

In an interview, Anne Garcia-Romero says, "I am excited when I go to the theater and see a play that is culturally complex, linguistically innovative, aesthetically adventuresome, impeccably produced and has a running time of less than two hours."[31] It's no surprise that her own plays are all of the above, tightly scripted explorations and journeys that reflect her own lived experience as a Spanish-American theatre artist who is the inheritor of a complex cultural legacy: she cites Federico García Lorca, Gabriel Garcia-Márquez, and Tennessee Williams as among her primary influences.

With characters who find each other across visible and invisible cultural divides—*Santa Concepción* is written in Spanglish—Garcia-Romero finds the ironic humor and humanity in these border crossings, offering her actors rich possibilities in performance. Often developing her plays through workshops and staged readings, the language of her characters is as much informed by the performance as vice-versa: "I can't see how a play works until I experience my words in the mouths of the actors and in their bodies on the stage," she says.[32]

LIST OF PLAYS:

Original Plays:
Santa Concepción
Earthquake Chica
Desert Longing
Juanita's Statue
Mary Peabody in Cuba
Paloma
Provenance
Land of Benjamin Franklin
Horsey Girl
Don Quixote de la Minny
Painting Velazquez

---

31   Anne Garcia-Romero, Interview with Adam Szymkowicz, "I Interview Playwrights Part 287: Anne Garcia-Romero," 21 November 2010. http://aszym.blogspot. com/2010/11/i-interview-playwrights-part-287-anne.html.

32   Eileen Lynch, "Playwright and Theatre Scholar Gives Voice to Lost Stories," *University of Notre Dame College of Letters and Sciences Newsletter*, 3 November 2011. http://al.nd.edu/news/27253-playwright-and-theatre-scholar-gives-voice-to-lost-stories/

Pandorado
Marta's Magnificent Mundo

Translations of plays by Jordi Galcerán:
The Grönholm Method
Cancun
Conversations with Mama

PLAYWRIGHT INFORMATION:
 Website: www.annegarciaromero.com

PERFORMING THE MONOLOGUES

The plays of Anne Garcia-Romero are a wonderful challenge because they demand full characterizations from the performers. Although the characters' realizations and confessions might border on the sublime, the images, sensations, and language used to reveal them are realistic and grounded in their lived experiences.

Notice, for example, how Reynaldo from *Santa Concepción* describes working with steel—how the long thoughts and images he describes in the first half of the speech have been earned through his experience working in a foundry. Engaging sensorially with those images will allow the actor to transition into the emotionally rich elements in the second half: his physical world is also informed by the stresses of providing for his family. The values and belief systems of a culture dominated by traditional Latino/a gender roles—*machismo* vs. *marianismo*—and what is at stake in this world of dangerous, hard labor, must be understood by the actor.

You'll find a similar challenge in Esmeralda's monologue from *Earthquake Chica*, where initial descriptions based on physical sensation soon reveal a much deeper truth. The performer would do best to avoid distortion or overplaying notes of desperation or resignation. Instead, the monologue works best when the actor can tap into her internal resources and search for the truthful struggle for answers as Esmeralda explores the poignant questions of why she should continue. Direct your energy towards the (unseen) other character, and keep the action of seeking those answers—of wanting those answers—at the forefront.

EXCERPTED FROM

SANTA CONCEPCIÓN

Anne Garcia-Romero

Character: Reynaldo (male), early thirties.

In a Spanglish land, a suitor seeks a wife. He fulfills his desires and his spirituality with the saintly Connie, but then finds a new way of being that feeds his soul in a completely different way. He is ready to move on to the big city and the land of promotions and steel.

Reynaldo: Connie. *Concepción. Mira. (beat)* The power of molten steel . . . a raw . . . sheer force. You can't comprehend the beauty of it. Only three weeks of training and I started working with this spectacular, gargantuan substance and making good money for us . . . such power and profit. Tons of red hot steel . . . it will burn you to death if it touches you, the steel will burrow inside your skin looking for carbon until you are a heap of smoking flesh. We corral death every day . . . we play god . . . supernatural power in our own hands. *(beat)* Through my glasses, I watch the sparks fly and I feel my bones quiver and my throat vibrates and the furnace pops and my whole chest spasms. And then the arc light heat grows and expands until the burning substance is almost twice as hot as the surface of the sun. These are ancient rituals, *querida*. Men have been melting metal since before the days of your *Virgen María* and *Jesucristo. (beat)* And a golden light fills the melt shop as the furnace gives birth to a shining, new heat of steel. *(beat)* They're going to promote me to melt shop manager. They see I have ease and confidence with this work. You can't even begin to comprehend the force of what I deal with daily. *(beat)* This is my power, *querida. (beat)* You have your spiritual Mass. I have my molten mass. *Es así. (beat)* No more worrying about money. We live a tranquil life. You are tired but you will regain your strength. *(beat)* I'll see you in the morning.

EXCERPTED FROM

EARTHQUAKE CHICA

Anne Garcia-Romero

Character: Esmeralda (female), thirties.

Physically extroverted, Esmeralda's life and love are not on stable ground. She is more comfortable in the bedroom, dancing, or shopping than talking about her feelings. Working as a secretary for law firm, she meets accountant Sam Reyes, her polar opposite, and together these star-crossed lovers look for ways to navigate their heritage, their history, and each other.

Esmeralda: You have no idea, Sam. I wanna finish things. I can't. I see my sister the physicist and I feel crazy. I think of my father and I wanna run. And then my heart starts pumping. And I can't breathe. And my feet feel like lead. And my stomach fills with glass. And my chest is like a lump of charcoal. And my hair and eyelashes start to fall out. It's not enjoyable. I have to keep moving. I have to. *(beat)* But if I stop for too long the empty lonely silence descends and I have no way out. Before, booze and boys were the great escape . . . but I don't want that anymore . . . so I have to keep moving. If I don't, my mind starts to earthquake. Starts to move and shift and get destructive. So I'm earthquake chica in a way, inside my head, I guess. (beat) Now you're going back to prison law firm land and I'm going off to this awesome travel world job and yeah I'm excited but like what if I can't stand it and the office smells like toxic chemicals and the travel people are horrible and I won't have you there to talk to and oh god . . . my breath . . . and then . . . *(beat)* And then but I'll be all alone. And I hate my tiny apartment. I lie in bed and I hear my nutcase neighbor screaming at his Siamese cat or playing electric bass at midnight and I think what's the point? Why live another day? I mean why have all this craziness inside my head? Oh god . . . my breath. *(beat)* No really, what's the point? If I'm an earthquake and I'm so destructive, why keep being here on this planet? Why not just leave forever? Everyone's left me. I'm not helping anyone apparently. I'm not really good at anything. I can't finish jobs . . . I can't even have relationships. Really, why be here? Why not just leave for good . . .who really cares anyway? *(beat)* You say you care but do you really? I don't think so. I mean you can't stand to be with me so much that you're going back to that horrible job in that far away land where large bellied secretaries roam. And then you're gone just like everyone else in my life. You don't care really. No one does. But that's okay. I can just leave this planet and no one will care. I mean I lie in bed and I fantasize about how I'd do it. Pills? Razor blades? Rope? And I think maybe. Why not? Who'd care really?

GUILLERMO GÓMEZ-PEÑA

ABOUT THE PLAYWRIGHT

A renowned performance artist, poet, and political activist, Guillermo Gómez-Peña is one of the most influential thinkers and practitioners of intercultural theatre in the world. Provocative, shocking, and outrageous, Gómez-Peña's art installations force audiences to rethink how we tell stories with bodies, sounds, and spaces. He has made himself a revolutionary force of history: the first Chicano to win a prestigious MacArthur Fellowship; director of the troupe La Pocha Nostra, which sponsors and creates "performance activism and oppositional art" all over the world; and pioneer of a raw, vibrant theatrical form that has been described as "Chicano cyberpunk" and "ethno-techno art."

Gómez-Peña frequently employs verbal as well as visual humor, and has written some stand-alone theatrical pieces that could function effectively as audition pieces or classroom work. Like much of his work, these selections reflect Gómez-Peña's rejection of traditional theatrical narrative or characterization: his performances are blueprints for transformational experiences, not escapist storytelling. Any actor approaching his work would do well to heed his advice regarding his understanding of his work as a performance artist:

> *We chronicle our times, true, but unlike journalists or social commentators, our chronicles tend to be non-narrative and polyvocal. If we utilize humor, we are not seeking laughter like our comedian cousins. We are more interested in provoking the ambivalence of melancholic giggling or painful smiles, though an occasional outburst of laughter is always welcome.*[33]

LIST OF PUBLICATIONS

Warrior for Gringostroika (Graywolf Press, 1993)

The New World Border: Prophecies, Poems & Loqueras for the End of the World (City Lights, 1996)

Temple of Confessions: Mexican Beasts and Living Santos (PowerHouse Books, 1997)

Dangerous Border Crossers (Routledge, 2000)

Codex Espangliensis (City Lights, 2000)

Ethno-Techno: Writings on Performance, Activism and Pedagogy (Routledge, 2005)

---

33   Guillermo Gómez-Peña, "In defense of performance art," pochanostra.com, n.d. http://www.pochanostra.com/antes/jazz_pocha2/mainpages/in_defense.htm. Retrieved 30 December 2013.

El Mexterminator (Oceano, 2005). Spanish.

Bitacora del Cruce (Fondo de Cultura Economica, 2006). Spanish and
 Spanglish

Conversations Across Borders (Seagull Books, 2011). Laura Levin ed.

Exercises for Rebel Artists (Routledge, 2011)

PLAYWRIGHT INFORMATION

La Pocha Nostra Live Art Lab Website: http://www.pochanostra.
com/

Gómez-Peña's Photoblog: http://interculturalpoltergeist.tumblr.
com/

PERFORMING THE MONOLOGUES

In recent years, Gómez-Peña has explored two distinct territories
in his solo work: the ongoing re-writing and re-enactment of some
of his classic performances (he calls this his "living archive"), and
writing and testing brand new material dealing with radical citizenship and what he terms "imaginary activism." In both cases, the
artist's unique format for revealing to an audience the process of
creating, languaging, and performing material becomes the actual
project. It is precisely in his new solo work where his literature,
theory, pedagogy and live art come together in a wonderfully strange
mix. Not one solo performance is ever the same.

For *Mexiphobia*, it is important that the words feel as if you are
coining them as you speak them. I suggest rehearsing as if you are
writing a letter, slowly, and then with intention, finding the word that
you need to say in that exact moment. This will give value to the words
as you frame your ideas. Also, note that you have a series of questions:
be aware of the progression of thoughts. This monologue utilizes direct
address to the audience. The host may be speaking to many people,
but, like any good infomercial host, he/she has the uncanny ability to
make you feel like you are getting advice from your best friend.

In *The Self Deportation Project*, you are taking the listener
on an adventure; make sure to see and deliver the structure in this
narrative. There is a clear proposal at the beginning: you move into
the main idea, which, once you start going, leads you on a path that
must keep going until you resolve with the pulse of your original
proposal and character. Note how in the concluding beat of this
selection, the line suspended: "Life is still marvelous in the Global
Barrio *que no*?" Trust the cleverly crafted and finely structured text,
and allow it to tune you into your characterization.

EXCERPTED FROM:

WHAT TO DO ABOUT YOUR ACUTE CASE OF MEXIPHOBIA

Guillermo Gómez-Peña

Character: Male or female, late night infomercial host

Host: *(Happy Latino accent)* Dear American citizen:
Do you feel like a minority in your own city?
Have you ever thought: "I didn't get that job or that grant because . . . I'm white"?
When you hear people speaking Spanish in a public place, does it ever cross your mind that we might be talking shit about you?
Don't you hate having to speak the *pinche* "Mexican" language to order your "fajitas without lard"?
Do you feel that "illegal" immigrants are getting free and immediate medical services, while taxpayers like you pay a fortune for health insurance and then spend weeks waiting for an appointment . . . to see a doctor named Gonzalez?
Where does this end? Let's go deeper into your subconscious . . .
Aren't you afraid that the Mexican crime cartels are already here operating in your neighborhood?
Has it ever crossed your mind that perhaps your Mexican nanny and gardener might in fact be members of the Tijuana cartel or even worse, a redundant 'sleeping cell'?
Do you feel that the Chicano intifada is about to start any moment?
Aren't you afraid of mysterious diseases such as the swine flu brought to the US by highly infectious aliens like me?
Do you often find yourself awake at 3:00 in the morning watching B-movies on TV with titles such as "Alien vs. Predator"; "The 50-foot Wetback from Mars", or "The Attack of the Killer Chihuahua"?
Do you have a hard time differentiating between a photo of Carlos Santana and one of Kaddafi?
Señor, aren't you scared that those sexy Latin boys next door might seduce your innocent daughter, or even worse, your wife?
And you *señorita*, when you encounter a Latino male in the street, do you feel he's undressing you with his gaze? Do you even know what the word gaze means?
If you answered positively to at least 3 of the above questions,

you are very likely suffering from "Mexiphobia," a seemingly rare psychosomatic condition created by xenophobic politicians and hysterical TV pundits with the sole objective of distracting you from the real issues afflicting contemporary America.

You know, the object of your fears may be fictional, but your fears themselves are real, amigo, and you must confront them *ahora!*

For information on how to join your local Mexi-phobia support group, go to www.MojadoUSA.wet

EXCERPTED FROM

THE SELF-DEPORTATION PROJECT

Guillermo Gómez-Pena

Character: Male/female, doing vocal impressions as indicated.

Speaker: What if H.G. Wells had been Chicano? Imagine one of the possible immediate futures in a typical US city, that is to say, a city full of immigrants, people of color, and people who speak other languages . . . like Spanish. You perceive yourself as an "angry white male," but no one knows about it. Not even your beautiful "Hispanic" wife or your gorgeous interracial kids. So, this is the set up: Close your eyes and just imagine:
(Pulp narrator voice)
You wake up one day and go to work. You need to stop for gas, but the gas station is closed. (You don't know that all the attendants went back to their homeland the day before.) You drive around looking for an open gas station until you run out of gas. You call a cab, but there are no cabs because the drivers, mainly Latino, quit the day before.
Somehow you make it to the office to find your colleagues watching TV in total disbelief. The president is pleading for all unemployed Anglos and African Americans to show up immediately to the closest emergency labor recruitment center. The country is paralyzed. Total Brown-out! The disappeared Latino labor force must be replaced overnight.
At lunch time you discover that most restaurants are closed, duh! Someone explains to you that the chefs and the waiters were all part of an epic self-deportation program. Since you are fairly apolitical, you still don't quite get it. Many stores and hotels are closed-for obvious reasons—and the banks are going crazy. All across the country, millions of Mexicans and other Latinos, with their suitcases in hand, are lining up at bank counters to withdraw their accounts, on their way back to their homelands.
You begin to worry about your family. You decide to go home, walking of course, cause, remember, your car is parked somewhere in the other side of town without gas. Your Hispanic wife is devastated. Most of her relatives chose to go back to the old country. She is also furious because Juan, the gardener and Maria, the baby sitter are nowhere to be found. She explains she had to stay home to take care of the kids, and missed all of

her work appointments. She even had to take the kids to do the shopping which Maria normally does. They stood in an eternal line at the supermarket only to find that there was no fresh produce. According to the supermarket manager, "there were no Mexican truckers to deliver it."

You go to bed in total perplexity, and you dream . . . in Spanish. Or better said, you have a nightmare in Spanish: You see yourself picking fruit under a criminal sun for 10 hours a day. Your hands covered with a monstrous skin disease produced by pesticides. You wake up sweating in the middle of the night and your kids are crying because . . . they miss Maria!

You turn on the TV. A panicked US president delivers the bad news: Very few people responded to his desperate call for workers. The unemployed "citizens" were clearly not inspired by the idea of working for minimum wage and no benefits. The nation's tourist, construction, garment and food industries, are all in disarray. San Diego, Los Angeles, Santa Barbara, San José, Fresno, San Francisco, Phoenix, Tucson, Santa Fe, Albuquerque, Denver, San Antonio, Houston, Miami, Chicago and a myriad other smaller cities have declared bankruptcy. And so have many national banks. And if this weren't enough,—the president concludes—within days, crops across the country will begin to rot because there's simply no one to pick them. Luckily Mexico has offered to send some emergency food supplies, humanitarian aid, and maybe even some Mexicans." A desperate president, proceeds to beg the remaining Mexicans to stay: *"Queridous amigous aliens: querremos que ustedis recapaciten y nou abandounen sus trajayos mas, les subiremimos el salary y les dareimos muchious benefits y su terjeita verdi instantánea. Por favour."*

Now, open your eyes and cool down. It's been a hard day que no? But don't worry, Maria is still here. She brings you a cup of delicious coffee . . . from Chiapas or Bolivia, while you listen to your new Putumayo CD. Life is still marvelous in the Global Barrio *que no*?

147

José Cruz González

ABOUT THE PLAYWRIGHT

José Cruz González is perhaps best known for his work in children's theatre; he is playwright in residence for the Phoenix-based company Childsplay, and a former writer for the children's television show *Paz*, but his credits also include beautifully constructed plays with mature themes that still manage to retain a childlike wonder about the world. In González' plays, the simplest of moments rendered honestly can create suprising delight. Elements of magical realism—sometimes subtle, sometimes spectacular—seem to resonate on a primal level that renders his stories and his characters somehow perfectly theatrical.

González has been active in supporting and promoting Latino/a theatre: he started the Hispanic Playwright's Project at South Coast Repertory in Costa Mesa, and ran the project for more than a decade. "The Latino community is not well represented in theatre," González said in a 2011 interview. "I have been trying to tell the story of the other, the outsider, the one we don't normally hear from. I want to bring culture not often represented on our stages. Hopefully, kids will see themselves portrayed positively on stage."[34] Whether aimed at families or adults, González continues to honor the traditions of his cultural and artistic communities, while reimagining the ways in which those stories can be told.

LIST OF PLAYS

Mariachi Tales
Los Velientes
The Sun Serpent
Super Cowgirl and Mighty Miracle
Invierno
Sunset and Margaritas
The Heart's Desire
The Blue House
North Country
The Guitar Maker's Children
The Cloud Gatherer
A House Named Eden
Tomás and the Library Lady
Old Jake's Skirts

---

34   Brian Guering, "An Interview with Seven TYA Playwrights." *TYA Today.* Spring 2011: 32-39.

Thaddeus and 'Tila (A Crane and Frog Tale)
Earth Songs
Waking up in Lost Hills (A Central California Rip Van Winkle)
Lily Plants a Garden
Fast and Loose
September Shoes
Always Running
Cousin Bell Bottoms
Two Donuts
Odysseus Cruz
Words from a Cigar Maker
Salt & Pepper
The Magic Rainforest (An Amazon Journey)
Marisol's Christmas
Manzi (The Adventures of Young César Chávez)
The Highest Heaven
Mariachi Quixote
Harvest Moon
La Posada
Spirit Dancing

PLAYWRIGHT INFORMATION

Faculty website: http://www.calstatela.edu/academic/musictheatredance/Josécruzgonzalez.php

PERFORMING THE MONOLOGUES

Invierno is inspired by Shakespeare's *The Winter's Tale* and set in the present day and in 19th century rancho California, along the Central Coast. Hermonia is one of the Chumash people who occupied the coast from San Luis Obispo to Malibu, including the Channel Islands, for thousands of years. She lovingly refers to her grandfather as K-popo"! [ke.po.po] in the language of the Santa Ynez Chumash people, Samala. Reading Shakespeare's is imperative to a full understanding of the play's dramatic structure and themes. Just as with Shakespeare, this text demands that the actor pursue the thought, and that whatever is said provokes the next thought. Falling inflections will not only impede audibility, but halt the thinking. The speech is cumulative, building word for word and thought for thought. The actor will need to balance the argument and the emotion. It is the act of thinking that gives Hermonia her strength.

151

González' *Sunsets and Margaritas* is a madcap, big-hearted comedy. Don't be afraid to explore the classic comic stereotype of the womanizer. This archetype can be described as confident and sexually charged. They like to chase the opposite sex and are often seductive and bold. While they are narcissistic and conceited, they are always well put together, smooth, and suave, exhibiting extreme confidence which can come off as arrogance. They aren't afraid to use sarcasm (think Charlie Sheen in *Two-and-a-Half Men*). Another fun archetype to play with while exploring Jo Jo is the Trickster[35], whose mantra is "maybe, maybe not." While rehearsing, you might sing the monologue as a love song. The goal is that shifting rhythm and pitch through these explorations can unlock your performance choices.

---

35   Term from *Acting and Singing with Archetypes* by Frankie Armstrong and Janet
      Rodgers (New York: Hal Leonard Publishing/Limelight, 2009).

INVIERNO

José Cruz González

Character: Hermonia (female), twenties.

Hermonia is wife to Don Leon, a prominent 19th century Californio, and she has just given birth to their daughter in jail. She has been falsely accused of conspiring to murder her husband, committing adultery, and aiding in the escape of Don Patricio, a 19th century Irish-American transplant y Californio. Speaking before the priest, her husband, and the town, Hermonia defends her innocence and pleads with dignity and grace for her life. (You can find the equivalent scene in A Winter's Tale *Act III, Scene ii.)*

Hermonia: You will hear me, Husband. I am no threat. I come from a proud people. My grandfather was chief. Long ago when your people first came here he reached out to help them. If he hadn't, they would have perished. K-popo"! (my grandfather) believed that we are all children of the Great Spirit. When I was born I was unwanted by mother's people, but K-popo"! (my grandfather) accepted me and raised me as his own. He taught me to have compassion and respect for all of God's creations. I was baptized in the holy church, but K-popo"! (my grandfather) taught me that God's church is the natural world. I am forever bound to the land and its people. That is where I find my truth. That is why you chose me. And loved me. Husband, I have never loved a man as I love you. I tell you I am innocent. You of all people should know me best. I have been your loving wife, true to only you. I stand here before you, stripped of everything. My children cry for their mother. My son's tears go unanswered. My infant's milk untouched. Look at me. Where is the man who called me "wife?" Where is the man who honored and vowed to care for me?

I am not afraid of your threats. You have stolen what I hold most sacred. My children and my honor are taken from me and I am disgraced. Tell me, my love, what power could Death hold over me? My faith is my family and my innocence. God, the land and the people are my judge. Let my confession reveal the truth. Padre, I give you permission to share what I confessed before God. Tell them.

Sunsets and Margaritas

José Cruz González

Character: Jo Jo (male), twenty-two.

*A 22-year old, U.S. born Latino who rides a fully
blinged-out lowrider wheelchair, Jo Jo is using his
considerable charm and his wannabe gangsta fashion
designer street cred to woo Bianca, a distant cousin and
a girl smart enough to see through his shenanigans. At
the back of the family restaurant, Jo Jo finds Bianca
crying because she feels she spoke out of line; Jo Jo
consoles and then pounces.*

Jo Jo: It's not your fault, Bianca.
I involved you and it was my bad. Sorry, home girl.
Everyone's been affected. I mean look at me. It put me in a
wheelchair!
Well, okay, that's not what put me in this wheelchair.
My peeps and me were cruising when this rival clica got all
over our shit. We went to lay flowers, and drink some beer at my
Nana Olivia's grave when they opened fire on us. My homies
and me went down in a blaze of bullets. I took nine rounds. Nine.
I saved my home boys. I knew first aid cause I was a Weebalo
back in the day. Our motto was "Be Prepared."
It was like Scarface with gunfire everywhere. I went Rambo on
them vatos. When it was all over it was just me standing.
The doctors messed up my spine, removing those nine bullets.
Nine. Ain't that some shit?
You ever heard of Sing Sing?
Rikers?
Leavenworth?
There's one for every place I did time.
Yeah, that's why I've got these tears tattooed on my face.
I don't want to talk about that. I was young and stupid, but I paid
my dues to society. I'm rehabilitated. Let's talk about you. You
got a boy friend? You ever thought of modeling? Here's my card?
"Trucha" means "watch out, shrewd, sharp." I design gangsta
cool. The clothes, tattoos, and earrings I'm wearing, I created
myself. My clothing line is going to be big one day. I got local

155

skaters and rockeros wearing my shit. Hey, Latinos need to be stylin'. There're millions of young people that got to get their look on. I'm going to be the Latino Calvin Klein.

VIRGINIA GRISE

About the Playwright

The work of San Antonio-raised (and now Brooklyn-based) playwright, director, and performance artist Virginia Grise takes many forms, and Grise admits to thriving on giving herself new and exciting challenges as a writer. "There are certain things that I am obsessed with as a writer, things that reappear in my work," she explains. "But I certainly hope that my work looks different— that each piece is radically different from the other . . . Each piece of writing reflects a different set of questions I am asking myself aesthetically, politically, and theoretically."[36]

Playwright David Hare, in awarding Grise the annual Yale Drama Prize, called her "blazingly talented and resonant."[37] Indeed, Grise's words seem to demand to be brought to life, an indication that Grise thinks as much about how actors and directors might approach her work as she does the work itself. Having collaborated with other artists on performance installations, dance theatre, community-based creation and solo performances, along with productions of her own original plays, her work manages to express profound truths in a rich, poetic style. Specifically reviewing *The Panza Monologues*, one critic made an observation that could well apply to any of Grise's plays: "The performance builds bridges across cultural lines that divide us precisely because it is situated thematically, linguistically, and aesthetically in the particularities of the USAmerican Latina experience."[38]

List of Works

blu
Making Myth
rasgos asiaticos
a farm for meme
ponme la mano aqui
The Panza Monlogues (with Irma Mayorga)
The Mexicans as Told by Us Mexicans (with Ricardo Bracho)
behind barbed wire (with Community Arts Partnership)

36 "Virginia Grise Looking Up at the Sky: blu," La Bloga, 23 October 2011. http://labloga.blogspot.com/2011/10/virginia-grise-looking-up-at-sky-blu.html
37 "Yale University: 'Blazingly Talented' Playwright Wins Yale Drama Series Prize." *Yale News,* 5 March 2010. http://news.yale.edu/2010/03/05/blazingly-talented-playwright-wins-yale-drama-series-prize
38 Karen Jean Martinzon, "¡Teatro Caliente!" (review), *Theatre Journal* 57:3 (October 2005): 485-489.

The Architecture of Becoming (with Women's Project)
would I then be . . . (dance theatre)
Passions (dance theatre)
Held by Dreams (dance theatre)

PLAYWRIGHT INFORMATION
Website: www.virginiagrise.com

PERFORMING THE MONOLOGUES

Making the college circuit much like *The Vagina Monologues*, Virginia Grise's *Panza Monologues* (co-written with Irma Mayorga) creates activista theatre about female bodies and the connections between bodies, culture, and politics. But instead of focusing on the *chochas* (vaginas), Grise writes about *panzas* (bellies). Grise puts bellies front and center: in a 2011 interview, she states,

> *I'm always really interested in questions of colonization, and in the United States the issue of food is completely interrelated to issues of poverty. In San Antonio, access to healthy food is hard. I love in [the monologue "Hunger for Justice"] where she says, "We were learning about the systems and in learning about the systems, why not center our body in everything that we do? Because if we can't take care of our own bodies, then how are we going to do all this work?" Throughout the entire piece there's definitely a political agenda, and that political agenda is about claiming authority for our selves. That's connected to class, race, sex, gender.*[39]

It is important that the actor approaching Grise's selection have a strong connection to their breath. Breathe into your *panza*, stay centered, and allow your voice to share the story. You are the narrator and the activist in this selection, and you need clarity in your communication and a relationship to your listener. It would support the narration if, when speaking the Cubano Spanish, the actor were able to find the distinctive placement and musicality of the accent. If the selection is too long, an internal cut can be found from "San Antonio" to "I am not an Americana." The stage directions from the original production, directed by Grise's co-author Irma Mayorga, are

---

39 Dahlia Grossman-Heinze, "The Panza Monologues," *Ms. Magazine*, 9 April 2011. http://msmagazine.com/blog/2011/04/09/the-panza-monologues/

included as inspiration to physicalize. The piece is complemented by strong physical action, but the actions here are suggestions, not requirements—explore your own physical journey.

Grise's 2010 Yale Drama Award-winning play *blu* has beautifully crafted urban poetic language. Soledad's story is rooted in real experience, but Grise did not conceive the piece in a naturalistic fashion. Magic and mysticism are intrinsic to the script. This is heightened language and a heightened situation, and the selection demands energy and emotional availability. Don't be afraid to add to the piece by letting the body spring to the aid of this metered language. Although recalling the past, the immediacy of Soledad's connection to her partner Hailstorm is what leads her to conclude that she is "done." It is her pursuit of a future that makes her recall the past.

EXCERPTED FROM

THE INTERNATIONAL PANZA

Virginia Grise

Character: Female, any age.

From *The Panza Monologues,* co-written with Irma Mayorga

Stage directions from original production directed by Irma Mayorga

Female: The International *Panza*!

"México! México! México!"

The cubanos shouted in the streets as we walked by, like sports announcers.

"México! México! México!"

They recognized us by our nationality before we even spoke. Confused *cuando yo metí la palabra.*

"Oiga, tu no eres de México."

And I tried to explain to them…

Chicana (points to herself)
Aztlán (raises one fist in the air, revolutionary style)
Broken Treaties *(crosses her arms in front of her, both fists clenched)*
Border Crossing *(moves her arms, still crossed, from center to the right of her in an arc)*
The Mexican American War *(uses her fingers to create two guns, points them at the audience)*
La Migra (flips her guns sideways, gangsta style)
The Treaty of Guadalupe *(gestures the ripping of paper)*
San Antonio! *(Raises both hands in the air, exasperated. Runs stage left, explaining the rest of the story to an audience member.)*

You see, my mom's *mexicana*
but her father was Chinese.
And my father?
Well, he's white.

"So that makes you what?" he asks.

The Mexicanas try to help, explaining that I am one of them, sort of, but then again I'm not. The Cubano seems to understand, "Oh, like the *gusanos,* you mean?"

"No, not at all," the *mexicanas* say, "*She* didn't have a choice."

You see, *Tejas* was once part of Mexico but overnight brothers became enemies, *paisanos* outsiders, and invaders *rightful* owners of a land they *stole* from the Mexicans, who stole the land from the Indians.

"She's a *Tejana.*"

"Americana?"

The *mexicanas* try again. This time breakin it down into its syllables.

"Chi-ca-na."

And I decide not to tell them that I was really born in Georgia because my father was in the military but I moved to *Tejas* when I was three and I've never lived anywhere else and San Antonio is my home. I decide not to tell them that my mother's family is not *chichimeca,* that the border didn't cross her, she crossed it and no, not during the Revolution of 1910 but in the 1960s. That she married a *gringo* so she could go to the u.s. of a's.

My father was from a farming town, Goshen, Indiana. My real name is Virginia, Virginia May. Not Victoria, Vicki, Kike, or *(spoken in Spanish)* Virginia even. My ways are a lot less *rasquache* and a whole lot more trailer trash. My grandmother's name was Córtez for god's sake. I decide *not* to tell them that the blood of the conqueror takes up more space than anything else inside my body but no, I am not an *Americana*. The u.s. of a's did not want me, *guerra*, *alta y gorda* anymore than it wanted my mother, *prieta, baja y gorda*.

I don't explain to the *Cubano* or the *mexicanas* why my Spanish is broken. That the reason I speak *pocha* has as much to do with assimilation as it does with oppression. That Spanish is also the language of the colonizers. This they already know. And just when I decide NOT to tell them all of that the Cubano looks at me and says...

"México is in your face. *Tú gente sí era mexicana. Lo ves en tu cara."*

I ask, "How did you know? Even before we spoke. How did you know to call them by their country of birth, me by my country of memory, us by the *tierra of nuestras antepasados?* How did you know that we were *México?"*

"Es que la cara de México está mas gorda, mas redonda. The face of Mexico is much fatter, more round."

I want to protest but first I take a second to look at my *compañeras* —all *flacas* not *gordas* like me and it's true! All our faces are round even when our *panzas* aren't. Our faces are round like the *luna,* who doesn't show her face in Cuba during the winter months. Our faces round like the *tortilla, pan* the *cubanos* do not eat. All of us – big, fat *Olmeca* heads, not like the faces of other Latinos, definitely not like the face of a Cubano, shaped long like *azucar de caña. Somos nosotras las hijas de Coyolxauhqui,* full moon faces. *Y yo con una panza* to match. Big, round beautiful full moon *panza* to match my *Olmeca* head.

You see, well yeah I guess you see, I'm a big woman. That's why I spell *Panza* with a "z" not a "s" cuz it takes up more space.

Gestures the "z" in the air, zorro style, showing exactly how much space it takes up.

And I'm a big woman goddammit.

EXCERPTED FROM

BLU

Virginia Grise

Character: Soledad (female), thirty-seven.

A mother, tired of the hard life, in present day barrio, USA. She is alone with her lover Hailstrom when she shares this memory of her past about her children's father, Eme, who is now locked up.

Soledad: there's that split second. you know. that split second before some one, some one hits you. you know it. know they gonna hit you before it happens. see it in their eyes. their body. whole body tenses up. hold it tightly. all the years of anger and rage. disappointment. being looked down on. thought less of. every time they got beat up. beat down. the broken dreams. not wanting to dream big because you might end up with big disappointments. not wanting to dream at all. hold it so tight. the bones caught in throat.

my dad use to beat the shit of my mom and we knew. knew when he was gonna hit her cuz the whole world stopped, stopped spinning. that moment. even before the fist is clenched. raised in air. that moment before. less than a second. the spinning stops. he'd bite down on his lip. open his hand. and pas. coffee table thrown. tv broken. on the floor. silently. eyes closed fist clenched. pas. pas. pas. and we'd sit there watchin. just watchin him wail on her just watchin. and we's the only ones screamin. my sister would hold me. i'd be all curled up in a ball. arms locked round her neck. so i wouldn't see. tried to keep me safe. i remember the sound of fist on face. and i knew. i was just a little girl but i knew. i was never gonna let a man hit me . . . until he did. until he hit me. gemini was just a baby, just a baby when it happened. kicked and screamed. wasn't gonna let her grow up like that. so when he got arrested. that was it. that was it. no more. i wuz done.

QUIARA ALEGRÍA HUDES

ABOUT THE PLAYWRIGHT

Quaira Alegría Hudes' advice to writers on how to approach dialogue would also apply to any actor picking up her work: "It's music. Each line is a melody. Vary the tempo and the pace. Create your own language. Listening to music reveals a lot about dialogue."[40] Hudes' plays are musicals: explicitly in the case of the Tony-winning *In the Heights* or the children's play *Barrio Grrl!*, or implicitly as in the mother-daughter road trip play *26 Miles* or the Pulitzer Prize-winning *Water by the Spoonful*. Playwright Paula Vogel, one of Hudes' mentors in the graduate program at Brown University, described this musicality as "an emotional honesty without sentimentality, and then effortless bursts of heightened lyricism."[41]

Regardless of whether or not the characters actually sing on stage, Hudes always manages to render her characters in perfect tune with language and deep emotion that crosses cultural boundaries. Born in Philadelphia, Hudes is half-Puerto Rican and half-Jewish, and her plays often reflect the dazzling possibilities of a mixed-race identity while crafting figures who seem to be transcendently human more than anything else.

Hudes reveals that her own method of writing is itself both intuitive and deliberate, and that the key to her work is the patient and often unknown exploration of the inner and outer world of the characters. "I liken this experience to walking into a dark cave without food or water," she says. "Or falling into the bottom of a well. Or getting lost in a dark wood."[42]

LIST OF PLAYS

The Elliot Trilogy:
　　Elliot, A Soldier's Fugue
　　Water by the Spoonful
　　The Happiest Song Plays Last
26 Miles
In the Heights
Barrio Grrrl!
Yemaya's Belly

40　　"The Craft: Quiara Alegría Hudes," *Dramatist* 12:2 (November 2009): 6.
41　　Alexis Soloski, "Quiara Alegría Hudes: An Interview with the 2012 Pulitzer Winner," *The Village Voice*, 18 April 2012.
42　　"The Craft," 7.

Playwright Information

    Website: www.quiara.com

Performing the Monologues

    Hudes' *Water by the Spoonful*, which won the 2012 Pulitzer Prize for Drama, explores the effects of addiction and poverty on characters struggling for human connection in a dissonant world. The beauty of her writing is that through crisp and pointed dialogue, she makes the invisible scars of the heart and psyche visible. In the male selection, Elliot, an Iraqi veteran, is reeling from his beloved aunt's death and still suffering from post-traumatic stress disorder as he illuminates the darkness of his childhood memories. This is a charged situation and it is impossible not to feel for him. Note the emotional shift and give time for the transition to land on the audience. ("Spoon. But you couldn't stick to something simple like that.") For the final line ("Cuz when you dehydrate you can't form a single tear"), make sure to choose an action that is not based solely in anger, as the strength of the piece lies in the opening of his heart, not the closing.

    Yasmina faced tremendous obstacles to enter the world of music and academia. She is a phenomenal teacher and this is her first job: and her eagerness to please is clear. It is imperative that the actor research and hear the John Coltrane piece that she is describing. In order to own the words, one must own the image and the aural experience.

EXCERPTED FROM

WATER BY THE SPOONFUL

Quiara Alegría Hudes

Character: Elliot (male), twenty-four.

In a Philadelphia diner, Elliot, a Puerto Rican, confronts his estranged mother (a former heroin addict) in front of one of her friends. Elliot makes it crystal clear that because of their history, their relationship is strained.

Elliot: My sister and I had the stomach flu, right? For a whole day we couldn't keep nothing down.
Medicine, juice, anything we ate, it would come right back up. Your co-worker here took us to Children's Hospital.
It was wall-to-wall packed. Every kid in Philly had this bug. ERs were turning kids away. They gave us a flier about stomach flu and sent us home. Bright blue paper. Little cartoon diagrams. It said give your kids a spoonful of water every five minutes. A small enough amount that they can keep it down. Five minutes. Spoon. Five minutes. Spoon. I remember thinking, Wow, this is it. Family time. Quality time. Just the three of us. Because it was gentle, the way you said, "Open up." I opened my mouth, you put that little spoon of water into my mouth. That little bit of relief. And then I watched you do the same thing with my little sister. And I remember being like, "Wow, I love you, Mom. My mom's is all right." Five minutes. Spoon. Five minutes. Spoon. But you couldn't stick to something simple like that. You couldn't sit still like that. You had to have your thing. That's where I stop remembering.
A Department of Human Services report. That's my memory. Six hours later a neighbor kicks in the door. Me and my sister are lying in a pile of laundry. My shorts was all messed up. And what I really don't remember is my sister. Quote: "Female infant, approximately two years, pamper and tear ducts dry, likely cause of death, dehydration." Cuz when you dehydrate you can't form a single tear.

EXCERPTED FROM

WATER BY THE SPOONFUL

Quiara Alegría Hudes

Character: Yaz (female), Puerto Rican, twenty-four.

Yaz is Puerto Rican, a first year adjunct music professor at Swarthmore College is in the middle of her class. They are listening to "Ascencion" by jazz saxophonist John Coltrane. Trying to impress to her students with the beauty of the music, she switches tactics and shares a lesson from her heart.

Yaz: Coltrane's *A Love Supreme*, 1964. Dissonance is still a gateway to resolution. A B-diminished chord is still resolving to? C-major. A triton is still resolving up to? The major sixth. Diminished chords, tritons, still didn't have the right to be their own independent thought. In 1965, something changed. The ugliness bore no promise of a happy ending. The ugliness became an end in itself. Coltrane democratized the notes. He said, they're all equal. Freedom. It was called Free Jazz but freedom is a hard thing to express musically without spinning into noise. This is from "Ascension," 1965.
Oh come on, don't make that face. I know it feels academic. You're going to leave here and become R&B hit makers and Sondheim clones and never think about this noise again. But this is Coltrane, people, this not Schoenberg! This is jazz, stuff people listen to *voluntarily*. Shopping period is still on—go sit in one session of "Germans and Noise" down the hall and you'll come running back begging for this muzak.
(Yaz turns off the music)
In fact, change the syllabus. No listening report next week. Instead, I want you to pinpoint the first time you really noticed dissonance. The composer, the piece, the measures. Two pages analyzing the notes and two pages describing the experience personally. This is your creation myth. Before you leave this school you better figure out that story and cling to it for dear life or you'll be a stockbroker within a year.
I was thirteen, I worked in a corrugated box factory all summer, I saved up enough to find my first music teacher—up to that

point I was self-taught, playing to the radio. I walked into Don Rappaport's room at Settlement Music School. He was old, he had jowls, he was sitting at the piano and he said, "What do you do?" I said, "I'm a composer, sir." Presumptuous, right? I sat down and played Mr. Rappaport a Yazmin original. He said, "It's pretty, everything goes together. It's like an outfit where your socks are blue and your pants, shirt, hat are all blue." Then he said, "Play an F-sharp major in your left hand." Then he said, "Play a C-major in your right hand." "Now play them together." He asked me, "Does it go together?" I told him, "No, sir." He said, "Now go home and write." My first music lesson was seven minutes long. I had never really heard dissonance before.

Lisa Loomer

ABOUT THE PLAYWRIGHT

Lisa Loomer has found success in all three major wings of the American entertainment industry: television, film, and stage. "I just write what I feel I have to write in terms of theater. I write about what I care about, what pisses me off," says Loomer of the writing process that results in stage work that can be both acerbic and emotionally resonant. "In writing for television and film, yes, I have thought more about the audience. It is a 'broader' audience and I do want to reach them."[43]

Of Spanish and Romanian descent, Loomer's work frequently explores issues of class as well as gender and ethnicity. She also writes with an insider's knowledge of the less glamorous side of Hollywood, whether behind the scenes on a TV sitcom (*Maria! Maria, Maria, Maria*) or in a community of female ex-gang members (*Café Vida*), never afraid to take on the power structure of a culture that by nature marginalizes women, immigrants and people of lower economic status. Her plays confront subjects as varied as what women endure for the sake of beauty (*The Waiting Room*), the frustrating relationship between a domestic worker and an employer (*Living Out*), and the impact of ADHD on a young family (*Distracted*). "I seem to have written a lot about balance or the need for balance," says Loomer. "The balance of masculine versus feminine, nature versus science, Anglo culture versus Latino culture, the powerful versus the powerless, life versus art."[44] Her ability to convey that balance with conviction and humor have made her one of the most visible and influential Latina writers of her generation.

LIST OF PLAYS

Birds
Looking for Angels
Accelerando
Bocón
The Waiting Room
Expecting Isabel
Broken Hearts
Living Out

---

43   Warren Etheridge, "Living Out—Screenwriter Lisa Loomer," *The Warren Report,* 18 January 2003. http://thewarrenreport.com/2003/01/18/living-out-screenwriter-lisa-loomer/
44   Scotty Zacher, "Interview: Playwright Lisa Loomer," *Chicago Theatre Beat,* 3 February 2010. http://chicagotheaterbeat.com/2010/02/03/lisa-loomer-interview/

Distracted
Café Vida
Homefree
Two Things You Don't Talk About At Dinner
Roe

PLAYWRIGHT INFORMATION
    Plays published by Dramatic Publishing:
        www.dramaticpublishing.com
    Theatrical Representation:
        Beth Blickers, Abrams Artists
    Film and Television Representation:
        ICM

PERFORMING THE MONOLOGUES

While she was writing *Café Vida*, Lisa Loomer spent 18 months speaking with the men and women of Homeboy Industries and Homegirl Café. Research into the production history is imperative to fully understand the impact the play had on its community. *Café Vida* offers the actor biting dialogue and plenty of opportunity for irreverence. The play tells the story of rival home-girls ready to leave gang life and begin anew. This LA story offers a glimpse into the choices we make personally and as a nation.

El Maíz, a five thousand year old man, who appears as a homeless man who frequents the café, can be played by an actor of any age who can connect with his un-socialized self, though it is best suited for actors over fifty. El Maíz is without shame and he cares not what the world thinks of him and he has a voice and will use it because he is mad as hell. Research into the practices of the international agricultural biotech seed company Monsanto and the debates surrounding NAFTA policies fueling the drug trade are necessary in order to fully digest El Maíz' rage.

In *Expecting Isabel*, Loomer's 1999 comedy about infertility, we are introduced to Nuyorican Lupe, a possible birth mother whose heart is breaking even as she gives advice to the adoptive parents. This is a performance-driven play and it is best that the actress who tackles this character have deep connection with her emotional life. Lupe is both winning and losing in this situation. She believes that she is providing a better life for her baby, but she is also giving up

173

her child. Note the dramatic shift when the adoptive parents offer her money for her services. How offended is she? When does she decide that she will not give up the baby? When do the possible adoptive parents know that she will not be giving up this baby? I suggest that the actor clarify and magnify the moment before she speaks and the moment after she finishes speaking in this selection. The bookend actable moments are imperative to making the monologue work since it was excerpted from dialogue.

<small>EXCERPTED FROM</small>

CAFÉ VIDA

Lisa Loomer

Character: El Maíz, looks like a regular guy of fifty, though he's five thousand.

> *El Maíz, a man whose skin is made of corn on the cob, enters and sits among recovering gang members in an anger management class. Asked if he has something he'd like to discuss, he vents his frustration about free trade and NAFTA.*

El Maíz: Yeah, I'll share, con mucho gusto. I'll share. Cause I been set up and disrespected and I'm mad as hell and can't take it no more! I'm gonna share, arright, so watch out, 'cause I'm gonna share.

(beat; controlling himself)

I was the biggest thing en Mexico. Numero uno for five thousand years. El Maíz!

(to someone in audience)

"The Corn"—in case you failed Spanish.

(laughs, bitterly)

Hell, I was a Creation Myth! The Mayans thought man came from me. I was a God, entiendes? Mohammed, Jesus, Moses . . . and El Maíz.

(to the group)

Your great great great great grandparents worshiped me.

(mimes patting tortillas)

Your abuelas patted me in their rough hands. Tortillas, tacos, enchiladas . . . ? Like to see you make 'em without me!

(beat)

Then came the biggest gang truce in the history of this pinche world.

(beat)

La NAFTA. North American Fucking Trade Agreement. And Mexico was forced to buy corn from the U.S. Y ¿porque? Because the pinche U.S. corn was "surplus"—which is English for "cheap!" Mexicans eating corn from Iowa? *Hijo de la gran chingada.*

175

I never saw it coming . . . Farmers that worshipped me couldn't even afford to grow me no more. The little farms shut down en Mexico—

(to white audience member)

Just like the independent bookstore that got wiped out by *pinche* Barnes and Noble, eh? The Mexican farmer had to sneak across the border—to slaughter chickens en Georgia for El Tyson. To the meat plant en Nebraska to kill their sick, hormone addicted cows. And if he made it to L.A. and tried to grow a few *pinche* vegetables in South Central? The *puto* politicos shut down the farm.

(beat)

Meanwhile, back *en* the old country . . . The farmer that stayed *en* Mexico worked the only crops he could make a few *pinche* pesos from . . . marijuana y cocaine. Or he went to work in the *maquiladoras*, or in the *fábricas* that make your meth. Our homies in the Mexican *gobierno* got in bed with Big Agriculture—and lemme tell you, Monsanto got a big GMO dick!

Monsanto tells the farmer what he can grow, who he's gotta buy seeds from . . . Them! And if you don't buy?

(mimes throat cutting)

They put you out of business! And what does your *gobierno* give Monsanto? Twenty to life? No, the government gives them "protection!" Protection under NAFTA! *Oyeme*! Monsanto's genetically engineered corn is sneaking over the border into Mexico and taking over! It's cornicide!

(enraged)

I've seen the fruits of NAFTA. I've seen Free Trade: "We choke on your corn . . . You die from our meth—!"

I claim my neighborhood! Michoacan, Oaxaca, Guanajuato, Juarez—!

I want my country back—!

EXPECTING ISABEL

Lisa Loomer

Character: Lupe Santiago (females), twenties or thirties.

A proud expectant mother who lives in a small East Harlem tenement apartment finishes up her interview with the possible parents of her child. She is a woman of dignity and struggles with her decision. Should she give up her baby?

Lupe: Oh listen—one thing I got to tell you because I might forget at the hospital. All my kids are allergic to milk. You better write this down. You need paper? So you got to use the soy formula. And two of my kids got bronchitis, so when they start coughing, you got to give antibiotic right away.

(Pats stomach)

This one's pretty active, moves around a lot . . . But don't let the doctor give you none of them hyperactive drugs. They see a Puerto Rican kid that's active, right away they want to put her on Ritalin.

(Upset despite, herself)

They don't need that shit—They're just kids, okay?

(Everyone is getting emotional now . . .)

You give them a lot of love, they'll be fine, okay?

(Nick takes out his wallet)

NO. I don't. I don't want money for this. I don't want nothing. You just . . . You just love her, okay? That's all. You just let her know that I loved her and—and this wasn't about her, okay? I want her to have a room that's hers! I want her to go outside! And you let her know about Jesus. You let her know that . . . she'll be fine.

JOSÉFINA LOPEZ

ABOUT THE PLAYWRIGHT

"Oral tradition is really how Chicano literature came to be," explains Joséfina Lopez of how she herself came to playwriting. "I was not exposed to the written word, but I had the greatest teacher. I always tell people that my mother was my inspiration because she was the best *chismosa,* and she had the best stories. And if anyone taught me about drama, it was my mother because she knew how to tell a story. And my grandfather also told stories."[45] Inspired by the productions of Luis Valdez and El Teatro Campesino, and with a lifetime's worth of stories, characters, and experiences shared by her family, Lopez knew from a young age that she would ultimately fulfill her calling as a playwright.

With a career that has blended her theatrical artistry, fluidity with the written word, and passionate activism, Lopez' self-determination and dedication to her geographical and artistic communities are exemplary and inspirational. Born in Mexico, and for many years an undocumented resident (living in the Boyle Heights area of Los Angeles), Lopez' journey across literal and imagined borders gives her work dimension and resonance, and the ability to shape painfully and playfully honest characters who are capable of deep intuition, wisdom, and poetry. Her first produced play *Real Women Have Curves* was later turned into a landmark HBO film (Lopez co-wrote the screenplay), earning acclaim from audiences and critics around the world. Lopez' passion for truthful storytelling has also led her to find success as a novelist, poet, public speaker, and playwright. Several years ago, she also founded CASA 0101, a company dedicated to promoting and producing culture in Boyle Heights through theatre, media and performance, for which she continues to serve as both as artistic director and teacher. "So much of writing is about healing the unconscious wounds," she says describing the guiding vision of her work, "Whatever the idea is, I know the attempt from the unconscious mind is to help me heal."[46]

45 "Joséfina Lopez—In Her Own Words," Latinopia, n.d. http://latinopia.com/latino-theater/Joséfina-lopez/. Retrieved 30 December 2013.
46 Meredith Resnick, "The 5-Question Interview: Joséfina Lopez," *The Writer's Inner Journey,* August 2009. http://writersinnerjourney.com/2009/08/Joséfina-lopez.html

LIST OF WORKS

Lola Goes to Roma
Hungry Woman (based on her novel)
A Cat Named Mercy
Queen of the Rumba
Simply Maria, or The American Dream
Real Women Have Curves
Unconquered Spirits
Confessions of Women from East L.A.
Food for the Dead and La Pinta
When Nature Calls
Trio Los Machos
Boyle Heights
Detained in the Desert
Hotel del Amor (short play)
Coming Out Party (short play)
The Latino Gay Ghost Whisperer (short play)
Botox Party (short play)
Pastorela Baby (short play)
Hungry Woman in Paris (novel)

PLAYWRIGHT INFORMATION

Personal Website: http://Joséfinalopez.co/
Company Website: http://www.casa0101.org/

PERFORMING THE MONOLOGUES

In these three very different plays you will clearly see the voice of the activist, poet, and playwright.

Detained in the Desert is a conversation play about the human price of immigration and migration. Set in Southern Arizona, the play provides a lens through which to view draconian laws like S.B. 1070 and the beliefs of the fundamentalist right. In this selection, we are introduced to Ernesto, based on Enrique Morones, founder of the nonprofit Border Angels. Research into the human rights defender's career and Arizona politics is imperative for an accurate portrayal. Pay close attention to the argument: Ernesto is effective because of his clarity of thinking, not his fervor.

When Nature Calls is a series of monologues played by seven actresses exploring the connection and relationship of women to nature. Lopez describes the piece as her "Inconvenient Truth," honoring *la tierra, la feminina,* and environmental consciousness. The selection below introduces us to Yolanda, a woman capable of great transformation. She may have become an accidental environmentalist, but in the retelling of the experience, she discovers the lessons of personal transformation. It is not clear to whom Yolanda is speaking: she may be speaking to her better self, a best friend, a therapist, or the audience. Make the strongest personal choice that will make the process of communicating the story powerful and evocative. Time, space, and place are also created in the actor's imagination. My suggestion is that you seek a relationship to your listener that creates a culture of participation. Put the test of your words in the imaginary other.

Boyle Heights is an autobiographical saga—Lopez's love letter to her hometown. In this opening selection, we meet a college educated poet named Dalia (based on Lopez) recalling her childhood memory of her journey to the city of angels, Los Angeles. A transformation from child to woman all happens in 27 lines. There is a natural pace and build-up to "I truly believed we were going to heaven." Allow the final two lines to linger and land on the listener. The second poem by Dalia is directed to Craig, her soon-to-be ex. In the play, Dalia speaks to Craig via her cell phone. For audition purposes, it would be best to not to use the device of a telephone, but to place the focus outward. Create the where, how, and on whom to focus the eyes (not the auditioners). Keep in mind that Dalia is not afraid to be herself, love herself, and if it gets messy so much the better—she is now home. Note the three different stanzas, and honor the poetic and emotional build.

EXCERPTED FROM

DETAINED IN THE DESERT

Joséfina Lopez

Character: Ernesto Martinez (male), fifties.

Ernesto is an activist who distributes gallons of water throughout the desert to provide aid for migrants crossing the border. He responds to a conservative talk show host.

Ernesto: Carl. I know who you are. You're a poor confused man who thinks poking holes into the gallons of water I leave out in the desert is a patriotic act. Or taking shotguns to the border and dressing up like G.I. Joe is an act of—that makeshift green uniform that you proudly wear, trying to imitate a Border Patrol Officer, is made by undocumented labor. I know that because I've visited those factories where undocumented people get paid pennies to make your uniform. That rifle that you use for target practice in the dessert, those parts are assembled in Mexico by Maquiladora workers who are exploited by NAFTA. That cap that you wear - now, that's made in China. Yes, it's made in China by forced prison labor. Gentlemen, I can see we are not going to come to any understanding, and I have a lot of water to deliver. This is going to be a very hot week, so I better get back to work. I just hope that one day you see the light, but hopefully not before you . . . finally see the light . . . goodbye.

WHEN NATURE CALLS

Joséfina Lopez

Character: Yolanda (female), early twenties.

Running away from an abusive relationship, Yolanda becomes an accidental environmental activist and "tree woman."

Yolanda: Do I miss that tree? Yes, and no . . . The first thing I want to clear up is that I am not an activist. I wish I were that conscious and selfless, but I'm not . . . That still doesn't explain why a perfectly sane woman would climb up a tree and live there for two months . . . . I was simply running away from my fiancé— ex-fiancé. One night after dinner at a fancy restaurant in Beverly Hills he got upset with me for correcting him in public. So when we were in private he slapped me. After he did that I just ran . . . I knew he would say he was sorry and he would never do it again and he would buy me flowers and like a love-starved idiot I would go back to him and he would do it again. So I ran, but something about this tree . . . It begged me to climb it. And I didn't want to go home and I didn't want to go back with him . . . You see I ran and I knew there was no future with this man, but I didn't want to have a future without him. So I stopped the world; my world. That's why I climbed that tree.

When I was on that tree . . . The moon kept me company while I contemplated my life . . . It only got lonely when I let myself feel sorry for myself . . . The next morning after I climbed the tree I was awakened by an argument. A police officer was arguing with an environmental activist about my right to be up there on the tree. So I was about to get off, but the young man ordered me to "Stay up there sister. You don't have to get off. We pay taxes. You enjoy that tree!" So I stayed up. Quickly the activists started comparing me to "The Butterfly Woman" and other women who have climbed and lived on trees . . . Coincidentally they were building yet another Starbucks right next to that tree . . . So the activists took the opportunity to make me a symbol of anti-globalization and anti-capitalism . . . I mean I don't mind Starbucks, but do they have to be at every corner? Okay . . . So the environmentalists would feed me and I wouldn't say anything, I wouldn't disagree or agree with them, I'd just take their food and blankets and toilet paper . . . I liked being on that tree, with my thoughts . . . At night when all the activists and police officers and TV Crews would go home, I would pee . . . and it was like making rain. I howled and it felt good to be part of the wind. I rubbed my hands and made fire. I stretched out and I felt connected to the earth. I became the four elements. Earth, fire, water, and wind . . . I envied that tree. It had roots . . . I had none . . . I felt so disconnected to everyone . . . Things really got serious when the manager from Starbucks wanted the whole fiasco to end before they opened the coffeehouse, so he hired a private detective to investigate my life and he dug up my fiancé and convinced him to come plead for me to get off. My fiancé said he would take me back and forget the whole thing. Basically forgiving me for being temporarily insane . . . After he was done begging and making a fool of himself I assured him that I would not be getting off and I would make the tree my permanent home. The activists cheered . . .but I didn't really mean it. I was just pissed off at him thinking he was coming to rescue me . . . After two months of being up on that tree, I begged God for a miracle . . . I didn't want to get off and disappoint all those wonderful people who devoted their lives to saving trees and the earth. I also didn't want to get off and face my life, but I couldn't go on pretending I was an environmental activist. I couldn't go on pretending I wasn't a coward running away from my life.

EXCERPTED FROM

BOYLE HEIGHTS

Joséfina Lopez

Character: Dalia (female), thirties.

An actress and bohemian poet recites one of her poems.

Dalia: My father came to the U.S., he entered not by
the island where the lady stands tall,
but by the dark and cold borders,
divided by rivers, fences, and wild mountains,
filled with rats, snakes, coyotes, and border
patrol officers waiting for you to fall.
It wasn't until the fourth attempt did he manage to
find work and not get caught.
The money he earned he sent back.
Back to the little *pueblo* where we remained.
On an unexpected night my mother came to my
bedside and said:
"We're going."
Going where?" I curiously asked.
"To join your father *en la ciudad de*
Los Angeles!"
"Angels?"
We left at night trying to stay out of sight.
We took a bus, then a train, then a bus again.
The journey took three days and a lot of hours
of dreaming, of my father, and the clouds, the
angels, the music, and the golden gates.
I kept staring at the wheels of the bus waiting
for them to lift us up to the sky.
I truly believed we were going to heaven.
We had reached Los Angeles, but we were still
on earth.
This isn't heaven, but it is my home.

EXCERPTED FROM

BOYLE HEIGHTS

Joséfina Lopez

Character: Dalia (female), thirties.

Dalia recites a poem to her estranged boyfriend.

Dalia: Craig, I guess I'm just shocked to hear from you. It's been
three months . . .You want me back? . . . Yeah, I love you too,
but I gotta tell you . . . I've been doing a lot of thinking and a lot
of writing and I wrote you a poem. You want to hear it? Okay.
Let me read it too you. This is dedicated to you.
It's called "My low Self-Esteem Days."
Si te quise fue porque I had low self-esteem.
If I swore I'd always be by your side,
Was because I had nothing better to do.
Si te dije you were a great lover,
Was because I had nothing to compare it to.
If I said you and me were meant to be,
Was because I thought I couldn't find any better.
Si te dije que te amaba con toda mi alma,
Was because I hadn't found myself.
If you think that now that time has passed
And my low self-esteem days are gone,
That I'm a bitch, a whore, a liar
Well then go ahead!
Cause you ain't my master, my father,
My hero, my lover . . .
Shit! I ain't even gonna bother . . .
To address your remarks.
Time has proved me stonger,
 I don't need your approval any longer.
So, today, I ain't even gonna bother . . .
To let you know how good it's been . . .
Without you.
Goodbye, Craig.

MATTHEW LOPEZ

About the Playwright

"I don't know if you need to belong to a certain group to tell a story," says playwright Matthew Lopez. "If you did, I would only write about gay Puerto Rican guys who live in Park Slope and have an obsession with stinky cheese."[47] Lopez' success as a playwright is unlikely: a native Floridian with equal parts Latino and European heritage, Lopez trained as an actor before stumbling upon an idea for a historical drama that would become one of the most-produced plays in the nation. That play, *The Whipping Man*, features a subject matter that would seem far afield from Lopez' background. Set just after the American Civil War, the play is about a Jewish Confederate soldier and two ex-slaves who were raised Jewish. The success of the play only underscores Lopez' immense talent as a playwright. His characters may or may not share his ethnicity, but he writes with a theatrical flair and a gift for character-based comedy that appeals to all audiences.

Lopez' subsequent work draws favorable comparison to his predecessors in the theatre, echoing the devastatingly skewered characterization of Christopher Durang (*Zoey's Perfect Wedding*) and the lovingly bittersweet nostalgia of show business days gone by (*Somewhere*) reminiscent of Neil Simon. As audiences and theatre artists discover that Lopez' work feels like a fresh take on familiar traditions, they'll also uncover brilliantly sensitive characters whose stories and relationships provide great rewards in performance for both actor and audience alike.

List of Plays

The Whipping Man
Somewhere
Reverberation
Zoey's Perfect Wedding
The Sentinels
The Legend of Georgia McBride

Playwright Information

Website: http://www.matthewlopez.com

---

47   Felicia R. Lee, "Writing the Play His Curiousity Led Him To," *New York Times*, 27 January 2011.

PERFORMING THE MONOLOGUES

Somewhere is a dance-filled, heartfelt drama, and its characters are not afraid to dream the big American dream, or break into to song or dance. Both monologues offer the actor an opportunity to dive into deeply felt dialogue and compelling storytelling. The actress who tackles Inez should be aware that the role was written for and originated by Tony award-winning Broadway veteran Pricilla Lopez (the playwright's aunt, and the original Diana Morales from the play *A Chorus Line*). This character is an upbeat dynamo, a Puerto Rican Mama Rose or Mother Courage, who drives the story. In the re-telling of her story, it is imperative to remember that Inez must get her children to dream with her. If the selection is too long there are alternative endings at "But you can call me 'Pepe'" or "And we dance."

Alejandro, Inez' son, is a dancer: make sure to physically engage while exploring this selection. Notice the active language: "swing, run, not stop." Honor the punctuation in this selection and you will begin to embody a man whose ideas are building one upon the other.

EXCERPTED FROM

SOMEWHERE

Matthew Lopez

Character: Inez (female), fifty.

Inez comes home to her tenement apartment on West 66th Street in Manhattan. It's a summer night in 1959, and she has been working at a nightclub, following her shift as an usher in the Broadway theatre where the original production of West Side Story is running. She shares a late night drink and a classic family story with her eldest son, Alejandro. They have done this before, but tonight she tells this story to open Alejandro's heart and convince him to return to his passion for dancing.

Inez: It is July 15, 1936. El Escambrón Supper Club in San Juan, Puerto Rico. My younger sister Juanita drags me there because she's in love with the new singer and she wants to sit near the front so he will notice her. In truth, I do not want to be there. I want to be home asleep, not dressed up pretending I'm having fun. I am ten years older than my sister. At this point in her life, she doesn't understand the importance of a good night's sleep. But I do.

I am what the people of the time call an "old maid." Twenty-nine and unmarried. It's not that I haven't had offers. Back home, on my father's small farm in the mountains of Puerto Rico, many young men wanted my hand. But none of them captured my heart. I knew there was only one man for Inez Maria Crespo de Victoria and that none of these *jíbaros* were him. My other sisters—there were twelve of us, all girls—laughed at me, called me a foolish romantic as one by one they married men who made them fat and miserable. But eventually I began to feel foolish. How was I ever to meet this supposed man up there in the mountains? Before I had time to answer that question, the Depression came to Puerto Rico. For girls like me—unmarried and poor—the only way to survive was to leave our farms and villages for the cities like San Juan and Ponce and look for work. I left with Juanita. We worked at a factory, scraping labels off of bottles in soapy water. My fingers were always cracked and bleeding and my back always ached. We lived in a rooming house and shared a double bed with three other girls, one of whom was always farting in her sleep. And I don't mean genteel little whispers of air but loud, bullfrog horn blasts that would shake the bed and wake you up to choke on the smell of rotten eggs and the promise of death. These were the kind of farts that made you lose your faith in God, do you understand what I am saying, *niños*? Anyway, on this night, Juanita wanted to go out and to show me her new love. There is no reason on earth why I should have said yes to her. But a voice inside me said "GO!" and I always listen to that voice.

And so we went, to hear this singer.

It is an elegant club, straight out of the movies. The lighting is perfect and the crowd is beautiful. Everyone is happy. And yet none of it turns my head. I am almost ready to tell Juanita I want to go home when the bandleader introduces the new singer we have come to see. A spotlight comes on and suddenly, through the curtains, out steps the singer. He walks to the microphone, his tuxedo so perfectly fitted, his smile powering the room with electricity. He starts to sing, and I am carried away. The rest of the world disappears. It is just him and me and the song he is singing.

Then, suddenly, I am pulled back to earth by my sister, who pokes me on my arm. I look around and see everyone in the room on their feet, applauding. The singer bows, blows kisses and walks offstage and people start to dance and Juanita tells me how rude I am for not applauding the man of her dreams. How could I tell her? How could I even try to put into words what has just happened to me? What I am feeling? What I am now certain of? That the love of her life is actually the love of my own? And that she brought me here not to meet her future husband, but mine?

Before I can answer any of those questions, I look up and standing there before us, more handsome than Douglas Fairbanks, is the singer. He introduces himself: Cristóbal Francisco Ubiles Candelaria. But you can call me "Pepe."

"I couldn't help but notice you weren't applauding. Did you not enjoy my performance?"

I look at him and tell him the kind of truth that sounds like a lie: "I enjoyed it so much I forgot to applaud."

"Perhaps you just don't care for my singing."

"If I didn't like it, I would have applauded."

And with that, he extends his hand, I take it and he leads me to the floor. I don't dare look at Juanita as we go.

The first thing I notice is his cologne, that magical smell that is Pepe. I've never met a man who smells like your father.

He guides me around the dance floor and in that moment it is as if we are the only two people in the world. He asks me about my past and tells me of his dreams for the future, his dream of being a big bandleader in New York. To be a great singer and dancer on Broadway and in films.

To be the biggest star the tiny island of Puerto Rico has ever produced. He has dreamed these dreams since childhood and you can tell, looking into his beautiful green eyes that these dreams are still just as real, still just as wonderful as the day he first dreamed them. How could anyone not fall in love?

He then asks about my dreams. He looks at me, smiling, staring deeply into my eyes and I answer with the truth: that my dreams were his dreams and that I started dreaming them tonight.

He smiles.

He laughs.

He stops dancing.

He kisses me.

"What dreams we'll dream together, my love."

And we dance.

We are a family of dreamers. We force the world to look like our dreams. We do not force our dreams to look like the world.

EXCERPTED FROM

SOMEWHERE

Matthew Lopez

Character: Alejandro (male), twenty-two.

Alejandro reveals his secret dream to escape New York City to his younger brother, Francisco. It is 1959, and they are on the fire escape of their soon-to-be-torn-down apartment in a tenement on W. 66th Street. The lights have been turned off, Alejandro is a little drunk, and they are escaping the summer heat.

Alejandro: Let's get outta here. I mean forever. Let's get out of this city. Let's go explore the world, like Pop does. I get it now. I get why he left. They came here so full of dreams. And look what it got them. This city beat him down, made him a dishwasher instead of the star he thought he deserved to be. Dream smaller, they told him. Dream smaller until you can't see your dreams anymore. Until they're so small they slip through your fingers. That's what this city does to a man with dreams.

(Pause)

When I was a kid, I used to think that all the fire escapes in this city were connected, that if I crawled out that window and out onto this fire escape, I could swing from building to building until the city ended and I was free. I wanna do that, Cisco. I wanna run up this fire escape and swing to the next one and not stop until I see trees. And grass. And wide-open spaces.

MELINDA LOPEZ

ABOUT THE PLAYWRIGHT

"I love actors, and for me the experience of going to the theatre is 98% about the actors and what they do to me as an audience member and what they are doing to each other," says Melinda Lopez, a writer and performer who is just as well-known in her adopted hometown of Boston for her many roles on-stage as her award-winning playwriting. "That's how I approach my writing. I'm always thinking about what would be fun for someone to do."[48] Born to Cuban parents and Spanish grandparents, Lopez integrates history and identity into plays that crackle with frank, humorous dialogue and fully realized characters that represent the complexity and contradictions of their particular historical situation. Lopez writes that much of her work is about "being Cuban and American at the same time. It asks the questions we ask every day: What's the cost of living in a free country? What do we owe our country? Decades ago, we asked them in Cuba; now we ask them here."[49]

Lopez also embraces a wide variety of genres and styles, with plays reflecting her own interests in science *(From Orchids to Octupi: An Evolutionary Love Story)*, the lives of teenagers *(the musical Gary)*, and traditional theatrical classics *(an adaptation of Blood Wedding)*. No matter her style or subject matter, her plays reflect her ability to hone instinct and intellect into rich and vibrant theatre: "August Wilson, who was a huge inspiration for me . . . said that when you're in that writing mode, everything becomes fuel. I think a lot of the way I write is like a Rubik's cube—I have all these pieces and I keep rearranging them and seeing how they might be fun together."[50]

LIST OF PLAYS

Midnight Sandwich/Medianoche
Sonia Flew
Alexandros
Caroline in Jersey
Orchids to Octopi: An Evolutionary Love Story
Becoming Cuba

48 Bobby Steinbach, "Meet Melinda Lopez: Playwright, Equity Actor, and Mom," Actors Equity Association News and Media, 1 December 2006. http://www. actorsequity.org/newsmedia/news2006/Dec1.MelindaLopez.asp

49 "Sonia Flew: Study Guide." Milagro.org. http://www.milagro.org/5-History/ Study-Guides/web_sonia_dramaturgy.pdf

50 Steinbach, "Meet Melinda Lopez."

PLAYWRIGHT INFORMATION

For all rights including amateur and stock performances, please contact: Mary Harden, Harden-Curtis Associates (212) 977-8502

PERFORMING THE MONOLOGUES

Both selections are from *Becoming Cuba*, Melinda Lopez' powerful drama about a family confronting the reconstruction of their country as it struggles for independence. Knowledge and research of the time is imperative to an understanding of the play and the characters' struggles. The play traces the history and conflicts of the birth of Cuba's independence from Spain and ends with events leading up to the Spanish-American War, 1895-1898.

The female selection introduces us to the imagined wife of legendary warrior, Hatuey—an important icon for Cuban independence. In the play, Hatuey's wife represents the marginalized. Melinda Lopez craftily constructs a monologue that comically explores the very serious consequences of colonization. Note the use of lower case in the opening thought, and be specific with this possible incantation, summoning, vow, and/or prayer. Make sure to find the tonal shift on "Everyone says that I was enamored."

In the selection for a male actor, we meet Manny, who is no stranger to fighting for a cause. Time or the lack thereof is very important in this selection. Manny, his sister Martina, and the American journalist (Davis) will leave tonight for the front, but not without first attending opening day for the baseball season. It is imperative that the actor keeps the stakes high. This is no ordinary baseball game they are going to, and baseball is more than just a pastime. Baseball is in their blood, and this might be there last bit of joy before returning to the front.

EXCERPTED FROM

BECOMING CUBA

Melinda Lopez

Character: Hatuey's Wife (female), thirty-five.

Hatuey's Wife, a Taino warrior queen with a Union City sensibility, testifies.

Hatuey's Wife: to understand me, you have to remember me
let me rest in a corner of your mind, as I was, dressed in leather and flowers, a warrior queen. A mother.
Everyone says that I was enamored of the men who landed that day. White as ghosts, with yellow hair and silver skin. That I thought they were gods.
Seriously? Have you white people looked at yourselves? Have you been to a beach lately? White people are so ugly. For real! Like they're radioactive. All skin peeling off and hair plastered to their faces by the sweat. Why do you sweat so much? Skinny, anemic looking, all pasty and pale.
Gods? What kind of god gets a sunburn?
No, I wasn't thinking they were beautiful. I knew they were men. I could see that. Deformed under all the armor. I thought they must be hideous to cover themselves like that. We have a man like that, and we never let him out of the cave where he lives. The sight of his body is offensive. I though the white men were like him. Maybe they had been cast off from their land of beautiful brown people—too many of them to keep tied up, so the queen sent them away in this spaceship, over the ocean.
I felt sorry for them.
I invited them to dinner. Cooked up a big vat of frijoles. 200 partridges on a spit. Wild boar. Yucca and maduros. Garlic and lime juice. They came, they ate. And then they killed us. Yeah. I know. For real. While it was happening, I thought, this is the worst party ever.

BECOMING CUBA

Melinda Lopez

Character: Manny (male), twenty-eight.

*Manny is a soldier and revolutionary on a supply run
to his sister's pharmacy/apothecary in Havana, Cuba.
The season opener baseball game is about to begin.
He recalls with delight the last time Madrid played
Havana, the last game before the war broke out.*

Manny: Picture it, Davis. Three years ago. Almost to the day. Stadium's full. Havana Club against Madrid. And that Spanish team—they're good. They got a guy from Canarias—Domingo—Domingo—
Domingo Santo—the guy is the size of a horse. Long arms. Reach up twelve feet to catch a ball. Guys from Granada, those gypsies are fast. But The Club, it's just their year, you know?
—Bellán is pitching better than ever. He's tall and dry, like a walnut tree. Carries holy rooster blood in his pocket—a little vial—and it gives his balls more balls.
Martinez and O'Higgins bat in 4 runs apiece, and the Club leads 8-3. Top of the ninth. Bellán strikes out the first guy looking. Second man tagged at first. The game is three hours old and the Spanish Vice Consul gets up to stretch his legs. He's not going anywhere, mind you, but the crowd doesn't know that. The Cubans— the fans, you know, don't like that. Someone boos. Someone else throws something—
—and all of a sudden, the militares are up, flanking this guy—guns out—Dead silence. We're about to massacre this Spanish team, and all of a sudden, assholes are pulling guns—
Dead silence. Everyone is holding their breath—and out of nowhere, this voice—just one voice—*Viva Cuba! Viva Cuba Libre!* The crowd goes nuts. Bellán pitches, the ball goes flaming past the hitter, strike three! Just as two Cubans in the crowd tackle these goons—take them out—and before you can say Jack Russell Terrier, there's a riot. People flying through the air, military trying to hustle the Vice Consul out-- The teams on the field—just stand and look at the crowd—don't know what

to do—until the Spanish bench rushes Bellán and the Cuban bench comes back swinging—

They called the season a draw. Our coach moved to Tampa. Within two weeks, we were back in the war.

Biggest mistake they ever made. Half the guys in my regiment? Baseball players. You run fast. You swing at anything that moves. What's the difference?

EDUARDO MACHADO

ABOUT THE PLAYWRIGHT

Born in Cuba, Eduardo Machado came to the United States as a child, his family fleeing the Castro regime and eventually settling in California. After studying as an actor, Machado eventually turned to writing and directing for both stage and screen, and since 2004 has served as the artistic director of the INTAR Theatre in New York City. A writer of over forty plays, he is a champion and pioneer of North American theatre, and influential as playwright, director, and teacher.

"There's always someone in my plays who is on the outside looking in," says Machado about his work.[51] His plays often focus on issues related to the cultural and political history of Cuba and Cuban-Americans. Machado, who maintains his Cuban citizenship, resides and teaches in New York City, and also lives as an openly gay man, is in many ways the ideal vehicle to articulate the many complexities of Cuban identity, as he has "repeatedly mined his complicated feelings about the island, Fidel Castro, his family's exile and the American embargo for material examining where the personal and the political become inseparable."[52]

But Machado's plays are far from didactic or academic: his stories are the places of ghosts and poetry, as much the stuff of dreams and memories as an actual time and place, overflowing with specific and sensual detail and with tremendous appeal to actors and audiences. "I think you can't teach anyone to be an artist," says Machado, "but I think you can have them concentrate on the essentials of art. [Ingmar] Bergman said that the reason why he can write all those movie scripts and direct all those plays and be who he is because he can close his eyes and remember every smell in his grandmother's house when he was six years old. And I think those are the essentials of art; having the sensorial ability to create a world." [53]

LIST OF PLAYS:

Rosario and the Gypsies
They Still Mambo in the Streets of Rio

51   Stuart Spencer, "Eduardo Machado," *BOMB Magazine 30* (Winter 1990). http://bombsite.com/issues/30/articles/1292

52   Daniel M. Gold, "Complicated Emotions, Spurred by a Trip to Cuba," *New York Times*, 13 April 2010.

53   Ulrika Brand, "A Master Playwright Teaches His Discipline: An Interview with Eduardo Machado," *Columbia News*, 28 June 2001. http://www.columbia.edu/cu/news/01/06/eduardoMachado.html

The Modern Ladies of Guanabacoa
Broken Eggs
Fabiola
When It's Over
Why to Refuse
Once Removed
A Burning Beach
Don Juan in N.Y.C
Wish You Were Here
The Day You'll Love Me (translation, adaptation)
Stevie Wants to Play the Blues
Related Retreats
In the Eye of the Hurricane
Across a Crowded Room
Breathing It In
Closet Games
Three Ways To Go Blind
Between the Sheets
Kissing Fidel
The Day You Left Me
Crocodile Eyes
Havana is Waiting (formerly *When The Sea Drowns In Sand*)
The Cook
Havana Journal
That Tuesday
The Flag
Rich Women
Sacred Rhythms
Poet Matador
Celia's Funeral (with Carmelita Tropicana)
The Conductor
Secret Tapes
In Old Havana
My Sister
Paula
Crossing the Border (one act)
She Could Not Weep
That Night in Hialeah
Embroidering
Fiancés
See Emma Run
The Spanish Lesson

When It's Cocktail Time In Cuba
The Perfect Light
Cabaret Bambu
Finding Your Way
How I Found My Way Back to Rosario
In Paradise

FILMS:

Exiles in New York (also directed)
Crossing the Border
The Ship

TELEVISION:

Home Free
Her Name Was Lupe
China Rios
Hung (HBO)
Magic City (Starz)

PUBLICATIONS:

Tastes Like Cuba: An Exile's Hunger for Home (with Michael Domitrovich)
The Floating Island Plays

PLAYWRIGHT INFORMATION

Faculty Website: http://ddw.tisch.nyu.edu/object/MachadoEd.html

PERFORMING THE MONOLOGUES

Time is the element the actor must pay attention to in the selection from *Havana is Waiting*. The plane is about to depart and Federico wants to board the plane; but as time to return to Havana approaches, his obstacles are revealed. The actor is given many rich opportunities to pursue actions towards his objective of returning home. It is clear that Federico wears his heart on his sleeve and his emotions are complicated.

In *Fabiola*, we meet an equally compelling character. Sonia's world is falling apart and the rules of her environment are changing quickly. There is no doubt that her pregnancy and leaving everything she has known behind is taking a toll on her. The important question for the actor approaching this selection is "Who am I?" Researching the upper class lifestyle and social rules of 1950s Havana, Cuba is imperative to understanding Sonia's relationship to status. Sonia is justifiably scared, and has a lot to lose.

EXCERPTED FROM

HAVANA IS WAITING

Eduardo Machado

Character: Federico (male), forties.

Federico is a writer and professor, a slightly flamboyant man. This is New York City, 1999. Fred has come to fetch Federico to the airport but fear has gripped him. Responding to his question, "Why can't you return?", Frederico answers:

Federico: Fred, I told this story too many times, to too many people. So many that by now it should have lost all its meaning, but it hasn't. Did they throw me out, or did I walk out. Was I abandoned or did I set myself free? I do not know the answer to that. Was I thrown out, or did I walk away from my country? Did I decide to leave, or was I tricked?

There is an airport in Havana where I learned the meaning of impotence. I saw my mother on the other side of the glass. She let me go on a plane without her. It could have been forever. I held my brother's hand. I was nine, he was six. I handed over my blue aquamarine ring to the militia. My brother wet his pants. My father did not treasure us. They searched my butthole for diamonds. My brother sucked his thumb. And the world spinned around in the opposite direction and the wind carried us away. And I floated. Without a voice . . . nothing was recognizable. And I made up somebody new. And I survived. That little boy with the militia prodding his ass. That's what's waiting for me. Back there . . . down there in Havana. That's home. You want me to get on a plane and go back and face that. Help me. Okay, buddy?

FABIOLA

Eduardo Machado

Character: Sonia (female), twenty-five.

A Spanish mansion in Guanabaca, Cuba, a beach town near Havana. Sonia, eight months pregnant, passes the time in the ballroom with the family servant and her mother-in-law. Sonia leaves for America the following day and is worried about her new life.

Sonia: I'm ashamed to arrive in Miami Beach in 1961 wearing clothes from 1954. Everything's changed so much. I wonder what color beach towels Osvaldo bought. And if we have dishes, do they match? Clara wrote me that her house was furnished with what other people didn't want, that nothing matched, not the towels or the dishes or the sheets. And Conchita, Miriam wrote me that they don't have bidets.

I was taught on what side the knife should be, what side the fork, how to waltz, how to butter my bread little piece by little piece, that you must have good penmanship, how to embroider, to be a good Catholic, to be kind to people who work for you, to have faith, to honor my husband, to obey my father . . .

What good is it going to do me in a country where they don't even have bidets?!

I will always remember how to make floating islands. First you make an egg custard with milk, cornstarch, and three eggs. And a teaspoon of vanilla, of course. Then, the syrup: a cup of sugar to two cups of water, and brandy to taste. While it's cooking you make the meringue: two tablespoons of sugar to each egg white and a little cream of tartar so they stay firm and fluffy. I know how to make them the right consistency so they stay firm. When the syrup starts to boil, you throw in the custard, one spoonful at a time. Then you put a spoonful of meringue on top. If you're lucky they'll float. Little islands, like Key Biscayne. I can always get them to float.

(she starts to cry)

And tomorrow, I'll go and when I'll see you again, I'll never know. Isn't that scary?

ROGELIO MARTINEZ

About the Playwright

In the program notes to one of his plays, Rogelio Martinez asks "How does one return to 'ordinary' life after experiencing extraordinary things?"[54] Born in Cuba, Martinez came to the United States in 1980 as part of the notably extraordinary Mariel boatlift. That profound shift in the life and mind of a young boy is something that he still connects to his playwriting:

> *As I was leaving the boat, I was given a can of Coca-Cola. I tried to open it but I couldn't figure out how to work the tab. Around me, dehydrated Cubans were all trying to figure out how to open these cans. That vision stayed with me for years. Twenty-five years later I wrote a play called Fizz about Roberto Goizueta, the head of Coke during the New Coke disaster and a Cuban immigrant himself. I realized that to tell Roberto's story I didn't have to look far. Roberto's story is my story. It's the story of finding your piece of the American dream and not being able to completely understand it or experience it.[55]*

Though Cuba, Cubans, and Cuban-Americans are a part of many of Martinez' plays, he's just as comfortable writing about the universal issues of his time: urban conditions, the end of the Cold War, imtimate relationships in a technological age, and sports from baseball to ping-pong. A former student of Eduardo Machado (who has directed many of Martinez' plays) as well as playwright Romulus Linney and director/deviser Anne Bogart, Martinez is now a teacher himself, while continuing to develop new work with companies across the United States. "Theatre needs people to come together at a certain time in a certain place," says Martinez. "The more technology distances us from one another, the more theatre becomes a necessity. It's not going to go away anytime soon. History has already proven this point."[56]

---

54 Jeff Foust, "Review: When Tang Met Laika," *The Space Review*, 22 February 2010 http://www.thespacereview.com/article/1567/1
55 "Rogelio Martinez, MFA," Goddard University, n.d. http://www.goddard.edu/people/rogelio-martinez. Retrieved 30 December 2013.
56 "20 Days with 20 Playwrights: Rogelio Martinez, Day #1," Kanjy Blog, 29 July 2013. http://blog.kanjy.co/20-days-with-20-playwrights/rogelio-martinez/

LIST OF PLAYS

Elk Cloner
Wanamaker's Pursuit
When Tang Met Laika
All Eyes and Ears
Fizz
Learning Curve
I Regret She's Made of Sugar
Arrivals and Departures
Union City . . .
Displaced

PLAYWRIGHT INFORMATION

Faculty website: http://www.goddard.edu/people/rogelio-martinez

PERFORMING THE MONOLOGUES

In each selection from Rogelio Martinez, we meet families turned upside-down by events in Cuba, and characters that have experienced betrayal. In *Arrivals and Departures*, we are caught in the tensions of family dynamics. Don't miss the absurdity within the play. The stakes are high for Celin and he is determined at all costs to be the one in his family of writers to tell their story.

Illuminating Veronica introduces us to a very pregnant Veronica who's willing to take part in Fidel's vision for Cuba. Hopeful for the future and yet not fully prepared for the cost of taking part in the experiment, she, like Cuba, is a work in progress. Within the monologue it is important that the actor approaching the text fully embody the words "duty," " leave," and "belong," as these are part of her complex and lived experience.

EXCERPTED FROM

ARRIVALS AND DEPARTURES

Rogelio Martinez

Character: Mayito (male), late thirties to early forties

*Mayito left Cuba when he was young. He's become
a successful writer in America, but has now returned
to his family home in Sancti-Spiritus, Cuba. He has
his father's ashes and he's hoping that recalling his
childhood will relieve his suffering from writer's block.
Speaking to his brother, who is also a novelist, he shares
a bit of his life and reveals the complicated relationship
he shared with his father.*

Mayito: Every few months father would have me over to read to him
from his work—the work he'd done before he left this country.
He was going blind and he wanted to know the sum of his life.
I felt sorry for the old man, but one day by his bed I saw a copy
of some new book he'd been reading. He wasn't blind after all.
Just wanted to make sure I understood I was only half the writer
he was. I said nothing. Instead, I read to him that night but more
than that, I listened. I listened carefully to his words. The old
man was a good writer. No doubt. What was I going to say? I
ripped a page out when he wasn't looking. Afterwards I called
my wife. We were already separated. I read it to her and told
her I'd written it. I wanted her to know just how good I was.
My wife left me for another writer—a food critic with a perfect
body, which doesn't make sense. On top of that he knows several
languages, loves to go riding and she told me all these things
the night we decided to separate as if to say, when you've done
all those things come back and then we'll talk.

EXCERPTED FROM

ARRIVALS AND DEPARTURES

Rogelio Martinez

Character: Celin (male), late thirties.

*Celin is a Cuban novelist returned to his family home
in Sancti-Spiritus, Cuba. He asks his estranged sister
to consider his brother's actions. He begs her to align
with him and let him return to the family home where
he might have a chance of writing.*

Celin: Look at all these reviews. His writing—according to the
critic—has only gotten worse from one novel to the next. Did
you know that? That attention to detail—the situation—not the
same as it once was. Our Writers Union. They keep files on
writes from abroad. I'm only using their resources. Look at this.
His last book. They didn't just say it was bad. They said it read
like a work in progress. Our brother is an opportunist. He thinks
that by coming back—they—the critical establishment—the
Public—will start to take him seriously again. I'm not going to
let him use us. He has no right to come in here and use us for
some novel and then just take off.

Love me. I want you to tell me that you love me more than
him. I saw this American film once. This woman- she had to
make a choice. One would live; one would die. If you had to
make that choice. There she was with her two children and only
one would live. The other would be taken from her. It's typical
American melodrama but I was bawling because at some point
in our lives . . . at some point someone chose . . . I can't keep
lying—all this crap about choosing to stay because I believed
in this thing, Marxism—they chose for us. We have been lying
to ourselves. They chose who went, and who stayed. So now
I'm just asking you to choose me—do what my father never
did. Would you please—

We have to stick together. Look; I want to move back in. As if
I never left. I think I can get work done here. I was happy once.
Let me come home. I want to be happy again.

EXCERPTED FROM

ILLUMINATING VERONICA

Rogelio Martinez

Character: Veronica (female), early twenties.

The Cuban Revolution has arrived and Veronica's family including her father have left for Miami. Veronica has chosen to stay behind. Living with strangers in what once was her family's home, she remembers and reflects.

Veronica: Isn't it funny how you can forget something that meant so much to you growing up? Waking Papi up every morning. Duty. The duty I feel toward my family. I haven't felt that way in a long time. Maybe I should move out. Let someone else live here. Funny thing is growing up I didn't want to be here. I saw a postcard of a town in the United States. There was some snow on the ground and I knew that's where I belonged. I ran to my father and told him I wanted to leave. I was five. I told him I wanted to leave this house. I wanted to go to a place where everyone walked on clouds. He didn't know what I was talking about so I showed him the postcard. He said it wasn't a cloud they were walking on but water. And I said, even better. So he smiled and took me to the ocean. He threw me into the water and yelled for me to walk. And as much as I tried I couldn't. He demonstrated the impossibility of what I wanted. There is no such place. This is it. I either sink or swim. My father must be senile. He now believes in things he once told me were false.

OLIVER MAYER

About the Playwright

"Love matters," says Oliver Mayer in an interview. "It's worth fighting for. It's also messy, unexpected, dangerous. If you don't get it right, people can get hurt."[57]

The plays of Oliver Mayer are at times brutal and surprising, aggressively masculine but never lacking in sensitivity and nuance. Writes one critic, "Mayer takes muscle, and spirit, and courage from his Latino/Chicano culture, a gift which informs the action of his dramas but which allows his dramaturgy to be closes to contemporary playwrights Sam Shepard and Edward Albee. His characters have music in their blood that comes from their playwriting creator."[58]

The son of an Anglo father and a Latina mother, Mayer's intercultural sensibilities allow his characters to emerge with a great complexity that is often even beyond their own comprehension. Best known for *Blade to the Heat (Filo el Fuego)*, set in the world of boxing, his plays reflect the real world of human relationships and identity that reach audiences from all walks of life.

List of Plays

FULL-LENGTH PLAYS:
Blade to the Heat
Members Only
Fortune is a Woman
Wallowa: The Vanishing of Maude
LeRay
The Wiggle Room
Dark Matters (Materias Oscuras)
Laws of Sympathy
Dias y Flores
Bold as Love
The Righting Moment
Conjunto
Joy of the Desolate
The Road to Los Angeles
Ragged Time
Young Valiant

---

57 William Anthony Nerrico, "One Last Conversation with Oliver Mayer and William A. Narrico," *The Hurt Business: Oliver Mayer's Early Works* [+] Plus (San Diego: Hypberbole Press, 2008): 208.

58 Howard Stein, "Oliver Mayer: An Appreciation," from *The Hurt Business*: 12.

Joe Louis Blues
Gog

SHORT PLAYS:
Flash Play
Gun Play
The Man
Vegetables
Bananas and Peachfuzz
Oki Dog
The Chess Machine

OPERA:
America Tropical (David Conte, composer)

CABARET:
Rocio! In Spite of It All

TRANSLATIONS:
Filoel Fuego (Blade to the Heat)
The Entremeses of Cervantes
Materias Oscuras (Dark Matters)

PLAYWRIGHT INFORMATION:

Website: www.oliver.mayer.com

PERFORMING THE MONOLOGUES

Oliver Mayer's work is very physical and demands that the performer engage his or her body throughout these monologues: mastering the process of tension and release will make these very effective audition pieces. The physical choices and presence the actor brings to the roles are imperative. The space must be defined by soul, body, and mind—in both the literal and abstract sense.

Vinal's monologue from *Blade to the Heat* features a boxer who has literally been backed into a corner because of his own verbal assault against some of his peers. His entire worldview is shaped in terms of combat within the ring, his focus clearly fixed on his opponent's weakness, and he's happy to hit below the belt (verbally) if it will give him an advantage. The actor playing this part must commit to the character's raw brutality, while not ignoring the subtle ways in which Mayer allows Vinal to betray his own deeply buried fear of inadequacy and failure.

The images of stillness and movement in Sherezad's speech from *Dias y Flores* help situate the character who lives in a world that seems to be spinning so much out of control she has become transfixed. The unexpected discovery of something beautiful, connected to a powerful childhood memory, has provoked both a literal and figurative purging, as she emerges from a place of safety and secrecy to a place of danger and honesty. Try to explore the ways in which strong, physical choices with your body and voice can illuminate this powerful transition.

Excerpted From

BLADE TO THE HEAT

Oliver Mayer

Character: Wilfred Vinal (male), twenties to thirties.

Vinal is a Nuyorican boxer who, despite losing in the ring to the beloved Cuban-born champion Mantequilla Decima, made news by calling his opponent a "maricón" on television. Adding to this, he called current champion Pedro Quinn a "maricón," triggering an explosion of gossip and innuendo. Cornered by Quinn's trainer, Vinal explains his reasoning.

Vinal: You mean that *maricóncito*? . . .It's obvious, man. You can see it a mile away . . . . Look, you in the ring with a dude, you get to know him all kinda ways. Like if he eats garlic, or goes heavy on the greasy kid stuff, or if he don't wash under his arms so good. You get to know these things. You was a fighter, you know this. Gimme a little credit here. You come to a stinky gym like this for a reason. It's always something. Some assholes, they just like to fight. Other guys, they got to prove something. The little ones, they got a complex. Big ones, they got a complex, too. Some of these clowns like to beat on other guys to impress the chicks, like it'll make their dick bigger or something. Then there's the other kind. They here 'cause they like the smell of men. They like to share sweat. They like the form, man. The way a dude looks when he throws a blow, his muscles all strained and sweaty, his ass all tight bearing down on the blow, his mouth all stopped up with a piece of rubber, and only a a pair of soaking wet trunks between his johnson and yours. They like it. And they like to catch a whupping for liking it. That's just the way it is. I'm surprised, man. I thought you knew the business, oldtimer. Evidence? What do you want? Pictures? Come on! I'd fuck him! I'd fuck you. I tell it the way it is. If some dude wants to go down on me, bring him on! I'll fuck anything! But ain't nobody fucking me. I draw the line, baby! . . ..You go for the other guy's weakness, right? Am I right? He got a cut eye, you gonna hit him in the elbow? Come on! You jam your glove in there, you rip the fucker open. Tell me I'm wrong. *(silence)* When I fought Decima, that piece of trash called my mamita some dirty-ass names. I got mad, I din't fight so good. Okay, he found my weakness. I can live with that. I love my *mami*. But I vowed to God I'd get him back one way or the other. That's how I turned the fight around. All it takes is a single word. Hey, one look at him and I knew that macho crap would make him go crazy. Guy like that is stupid enough to think we really care where he sticks his two-incher. He ain't so great as everybody thinks. So, a little word, I got his mind messed up. And then I kicked his ass! I shoulda got that decision, too! I wuz robbed, baby! I wuz robbed! *(beat)* But the guy to worry about is Decima, not Quinn. Quinn is what he is. But I'll bet Decima is a little confused . . .Only need to say that kinda shit once. It sticks. Like glue. Like a cheap suit. Hey man. It's business. You talk to me when I'm champ, maybe I'll throw a few bucks your way . . . if you bend over. *(blows a kiss)* So long, *maricón. (exits)*

EXCERPTED FROM

DIAS Y FLORES

Oliver Mayer

Character: Sherezad Diaz (female), thirties to forties.

Reeling from yet another romantic failure, Cuban-American Sherezad visits her brother in New York's Loisaida (lower east side). There, on 13th Street between Avenues A and B, she finds herself at the Dias y Flores Community Garden, where she meets Silvio, a beautiful young Cuban trovador with a guitar who sings songs of love. Sherezad, behind bushes, pees.

Sherezad: *RABIA*. Oh what a filin. Like this kid in junior high, wore a long coat even in the summer, acne, the whole shebang. He never spoke. Lunchtimes he'd take his sandwich into the bushes and eat it like an animal. He was a freak, except . . . . except he could play. Rachmaninoff. Liszt. When he thought no one was listening, he'd play the piano till he was drenched in sweat. Nobody knew but me. Because I was hiding in the bushes, listening! Lost in the romance, the filin! And here I am back in the bushes. Like an animal. Listening to the romantic stuff. Lost in the music. I'm in the middle of an ocean of stories and I can't fucking swim! Fate is a bitch. With this *RABIA* stuck in my throat. And I can't stop talking. Something wants to come out of me but it's stuck in the back of my throat and it won't let go!

(She hacks from behind the bushes. Silvio stops playing.)

I think maybe we're moving a little too fast. I mean you're beautiful, marvelous, fantastic. But I'm coming off a major crack-up. I'm in shock, I'm concussed. I'm NUMB! My heart is . . . FUZZY, and my head never was too clear to begin with. Plus I'm not really there. So we're definitely moving way too fast, aren't we?

(She emerges.)

Or are we moving anywhere at all? I talk and talk and all you do is play Cuban songs in the sun like any young man should. I came in here of my own accord. I brought my pain in here. And I'd never in my right mind think of you . . . the way I'm thinking of you. It's the song! The song is in my blood! And I'm a Jersey Girl! I thought Billy Joel was in my blood, I mean, SING US A SONG YOU'RE THE PIANO MAN, right? I'm the piano man! But I'm feeling shit I haven't felt since, I dunno, a long time!

RICHARD MONTOYA

ABOUT THE PLAYWRIGHT

"We can dance and sing and do musicals which is fine, because we're going to need that," says playwright, filmmaker, actor, and theatre artist Richard Montoya. "Or we can be artists that reflect our times."[59] Drawing inspiration from a wide array of contemporary writers and traditions, his plays come to life as a kaleidoscopic array of iconographic characters, poetry and music, theatrical and philosophical in-jokes, historical resonance, political skepticism and a dignified respect for both human suffering and hope.

Montoya is an eighth-generation American who grew up in an artistic and activist family: his father José was a noted poet and founder of the Royal Chicano Air Force, a Sacramento-based art collective that has been producing and presenting work since 1970. Montoya himself is one of the founders of the theatrical company Culture Clash, who began performing in San Francisco's Mission District in the mid-1980s. The combination of performance art, sketch comedy, and ironically rendered representations of cultural types gave unique voice to the tensions of the time. "There were Nicaraguans. Salvadorans. It was the height of civil strife in those countries," Montoya recalls. "The Farm Workers Movement, the Chicano movement . . . nobody really wanted clowns."[60]

The work with Culture Clash has blossomed into a career across film, television, and theatre. A frequent collaborator with other writers and companies, Montoya's plays combine the raw energy of patiently and precisely devised ensemble work, a nuanced understanding of the world of the audience, and the singular and compelling vision of a playwright dedicated to the beauty and betrayal of language. They are also intricately tied to their settings—neighborhoods, cities, and borders—while still managing to speak to our most profound connections to the imagined and possible spaces of theatrical storytelling. "In a hundred years, these all might be empty, cavernous places," says Montoya of theatres. "I don't think the future is that bleak. But I'm ready for that. And I'm ready for a mansion on the hill. I don't know which one is coming, but I'll be writing plays still."[61]

59   Anthony Werner, "Interview with Richard Montoya," *Howlround*, 11 February 2011. http://www.howlround.com/interview-with-richard-montoya
60   "Richard Montoya: 25 Years of Laughing About Race," *All Things Considered*, 14 August 2009. http://www.npr.org/templates/story/story.php?storyId=111893905
61   Werner, "Interview."

LIST OF PLAYS

Solo works:
Water & Power
The River
Palestine, New Mexico
Federal Jazz Project
American Night
The Ballad of Juan José
Anthems
Culture Clash in the District
With Culture Clash:
Radio Mamba
Nuyorican Stories
Chavez Ravine
A Bowl of Beings
Bordertown
Mission Magic
Carpa Clash
The Mission
Culture Clash in Americca
The Birds
Peace
Film and Television:
Water & Power (Sundance Institute)
A Bowl of Beings (PBS)
Culture Clash (Fox)

PLAYWRIGHT INFORMATION

Company website: http://cultureclash.com/
Nola Mariano: nola@circuitnetwork.com

PERFORMING THE MONOLOGUES

Montoya's unique storytelling weaves together music, spoken word, dance, and humor to highlight the social, cultural, and economic diversity that is past and future California. His characters speak poetically— fewer words, stronger images—and he arranges words to have the most impact, making for unforgettable characters and selections that are sure to wow. There are ghosts in these works—colonial ghosts who continue to haunt the continent of the

Americas. This is not just a poetic idea but a real and practical one when thinking of border towns, Indian reservations, barrios, and prisons. When performing poetry, remember that the actor needs to be able to handle the ordinary and then extraordinary within the space of one line. Honoring the punctuation and noting when lines are short and/or then long will create the music in the selections. Balance the musicality without losing track of the thought.

In *The River*, we meet Esme, whose journey begins and ends at a river of mourning. Her story carries with it the weight of all those who have made the journey north. Note when she becomes poetic: normal language is not sufficient for her metaphysical and emotional needs. *Federal Jazz Project* is Montoya's love letter to San Diego, honoring the musicians, war veterans, and two sisters named San Diego and Tijuana and their FIVE SONS all named RAFA and their relations ship to each other. Experiment with as much range as possible because JR is speaking from the heart about war, loss, anger, and grief. There should be swirling build and a place to go. Unlike *The River*, THIS IS NOT POETRY. It should be treated as a stream of connected thought and monologue-like in its peaks and valleys. For audition purposes, an alternate ending can be found at "I was a fool."

EXCERPTED FROM

THE RIVER

Richard Montoya

Character: Esme (female), twenties.

Esme, still in Mexico, longs for Luis, her husband—a day laborer gone missing.

Esme: The River he left me standing in the middle of . . .
 (There is a sound: Real. Lovely, low tones, waves, water . . .)
The River that ran north from here
from the dirt of our front door
stained with tears of my hope and my LUIS long gone.
The River that runs past the dull rows of buses with
people without destination hidden deep in song.
From the still water I weave only loneliness and want.
Measuring the distance of memory plowed into faithless air,
waiting for the day when he will return or the day I must
leave.
And no one will know my name.
When the night comes calling you cannot hear me then Luis,
Amor, it won't be the same.
Water in his lungs when he wrote his final letter to me.
The road that runs North from my door stained with yesterday,
and my dream gone wrong.
Words and River joined together.
Each breath haunted, ghosts within . . . Luis? Si mi amor . . .
Luis?
Do not allow the current to carry you away . . .

EXCERPTED FROM

FEDERAL JAZZ PROJECT

Richard Montoya

Character: JR (male or female), twenties.

> *JR is a young marine and the grandchild of "Tijuana"
> who ends up in an opium den in the Chinese Quarter
> Mexicali, Mexico. In response to El Poeta, the narrator,
> who asks, "Your Tíos, these men the RAFAS they want
> to know how have you been?" JR responds:*

JR: How have I been?
Oh I'm okay but let's see . . .
I medicate.
I hurt.
I destroyed.
I defended.
I protected.
I serve.
I honor.
I pledged.
I occupied.
I colonized.
I know.
I was there.
I am a ghost.
I buried.
I eulogized.
I apologized.
I agonized.
I secured . . .
I covered . . .
I inoculated . . .
I have no fucking iPhone apps for any of this!
I abide.
I carry your cross.
I submit.
I soldier.
I survive.

I cannot breathe.
I suffocate.
I believed.
I don't care.
I blessed.
I objectified.
I care too much.
I yearn. I hunger.
I bleed.
I cut.
I don't exist . . .
I fix.
I stay jacked up.
I stay down.
I concuss.
I wait.
I hurry.
I yearn.
I don't care.
I care.
I took life.
I gave life.
I no feel pain.
I feel.
I lay in excrement in VA hospitals . . .
I don't want to live.
I can.
I can sir.
I'm cancer.
I am left behind.
I can't get out.
I was hope.
I pinned the badge.
I was crushed.
I was a fool.
We will pray for you son . . .
Fuck that.
I shit on you.
I don't forgive you.
I have guns.
I am fully loaded.
I am ready.

I sing death-songs.
I gave life.
I took life.
I have killed.
I am obsolete. Expendable.
I could not pull it off.
I am a shadow.
I took the long way home.
I was cannon fodder.
I busted a nut.
I got this.
I don't got this . . .
I carry the world in a rucksack
I possess the junkie seed.
I am a junky. Just like you. Abuela . . .
I hurt my son.
I hurt my wife.
I hurt my Family over and over . . .
I'm by myself,
I am good to go then,
To drive my bike into a wall going one hundred
And twenty fucking miles an hour so I can feel
something.
Rip flesh from my bones and feed a
Hungry Memory built of lies . . .
Lies over there. Lies brought back here.
Here. *(pointing to his temple)*
Oh yeah! Fuck it. *(laugh)*
I can hear my Master's voice.
He says I died over there but didn't know it.

CHERRÍE MORAGA

ABOUT THE PLAYWRIGHT

A poet, essayist, and activist who grew up in Southern California, Cherríe Moraga is known in cultural circles far beyond the world of theatre. Her characters are often driven by equally important but sometimes conflicting impulses, passions, and truths, partially reflecting Moraga's own interest in exploring issues of sexual identity, ethnicity, and culture. She proudly identifies herself as a Xicana, a term which signifies that her lineage is not one of a foreigner in a strange land. "It is way for Mexican-Americans to claim their indigenous origins here," she explains in an interview, "as opposed to being Italian-American, for example, an immigrant population. We are actually native to the Americas . . . it's framed my feminism, it's framed my queer identity."[62]

Identities that emerge through the collision of internal and external forces are central to Moraga's plays, many of which feature characters who undergo profound transformation. As a result, her plays have proved popular and resonant beyond their initial publication and production. Writing about her play *Giving Up the Ghost*, one critic explains how the play "continues to acquire critical social meaning precisely because Moraga utilized the stage not as a place for forgetting, but for remembering, for drawing attention to the continuing erasure of Chicana/o cultural landscapes and presences by policy makers, popular culture, and the public at large."[63] Her characters literally and figuratively embody their own individual and collective stories, revealing themselves not through happy endings and answered questions, but through a constant redefinition and rediscovery of the self in the moment.

LIST OF PLAYS

Giving Up the Ghost
Coatlicue's Call /El llamado de Coatlicue
Shadow of a Man
Heroes and Saints
Heart of the Earth: A Popul Vuh Story
A Circle in the Dirt: El Pueblo de East Palo Alto
Watsonville: Some Place Not Here

62 "Cherríe Moraga Talks About Identity," LINAR, Rutgers University, interview by Patricia Munoz. http://www.youtube.com/watch?v=1UF2fu5GZtw

63 Lorenzo Garcia, "The Border Logics of Adolescent Development in Cherríe Moraga's Giving Up the Ghost," *Youth Theatre Journal* 23:2 (2009).

The Hungry Woman: A Mexican Medea
The Mathematics of Love
Digging up the Dirt
New Fire

PLAYWRIGHT INFORMATION

Website: http://www.cherriemoraga.com/

PERFORMING THE MONOLOGUES

Moraga's *Watsonville: Some Place Not Here* is set in California
in the 1990s and was created after a series of interviews with members of the Watsonville/Palo Alto community. The play addresses
the treatment of immigrants and their families. The ultimate *cuen-
tatista* (storyteller), Moraga captures the politically charged situation
through the eyes Jo Jo. Notice the gliding together of words such
as "allovasudden." This not only gives the actor an idea of how the
character speaks, but also insight into Jo Jo's mind, which is racing
a mile a minute. This selection is extremely active, and has a great
progression to the final moment, where Jo Jo's thinking shifts and
he reveals his greatest fear (note the shorter sentence structure).
There is a great opportunity for the actor to effectively showcase
his versatility within this piece.

In *Shadow of a Man*, we are introduced to an equally compelling character. Leticia is on a mission: she must break free from the
confines of the "Marianismo"[64] values of passivity and sexual purity
that her mother has imposed on her. She is not afraid of challenging her mother's ideas and choosing her own path. Note the poetic
description of her act, "like a person opens their arms to take the
whole world in," and the repetition of the word and play on being
"worthless."

---

64   For more on Marianismo, see *The Maria Para*dox, by Rosa Maria Gill, D.S.W.,
      and Carmen Inoa Vazquez, Ph.D. (New York: Penguin/Perigee, 1997).

EXCERPTED FROM

WATSONVILLE: SOME PLACE NOT HERE

Cherríe Moraga

Character: Jo Jo (male), fifteen.

Jo Jo, Mexican-American, is speaking to an older family friend, Chente. The stress of the ongoing strike—and the new law which prohibits illegal immigrants and their children from obtaining employment, education, social services, and non-emergency medical care—has closed down his school and threatens his family's future.

Jo Jo: Our principal's a punk man. He said he was trying to prevent "further violence." Shit, we didn't even really wreck nuthin, not compared to how we was feeling. I dunno we were just kinda stunned. After they made the announcement, everyone just dropped and looked around the room at each other. It was like allovasudden we were trying to read in each others faces who was "legal" and who wasn't. Thinking real quick about who had an accent and who didn't, who dressed like a Mexican, who brought tacos to school, stupid stuff like that. It was crazy the stuff going on in our minds. And then it was like everybody in the class jus allovasudden got scared and really pissed off all at once. And I could see that the teachers was kinda scared too, like he didn't know what to expect from us. And without sayin' nothing, we all just got up out of our desks and ran out to the grounds outside, and then into the streets. Everyone was shouting and crying and hella pissed off and hurtin'. The whole school was out there. Just kickin' down trashcans, climbin' up on bus shelters, jus' screamin' and hittin' things out of bein' so mad. My mom's only got fake papers. I'm scared Chente. I don't wanna go back to Mexico. I never even been to Mexico.

EXCERPTED FROM

SHADOW OF A MAN

Cherríe Moraga

Originally published in *In Heroes & Saints and Other Plays*.
Albuquerque, NM: West End Press, 1994. © 1994 by Cherríe
L. Moraga. All rights reserved.

Character: Leticia (female), seventeen.

*A Mexican-American college student arrives home very
early still wearing her outfit from the evening before.
Her mother inquires about her activities and Leticia
opens up about this milestone in her life.*

Leticia: I thought of you tonight. I thought of no longer being your
daughter, that what I was gonna do . . . would turn you away
from me.

There they were, the Raza gods with their legs spread, popping
beers, talking *revolución* and those things, each with its own
life, its own personality and I wanted to taste them all. Each
and every *fruta*. *Una joya*, you would say.

(Pause.)

So, I opened my legs to one of them, Mamá. The way a person
opens her arms to take the whole world in, I opened my legs.

It's not about love. It's power. Power we get to hold and caress
and protect. Power they drop into our hands, so fragile, the
slightest pressure makes them weak with pain. I was tired of
carrying it around . . . that weight of being a woman with a
prize. Walking around with that special secret, that valuable
commodity, waiting for some lucky guy to put his name on it.
I wanted it to be worthless, Mamá. Don't you see? Not for me
to be worthless, but to know that my worth had nothing to do
with it.

CARLOS MORTON

ABOUT THE PLAYWRIGHT

"Too often play development and theatres in general are all white or all black or all Chicano," said Carlos Morton in 1989. "If we are truly to become a multicultural society, then we need to begin mixing in our art. What better place to see the new humanity than on that stage that reflects all the faces with all their beautiful colors."[65]

Morton was born in Chicago (his family name had been changed from "Perez" by his Mexican grandfather). As a young man, he studied improvisation with Second City, where he realized that "the actor could also be the playwright."[66] Morton became involved with the Chicano movement in El Paso before discovering El Teatro Campesino and studying with Luis Valdez, and later found work with the renowned San Francisco Mime Troupe. With his background in comedic theatre, journalism, poetry, and activism, Morton's early work is playful and political, a "high satire of Mexican and Chicano history . . . exploiting all the humor that can be derived from outrageous stereotypes and linguistic and cultural misinterpretation."[67]

The breadth of Morton's work reveals a playwright who is equally comfortable with drama and the reality of everyday life. Whether the intent is comedic or dramatic, Morton aims to provoke his audience to a deeper understanding: "An author writes because he has something to say to the audience, there is something the community has to deal with . . . that's part of my political theatre training. I don't write just to make money or get laughs, although I don't mind getting laughs or making money. But these reasons are not why I write."[68]

LIST OF PUBLICATIONS

The Many Deaths of Danny Rosales and Other Plays
  (Arte Publico Press, 1983/1987/1994)
Johnny Tenorio and Other Play (Arte Publico Press, 1992)
The Ficle Finger of Lady Death and Other Plays \
  (Peter Lang Publishing, 1996)

---

65   Carlos Morton, "Celebrating 500 Years of Mestizaje," MELUS 16:3 (Autumn, 1989-Autumn, 1990): 20-22.
66   Lee A. Daniel, "Interview with Carlos Morton," *Latin American Theatre Review* (Fall 1989): 143-150.
67   "Morton, Carlos (1947—), *The Greenwood Encyclopedia of Latino Literature*, (Santa Barbara: ABC-CLIO, 2008.
68   Daniel, "Interview."

Rancho Hollywood y otras obras del Teatro Chicano
(El Milagro/Arte Publico Press, 1999)
Dreaming on a Sunny Day in the Alameda (University of Oklahoma
Press, 2004)
Children of the Sun: Scenes and Monologues for Latino Youth
(Players Press, 2008)

PLAYWRIGHT INFORMATION

Faculty website: http://www.theaterdance.ucsb.edu/people/
academic/carlos-morton

PERFORMING THE MONOLOGUES

The female selection is from *El Jardin*. The play is an excellent example of the short dramatic form popularized by Teatro
Campesino. Morton created the "superacto," short plays with a
powerful political punch and superb writing which any actor would
love to wrap their minds and hearts around. *El Jardin* is based on
the Christian story of Adam and Eve, but in this form it is ahistorical
and timeless. Note the contemporary language and how Morton's
dialogue flows easily from English to Spanish. The setting is anywhere that the realities of the cultural experience exist—maybe El
Paso, Nogales, Chicago. Although Eva could be played like a stock
character, Morton's writing requires an actor capable of finding the
playwright's wit and the truth.

Silvery Night is Morton's adaptation of a short story by Tomás
Rivera. Tomás is a young Mexican boy in a migrant camp somewhere in Texas. The moon is full and his imagination gets the best
of him. It is important to remember that there is another character in
this selection, the audience. Tomás confides, performs, and reveals
moment-to-moment the events of the night from a child's eyes. His
world is heightened. The moon is a bit more silvery, the grass a
bit taller, his home a bit further, and the devil a bit scarier. Trust in
Tomás's world by allowing curiosity to lead you. The child has very
little past and does not fret much about the future. No affectation
of child behavior is necessary but rather a deep understanding of
motivations and perspective. Be sure you understand and pronounce
the Spanish without a *gringo* accent.

EXCERPTED FROM

EL JARDÍN

Carlos Morton

Character: Eva (female), child bearing age.

Eva is in paradise with Adán, but she is curious; her hormones and a deep need to go shopping are more powerful than the voice of God.

Eva: "In the beginning there was nothing . . . " just what is that supposed to mean?
Why can't I eat the Fruit?
I'm tired of eating nothing! Why can't I have some carne asada and some hot salsa, frijoles and arroz? I'd even settle for a hamburger with French fries. Or a tequila sunrise! He said I could start with dessert.
Don't you see! He's the big ranchero. We're nothing but peons!
I love you, *te quiero mucho*. But it is only a love between brother and sister. I want to love you more, I want to love all of you!
Why are you blushing?
No, don't go, stay here with your *mamasota*!
Why can't I have my own way
Why do I have to stay
Here in the green *jardín*
Sure it's a calm place
Larks sing, gazelles race
It hardly rains at all
Fruit from the trees do fall
Creatures both large and small
Love one and they love all
We always sleep late
Angels guard the gate
It never gets cold here
Nothing can be sold here
But I need more than this
More than complacency
Or smug security
I want to dance, I want to shout
I want to leap, I want to fly out

But more than wanting to go
Most important, I want to know!

EXCERPTED FROM

SILVERY NIGHT

Carlos Morton

Character: Tomás (male), ten, Mexican.

Tomas: I always wanted to know what the devil looked like. In the Christmas pastorela Don Rayos played the *diablo*. He wore a black cape with a black mask made of tin and red horns. *¡¡Hijoles!! ¡Que susto!* If you saw him in an alley, you'd run like hell! *De volada!* But I'm not afraid of *el diablo*, and tonight, I'll call him out, van a ver.
(He starts to walk.)
First I have to walk out past the other shacks in the migrant camp, past the outhouses, out by the alamo grove. I can't even see our house from here. Que house *ni que mi abuela*, it's more like a chicken coop. *¡De veras! Mi familia y yo somos* migrant workers, who follow the pisca from Tejas to "Iuta." That's where we're headed, Iuta. Where is Utah? *No sé, dicen que está* somewhere near Japan, *por allí.* Better be careful where I step in this tall grass, could be . . . Uhh ohhhh! Something swirling around the grass! Is it a snake! *¡¡Hay diosito!!*
(looks at the clock)
It's midnight. *A ver, ¿cómo lo llamo?* God, what if he appears? No, it can't be. Besides, he can't do anything to me, I'm not dead yet! All I want to know is if the devil really exists or not. Because if the devil doesn't exist, then there's no . . . . I'd better not say that. I could be punished. *Chihuahua!* How do you call the devil? *(clearing his throat.) Diablo! Pingo! Chumuco! Lucifer!! Satanas!! Chupacabras!!!*
I don't hear anything, do you? Maybe I'm not trying hard enough. I got to get into it. Come out *mentiroso, atascado, borracho, asesino! Chingate pues! Yo tu madre, que está en vinagre!! Nada, absolutamente nada.* I knew it, there's no *diablo*, he doesn't exist!

christopher oscar peña

ABOUT THE PLAYWRIGHT

christopher oscar peña can't help but defy easy labels, with plays that range from short monologues to multi-ethnic ensemble pieces. "As American playwrights of color, we are often told what we should be writing, restricting our work to simplistic ideas of race and class politics," he says. "That expectation assumes we're all the same, and—most problematically for me—it creates a theatrical culture of inauthenticity. There are amazing Latino playwrights writing about these subjects; they're true and important to them. But when you force me to do that, you're perpetuating a lie."[69]

peña was born and raised in the San Francisco Bay Area, "a land filled with the children of all types of immigrants who didn't feel different from each other because our differences made us alike."[70] Educated in Southern California and now residing in New York City, peña's work focuses on the complex cultural and interpersonal struggles of his own generation, urban and suburban Millennials who struggle with relationships, technology, ideology and identity with both brutal clumsiness, and unexpected grace. Perhaps one day, peña will be recognized as one of the first playwrights to see a character's fluidity as a central defining element: they yearn as much for the journey as the resolution, and seem to find peace in the perpetual surfing of transience as much as they might in traditional notions of stability and constancy.

LIST OF PLAYS

Full-length:
maelstrom
the suicide tapes
i wonder if its possible to have a love affair that lasts forever? (or thingsi found on craigslist)
l(y)re
icarus burns
a cautionary tail
alone above a raging sea
TINY PEOPLE (or, it gets better)

69   A. Rey Pamatmat, "My Parents Were Tiger People: christopher oscar peña chats about writing race with A. Rey Pamatmat," *Howlround*, 19 May 2013. http://www.howlround.com/my-parents-were-tiger-people-christopher-oscar-pe%C3%B1a-chats-about-writing-race-with-a-rey-pamatmat

70   Pamatmat, "My Parents."

awe/struck
Short Plays:
snow storm
(inhabit) the same place
and the rain . . . and the rain . . . and the rain . . .
DIRTY DEEDS
however long the night
we support the troops
what came after

PLAYWRIGHT INFORMATION

For all rights and inquiries, please contact:
management:
Henry Huang, Station 3
1051 N. Cole Ave, Suite B
Los Angeles, CA 90038
310.204.4444
henry@stationthree.com

PERFORMING THE MONOLOGUES

"You are the master of your own destiny. You want something. You have to go out there and grab it by the balls," is Liam's credo in *icarus burns*. peña's pointed and phrased contemporary writing provide the actor with a wonderful opportunity to do just that—jump in and take the thought on. This is not a speech to linger in, but to allow the thoughts to build, one upon the other. This character is smart and witty and his thinking is fast. The pace of monologue will reflect his clear forward thinking. He only slows down towards the end as he reflects on his family and his identity.

In *(inhabit) the same place*, peña takes us to maybe a memory, maybe a dream, and maybe to a world not as we imagine it but as it is for the person living in it in that moment. In the play, peña describes this woman's experience as:

> *she hears the birds chirping*
> *and feels the cool breeze even as the sweat suffocates her*
> *she sees the clouds moving and feels the warmth of the sun*
> *and feels the presence of GOD*
> *and hears the voice of her child*

247

the voice that brings a smile to her heart
the voice that brings a smile to her face
because this woman
she hears the hope in everything we don't.

It would be wise for the actor to note the use of the poetic and the ordinary in the space of one line and how this adds rhythm and texture to the piece. The associations of words and images cannot be just literal, but should allow us to enter this woman's exhilarating emotional life. If the selection is to long an alternative ending can be found at, "and I am everywhere."

EXCERPTED FROM

ICARUS BURNS

christopher oscar peña

Character: Liam (male), thiry-six.

*A wealthy investment banker of Latin American descent,
possibly Honduran, Liam is a first generation American
with no distinguishable accent. It is right before and
right after the 2008 election, in Los Angeles, California.
He is having lunch with his liberal gay brother and his
brother's partner. Tension runs high, and Liam turns
to the not-so-safe subject of politics.*

Liam: No, of course not
    Im not a total racist
    I like the guy
    He seems smart, ambitious
    Heart in the right place
    But that hope thing?
    I don't buy into that bullshit
    It's too much for me
    He may be a nice guy
    But you know what he still is?
    A politician
    And yea yea, I'm a liberal
    I believe in abortion, and gay rights, and all that jazz
    But at the end of the day I believe in capitalism
    I believe in red, white and blue and green
    But above all, i believe in green
    This isn't about race any more kids
    It really isnt
    Some of us like black people, some of us like white people,
    some of us like the asians and
    the mexicans
    And some of us dislike each other
    But you know who EVERYONE hates?
    Poor people
    Everyone hates poor people

Even poor people hate poor people
At the end of the day
It doesnt matter what color you are
Or what your accent sounds like
Or who you're fucking
At the end of the day
All that matter is how much you're packin'
Im talking dick and balls but i'm mostly talking wallet boys
That's the way of the world boys
Nothing will ever command respect the way the dollar bill will
So at least when it comes to money
Im staying republican
I'm a darwinist
Survival of the fittest
Our father immigrated here
From a third world country
Honduras
One of the poorest in the world
With no high school education and no connections
And no money and no jobs
And look at us now
If he could do it
Anyone could
Survival of the fittest

EXCERPTED FROM

(INHABIT) THE SAME PLACE

christopher oscar peña

Character: Latina (female), twenties to thirties.

An indeterminate Latina, with a heart of gold, in an indeterminate country, working in a sweatshop and taking a break. She lets us in on the secret of why she works happily for pennies a day.

Latina: One day I saw a picture
    And in the picture there were these kids
    And these kids
    They were
    They were somewhere beautiful
    Somewhere with clouds like cream
    Somewhere with mountains like giant sculptures
    Somewhere that is not hot like here
    But cool
    Cool like water
    Como agua en mis labios.
    Cool like the breeze after your first true kiss
    And the boys they were wearing the hats
    Hats like the ones I make
    And I thought—I thought maybe I made that hat
    That hat is mine
    So now when I make hats
    They are like my babies
    Mis chicos
    And I hold them gently
    I pull the thread carefully to make sure that it is tight
    That it is strong
    So that it can live a long time
    Survive
    You understand that
    survival
    And into every hat I put
    I put my soul
    my life
    My being you know

Into it
With a kiss
Un beso
You see
I may not be able to afford traveling from this place
See Washington
or paris
Or españa
Or nueva york
But when my hats leave
They travel
Everywhere
And they take me with them
I am in those hats
I AM those hats
In this way I am here
I am nowhere
And I am everywhere.
　　　(She pulls out a hat she has been working on)
This hat says padres on it
And my son
Mi hijo
He says padres are a team
Un grupo
In San Diego
He says they are *fútbol*
Or I think *béisbol*
You know the *béisbol*
Padres
But I think he is wrong
Padres
Fathers
I think this hat
This hat is a guide
A father
Maybe it will take care of somebody one day
I wonder.
　　　(A loud horn announcing end of break)
Lunch is over
Thank you for listening
Vaya con Dios.

GUILLERMO REYES

ABOUT THE PLAYWRIGHT

Born in Chile, Guillermo Reyes' twenty-plus years of successful playwriting can be partially attributed to his enthusiastic and irreverent embrace of culture as seen through the eyes of a bold and determined immigrant. Much of his work focuses on characters who consider themselves larger-than-life figures who seem more interested in revealing their imagination through role-playing despite living otherwise normal and mundane lives in the American southwest. Although it might be easy to see these figures as comedic stereotypes, Reyes ensures that his characters remain dignified and filled with emotional dimension. "Although he may use kidding as an effective cover-up," writes *The New York Times*, "Mr. Reyes is dead serious when writing about the artist's spirit, determination and resilience, especially in the resistance to lures, distractions, and dopey criticism."[71] That statement also speaks to Reyes' characters who don't necessarily inhabit comedic landscapes: he's written with equal passion about the political history of Chile, the shooting of Arizona Representative Gabrielle Giffords, and issues of civil and human rights.

A professor at Arizona State University who teaches courses in playwriting, screenwriting, and the history of the Academy Awards, Reyes is also focused on the development of new work by younger writers, serving as Director of the Arizona Centennial New Works Series. As both a writer and teacher, he believes that to be effective, an artist must be attuned to all the possibilities of the present moment. "Versatility is key," he says in an interview. "In an age when it's possible to post your dramatic writing to YouTube, we need to learn beyond genres and understand the core of the dramatic—and not develop prejudices against one genre or another."[72]

LIST OF PLAYS AND PUBLICATIONS

Published in anthologies
We Lost It at the Movies, published in Vaqueeros, *Calacas and Hollywood,* Bilingual Press, 2013
Deporting the Divas, published in *Gay Drama Now*
Cambria Press, 2013

71   Aivin Klein, "Where Writers Really Live: In the Imagination," *New York Times,* Nov. 9, 1997.
72   "Interview with Guillermo Reyes—ASU Centennial Project." July 12, 2011. http://ptnewworksfestival.wordpress.com/2011/07/12/interview-with-guillermo-reyes-asu-centennial-project/

Miss Consuelo and Places to Touch Him, published in *Borders on Stage,* L&S Books, 2008

Chilean Holiday, published in *Humana Festival 1996* Smith and Kraus, 1996

Deporting the Divas, published in *Asking and Telling: A Collection of Plays the New Century.* Applause Theatre and Cinema Books, 2002

Other Published Plays

The Hispanick Zone (L&S Books, 2014)

Men on the Verge of a His-Panic Breakdown (Dramatic Publishing Company, 1998)

Men on the Verge Two (*Gestos* magazine, *Theatre Journal*, 2007)

Saints at the Rave (in *Best Stage Scenes,* Smith and Kraus, 2003)

Dead Bolivians on a Raft (in *Coming to America: The Immigrant Project,* Smith and Kraus, 1999)

Produced Plays

Mother Lolita

Madison

Sunrise at Monticello

Little Queen

A Southern Christmas

Sirena Queen of the Tango

Book

Madre and I: A Memoir of Our Immigrant Lives (University of Wisconsin, Madison, 2010)

PLAYWRIGHT INFORMATION

Faculty website: http://herbergerinstitute.asu.edu/directory/selectone.php?ID=370

PERFORMING THE MONOLOGUES

Reyes' pieces usually feature long-form monologues. The characters' point of view conveys the story to the audience—so the actor plays the role of narrator as well as character. Thoughts are revealed through an objective, subjective, and sometimes omniscient voice. His monologues are best suited for actors with presence and personality to spare as there are lots of quick changes in body language, attitude, and gender. Honor the punctuation in Reyes' selections; use it as a guide to unlock the comedic timing. Also, all roles in the pieces provided are played by male actors (even if the characters are female).

The first two selections are from Reyes' 1996 play, *Deporting the Divas*. Reyes gives a brief synopsis of the play in the text of the playscript:

> *A Border Patrolman finds himself in an affair with an un-documented young Mexican man, making him question his various assumptions about masculinity and legality. The Divas in his imagination are beautiful and fabulous and give him refuge from his life as a closeted, married man, also challenging him towards a new form of thinking.*

Deporting the Divas is a quick-witted and chock-full-of-one-liners comedy. This comedy is based in truth, not contrived invention. This teacher really needs this job and she would defend her thesis with her dying breath. Don't allow this clever writing to usurp the actor's process. The actor should be specific about whom they are speaking to, and choose strong actions in pursuit of the character's objective. Trust that the laughs will come from the actor's ability to emotionally reveal, not sell the joke.

Reyes' *Men On The Verge Of A His-Panic Breakdown* is a series of comedic monologues offering a panorama of Latino gay life. Thematically, the piece chronicles the lives of various Latino immigrants dealing with transcultural shock of race and gender identity known as the "Hispanic breakdown." Edward's breakdown consists of not being Hispanic enough. It's tough to be a fabulous Latino actor passing for Anglo who gets a Latino part and now has to come to terms with his real identity. In order to nail the truth of the piece, it is best to not be cool, or small. Edward is passionate and his truth is big. The piece will move quickly: don't let the inherent speed and rhythm override the understanding of the piece. Find and honor the timing and stay grounded in the moment. If auditioning with this selection, it is not necessary to mime or use a phone. The hotline can be directed outward as if one was talking to an omnipresence. The accent can be flavored, but as in any good acting the audience is much more interested in *what* you say not *how* you say it. Audiences do not want to see your skill with the accent (although that is good too). They want to see and meet Edward, who happens to speak like a Californian.

EXCERPTED FROM

DEPORTING THE DIVAS

Guillermo Reyes

Character: Teacher (female, played by male actor); twenties to forties.

Desperate for a job, the teacher seeks employment in the San Diego Border Patrol office. She pleads to border patrol rookie Michael.

Teacher: Sorry. I've tried so hard to get Americans to learn English, but they refuse to. Now look, look, look, I'm sure you got a lot of depressed, resentful immigrants being kicked back across the border. But that's where I come in—the friendly Puerto Rican! Mainland Puerto Rican. A Nuyorican. While they wait to get deported, I give my lecture. It'll boost their self-esteem, and these people can then leave the country with a renewed confidence and vigor that'll make them contribute to the society where they came from, and they may no longer need to migrate illegally to this country because a new life-enhancing attitude will give them the focus, the energy, and yes the self-esteem needed to make it in their own country. It's good for you, good for the country, the taxpayers will love it.
So I get the contract?
It's my most innovative workshop since "Reempowerment for Liberals," "Celebrating your Celibacy," "Embracing your Inner Foreigner," and "Joan Crawford for Beginners," very popular in San Francisco. But this time I think I've really done it. This is it! My claim to fame: "Self-Esteem for Immigrants."
Waddy you think, mister?
Please, I need to supplement my income. I teach Spanish for Assimilated Latinos at the City College, never enough enrollments though.
You won't be sorry, mister. You won't be. Thank you, thank you.
I'm . . . I'm an illegal alien, OK? I'm a Guatemalan of German descent, so I pass as they say. I've got no papers.
And move over—I prefer this light.
(light sparkles above her)

That feels good. Reminds me of my days in the sun watching mommy pick lettuce.

Mommy's the one who discovered my unusual talents. On her deathbed, she held my hand and whispered in my ear: "You look like a white woman, *mija*, use it."

EXCERPTED FROM

DEPORTING THE DIVAS

Guillermo Reyes

Character: Teacher (female, but played a male actor); twenties to forties.

Act II of Deporting the Divas opens with Teacher defending her thesis.

Teacher: I'll take a few minutes now to address a very pressing matter—this is the cause of my life, mind you—and I've got petitions for you folks to sign outside—so I'm here to protest the shameful exclusion from the university curriculum of an ignored, cultural minority—no, I'm not talking about Chicano poets. Forget literature, honey. I'm talking about the grand culturally advanced aesthetics of . . . Carmen Miranda.
Who? How dare you? Who, she says. I'm tired of how the film schools of this nation have taken it upon themselves to exclude Carmen—such a shame, such a scandal, it's discrimination against Brazilians, it's plainly Eurocentric. Is it because of the hat? The hat!
Carmen . . . .Oh, Carmen, where is she now? Carmen Miranda. Brazilian bombshell, samba dancer and singer. Big star in the 1940s. Most people don't know this but . . . she was a woman. Yes, she was. No drag queen could have done what she did, awaken the inner goddess in me, well, *(self-conscious)*, in all of us, I mean. All that energy released upon a simple hat.
(wipes away tear of emotion.)
You see, for her it wasn't just a hat. For her, this was an extension or shall we say a cranial appendage much more powerful than any phallus. As you see here, the hat came adorned with rich, ripe, juicy tropical fruits which were, in my opinion, a precursor to the Stonewall riots. The Stonewall riots? As in New York City-queens riot after Judy Garland's death—you see, that bar at Stonewall was well-represented by Puerto Rican drag queens well versed in the Carmen Miranda tradition of fruity hats.
You see, I'm convinced Carmen is the key to finding the answer. Yes, the answer to one of the great mysteries of sexual identity: what's the connection between the gay male and the

259

female DIVA? Carmen, Madonna, Ertha, Diana, Evita, Barbra, Judy, Eartha especially Judy! My theory is: the Diva has been battered, trashed around, used and spat out like a queer or like an illegal alien, or combinations thereof, and yet she has fought back with sweat, guts and tears and continues to occupy a space in our collective.

She's fabulous! Occasionally, she falls from grace, but only to blast from a stereo yet again! She deserves to be worshipped as the spiritual androgynous force of nature that she is!

She is there to redeem our genders and to bless and coalesce them and, at last, we are free to love and dance and taste forbidden fruit.

<small>EXCERPTED FROM</small>

MEN ON THE VERGE OF A HIS-PANIC BREAKDOWN

"HISPANICALLY CORRECT,"

Guillermo Reyes

Character: Edward (male), mid-twenties.

A glamorous man with a California San Fernando Valley accent.

Edward: Hello . . . Is this, like, the Hispanic Hotline?
OK, this is my first time, you know. So, like, I'm supposed to give you the dirt and you're, like, supposed to tell me it it's like Hispanically Correct. Is that right?
OK, so I'm, like, young and I'm like glamorous, OK? And when I first came to Hollywood a couple of years ago I, like, changed my name, I bleached my skin and I started frequenting the trendiest straight bars in town. My name now is, like, Edward Thornhill the Third. Well, never mind my real name. I can barely pronounce it, OK?
OK, so, like, recently this famous American movie actress whose name I couldn't possibly reveal—she like bought the rights to a well-known Mexican novel. And all of a sudden there was this wonderful part for, like, a Hispanic actor, OK? But my agent doesn't even know I'm, like, ethnic. And I have to sneak off to the audition all by myself and I'm really nervous, OK? But once I get there, I'm like really good, OK?
I have a degree from Trish School of the Arts. No, not Tisch School of the Arts—but my friend Trish Lopez from East L.A. has this little studio, where we learn our basic stereotypes, OK? . . .
So Rodge, the Casting Director for the movie, like, he comes up to me and he says, "Wow, we've never seen an Anglo do a Hispanic so good. How do you do it, kid?"
He says, "Congratulations, kid! You're going to become a star!" But then he says, "And all you have to do is change your name to Hispanic."
"But, why?" I ask.
"Because," he says, "all these Hispanic activists will be upset if they found out an Anglo got a top Hispanic part. The only one for the year!"

261

And I have to think on my feet. Think, think, think. Then I finally tell him, "OK, I'll change my name to Eduardo Troncos." And he says it doesn't sound Hispanic *enough* and I can't even tell the asshole it's my real name.

(Begins to become frantic.)

So he goes around the room asking people for better-sounding Hispanic names. And they're all calling: Eddie, Eddie, Eduardo, Eddie, Eduardo, Eddie, Eduardo!

And I finally snap and start shouting at all these people in this horrible high school Spanish— *"Va fuera, va fuera, fuera!" "Va fuera, va fuera!,"* I keep shouting, and someone complains that I'm using the imperative interchangeably with the indicative! "This is no time for a grammar lesson, asshole! *Fuera! Fuera!"*

(Beat.)

And what I'd really like to know is, Hispanic Hotline: Is it, like, Hispanically Correct to, like, shut out the world and deny it all?

(He gets progressively more nervous, as they come to get him.)

I don't want to be connected to all this mess, all these rivalries between people like Mexican versus Anglo, English versus Spanish, woman versus man, gay versus straight, Armani versus Polo. Could I, like, become neutral to history itself and, like, make believe the Treaty of Guadalupe was just another crazy zoning law? Tell me it can be done, Hispanic Hotline! Give me a sign!

CARMEN RIVERA

ABOUT THE PLAYWRIGHT

Her craft honed at Latino-centered theatre organizations such as INTAR and Repertorio Español, Carmen Rivera's plays emerged as part of the burgeoning Nuyorican theatre community that gives unique voice to the cross-cultural experience. "It takes genius to make a dollar stretch," writes Rivera about the heroic nature of her characters. "It takes incredible discipline and courage to stay in school and not go the way of street life; it takes faith and strength to hold on and NOT slip into the cracks."[73] Whatever their situation, the vibrant characters who inhabit Rivera's plays possess fiery self-determination and a passion for connecting to their family and culture.

Embracing a wide array of genres and always exploring the possibilities of the stage to convey real-life characters through heightened emotions and unexpected twists of fate, Rivera made an immediate impression with her OBIE Award-winning debut full-length play, *La Gringa*, which has been produced in both Spanish and English versions, and is the longest-running Spanish language play in Off-Broadway history (*17 years as of 2013*). *The New York Times* noted how the play "captured the spirit of the Puerto Rican experience."[74] More recent plays have drawn inspiration from historical figures in poetry (*Julia de Burgos: Child of Water*), music (*Celia: The Life and Music of Celia Cruz, co-written with her husband Cándido Tirado; La Lupe: My Life, My Destiny*), and politics (*America's Dictator: Rafael Leónidas Trujillo Molina*). Whether drawn from real life, Rivera's own personal history, or from the playwright's raw imagination, the connection between her characters' dogged determination and their quest for finding comfort in their heritage and identity makes them ideal characters to both watch and inhabit on the stage.

LIST OF PLAYS

Full-length plays:
La Gringa
To Catch the Lightning
The Next Stop
La Próxima Parada (Spanish version of The Next Stop)
Julia de Burgos: Child of Water
Under the Mango Tree
Ghosts in Brooklyn

---

73   From the playwright's notes on the original production of *The Next Stop* at INTAR, 1997.
74   D.J.R. Bruckner, "Theater in Review," *New York Times*, 7 March 1996.

Palladium (co-written with Cándido Tirado)
Celia: The Life and Music of Celia Cruz (co-written with Cándido Tirado)
The Transporter of Souls (co-written with Cándido Tirado)
The Magic of the Salsa Kingdom (Dance Theatre)
America's Dictator: The Rise and Fall of Rafael Trujillo
Riding the Bear
LaLupe: My Life, My Destiny
The Loves of My Life

One-act plays:
Julia
The Universe
A State of Bliss
Elena
ameRICAN
Caravan of Death
Plastic Flowers
A Song in the Heart
The Power of Words
Urashima
Betty's Garage
The Nurse
At the Mango Tree
Delia's Race
The Next Cycle
this really happened in Brooklyn
The Park
An Enemy of the People (Adaptation)
Reporting Is Not Snitching
Can't Take It Anymore
Vito Marcoantonio
Rebirth
The Ring
Water Wars

PLAYWRIGHT INFORMATION

Website: http://www.carmenrivera-writer.com/
Agent: Ron Gwiazda, Abrams Artists Agency
275 Seventh Avenue 26th Floor
New York, NY 10001—646-486-4600

PERFORMING THE MONOLOGUES

In *The Next Stop*, Rivera writes about what she describes as the strongest and most valiant people – the people that live in the ghetto, the 'hood, the barrio. The characters in *The Next Stop* speak to the struggle against poverty in America.

When asked about performing the monologues, Rivera offers:

> *In certain circumstances, the characters from The Next Stop might be perceived through a stereotypical lens, one that is incessantly promoted in the media. I created the characters from The Next Stop, with love, admiration, intelligence, humor and respect. They are full-realized, three-dimensional human beings with dreams and fears. I believe that if one is able to capture the dreams and fears of a character, stereotyping is impossible.*[75]

Pay attention and allow breath into the shifts of Tony's thinking. It would be much better to find internal cuts to the monologue than to rush the strong emotional transitions.

In *Julia de Burgos: Child of Water*, we are introduced to the words, imagination, and psyche of iconic Puerto Rican, Julia de Burgos, considered by many one of the greatest poets of Latin America. She died tragically in 1953 at the age of 39. The play occurs between worlds, a surreal place where the dead and living meet, where souls live and die.

In this monologue, we meet Julia at her best—chasing dreams, full of life and excitement, ready to feed the oppressed, feed the hungry, protest injustice, and win a Nobel Prize. Rivera clarifies Julia's position and background for the actor:

> *Julia must leave Puerto Rico. Her mother, whom she loved dearly, has been dead for several years. She taught Julia about the magic and sacredness of nature. Julia's political activities, especially her involvement with the Puerto Rican Nationalist Movement, has forced her to leave Puerto Rico. She goes to the river by her house to say good-bye to her mother. Julia believes that through the river she is able to communicate to her mother. This monologue is based on the historical fact, that Julia did indeed throw her published*

---

75   E-mail correspondence with Micha Espinosa, 2013.

book of poems into the river as a gift to her mother. The Julia we see here is young and wide-eyed but also brave, passionate and sensitive. She willingly faces the consequences of her actions and doesn't back down from the struggle. Julia is a woman who lives her pacifist philosophy and cannot turn a blind eye to the injustices she sees around her.[76]

---

76   Ibid.

EXCERPTED FROM

THE NEXT STOP

Carmen Rivera

Character: Tony (male), early thirties.

Tony is Puerto Rican, a recovering drug addict recently separated from his girlfriend, with whom he has twin sons. Dressed in his best, he hopes today will be the day his luck will turn around. He is en route to win back the affection of his lady. As luck would have it, Tony finds himself delayed on the subway. He is hopeful for his future: if he can just get there, he knows he has a lot of love to give. He shares his story and his plan of action.

Tony: Fighting's not good for kids. Gladys, that's my old lady we tried to not fight in front of the kids. But sometimes it didn't work. You know people just lose it, it's natural. We have twin boys! It feels like a million years ago you know. My Gladys and I fuckin' freaked out, TWINS! You know . . . how we gonna take care of two boys? But it was okay. I didn't leave her, another motherfucker would of but not me, that's my responsibility you know . . .
(pause)
. . . I stuck by her . . .I was even there when they were born, all bloody and shit . . .I was there when they took their first breath . . .here . . .
(Tony takes out photographs from his wallet.)
Here this is Danny, he's like me, friendly, you know, we talk to people, like a good time . . .he's two minutes older than Alex, this is Alex. Alex is like his mother . . .shy . . .quiet, good people. I love my boys . . .And I love her . . .They look like me, right mama? They're fine if I say so myself huh? Man, these guys they're my pride and joy . . .You see Danny and Alex.
(Points to the balloons.)
They ten years old tomorrow. I'm bringing them their presents. I miss them too much. They live up in Boston . . .that's where Gladys went when we split up and everything . . .
(pause)
Yeah . . .Sometimes in life you just mess up you know . . .They

268

been up there for awhile you know. You know I know it's me that fucked up . . .that's what I'm going to tell her, I fucked up and I cleaned myself up.

(He holds back tears.)

That's exactly what I'm gonna to tell her, I admit what I did was wrong, and I'm gonna change. No, no I changed and I'm gonna be responsible . . .That's what a man does.

Gotta be a man you know what I'm saying.

One day Gladys went away and didn't tell me where she's was going. She just disappeared. She finally called me and told me she was in Boston. Then with the birthday of my boys' man, she finally said I could come up and see them. They miss their pops. This is my chance man. To show her that I changed, that I'm clean, employed and we should be a family again. I gotta good feeling about Gladys, you know. Got her roses and candy.

She's my woman, I can't live without her. After all this time and after what we've been through I know it's gonna happen; she was concerned about me . . .what bus to take, where to get it. She wants the family to be together. This is gonna be a great party . . .You know . . .Let me show you something . . .

(He takes out a little box, with a ring in it and he opens it.)

Look at this. It's nice right, this is it, now, I'm a gonna ask her to marry me. I'm a make everything legit.

EXCERPTED FROM

JULIA DE BURGOS: CHILD OF WATER

Carmen Rivera

Character: Julia de Burgos (female), twenty-five.

Puerto Rican Julia speaks to the river and to her mother who has been dead for several years. She carries a book of her published poems and a suitcase. The year is 1939, and she has news to share of a new love, the changing times, and an adventure to come on an island called Manhattan.

Julia: *Mamí, mamí,* I can't believe you're been gone for only several months. I still hear your voice; smell your perfume; I can't fix my hair the way you used to . . . I'm sorry I haven't visited you for two weeks—I've been busy in San Juan. A lot has happened. Look *mamí,* my second book—*Song of the Simple Truth.* I won a prize for it. People in San Juan think I'm pretty good . . . . I can't believe that. I've been meeting all these amazing artists: The Chilean poet Gabriela Mistral and Luis Palés Matos and Clemente Soto Vélez, Juan Antonio Corretjer and Luis Llorens Torres. Can you believe it? A little country girl from the mountains in the same company as Palés Matos. Luis Llorens Torres—he became my mentor—he said he would edit my poems. This is almost too good to be true. Our national poet is going to help me . . . I am spending a lot of time with all these great Puerto Rican artists—we drink coffee, talk about politics, poetry, philiosphy . . .
   (The Mother appears behind the scrim and looks lovingly at Julia.)
—oh—there's going to be another war in Europe—things aren't getting better in the world – ANYWAY um . . . you might not like this – but we are all *nacionalistas* too—we dedicate our writing to the cause of Puerto Rican Liberation—I even got a promotion in the Nationalistic party. I'm the secretary of the party, the whole party. I get to work directly with Don Pedro Albizu Campos, our great leader . . . That's not the only news I have . . .
   God I miss you *mamí* . . . I have something very important to tell you—Um . . . Don't be worried, but I'm going to New

York City. A lot of strange things are happening in Puerto Rico now . . . Don Albizu was arrested and seven other Nationalists . . . it's a little dangerous now, so I think I should leave—for a little while anyway. But don't be concerned for me, really, I won't be alone, I met a wonderful man. He's a doctor from the Dominican Republic, Juan Isidro. He's smart and charming. He's a socialist—committed to the struggle for a better world. I know you say things don't change, BUT I have faith they can. So does Juan. He also says he loves me a lot. We could do a lot of work in New York City . . . The Nationalist movement is very strong there and I can meet many more artists—and I'll have a bigger audience for my poetry. AND Manhattan is also an island—they have rivers . . . this is not really a goodbye— more like I'll see you later. I'm a little scared, but I know it's the right thing to do.

(Pause)

So I'm certain that I'll find you there.

(Julia throws book in the river.)

This is for you *mami*.

(A car horn is heard.)

That's Juan. I'll see you in New York. Meet me at the river *mami* . . .

(Julia takes one last look.)

Benedición mamí . . .

JOSÉ RIVERA

About the Playwright

"I have been able to carve out a niche as a writer of 'magic realist' plays (whatever that means)," writes José Rivera, "exploring the experiences of a Latino mind and soul set in a non-Latino world."[77] Rivera has emerged as perhaps the foremost Latino playwright of his generation, having worked for nearly thirty years in television, film, and theatre. Born in Puerto Rico, raised on Long Island, and now residing in Brooklyn, his plays are equally influenced by American popular culture and Latino literature, with a tendency towards the mystical and miraculous events that are rooted in human relationships and historical struggles for personal integrity and identity. As one critic notes, "he's a writer steeped in Hispanic culture who clearly often thinks in Spanish, which can sometimes give his dialogue a faintly stilted, transliterated sound. At the same time, he's wholly at home in North American culture, so that almost as many passages flow colloquially."[78]

A lifelong lover of film, Rivera was the first Puerto Rican screenwriter ever nominated for an Academy Award (for *The Motorcycle Diaries*). He remains committed to a bold style of writing that transcends boundaries of class and national origin and reaches audiences of any background. "When theatre language is hot," Rivera writes, "it blows your mind and kicks your ass and takes you to sublime, terrifying, and sexy places."[79]

List of Plays

187
Adoration of the Old Woman
The Book of Fishes
Boleros for the Disenchanted
Brainpeople
The Hours are Feminine
The House of Ramon Inglesia
Human Emotional Process
Kiss of the Spiderwoman (adapted)
Lessons of the Unaccumstomed Bride
Massacre (sing to your children)
Pablo and Andrew at the Altar of Words

---

77   José Rivera, "Split Personality: Random Thoughts on Writing for Theater and Film," *Cinema Journal* 45:2 (Winter 2006): 89-92.
78   Michael Feingold, "Diction and Contradiction," *The Village Voice*, July 4, 2006.
79   Rivera, "Split Personality."

Cloud Tectonics
Each Day Dies with Sleep
Flowers
Lovers of Long Red Hair
Maricela de la Luz Lights the World
Marisol
The Promise
References to Salvador Dali Make Me Hot
School of the Americas
Sonnets for an Old Century
The Street of the Sun
Sueño
Giants Have Us in Their Books (collection of shorts)
Gliese 58ld
Golden
Lunatic in the Trap Room
Yellow
Another Word for Beauty (music and lyrics by Hector Buitrago)
The Last Book of Homer

Screenplays
The Motorcycle Diaries
Letters to Juliet
Trade
On the Road

Television
The House of Ramon Inglesia
Family Matters
The Jungle Book: Mowgli's Story
Night Visions
Eerie, Indiana
   (co-created and co-produced)

PLAYWRIGHT INFORMATION

   Agent: Jonathan Looma, WME
   1325 Avenue of the Americas, New York, NY 10019
   (212) 586-5100.

   Manager: Rick Berg, Code Entertainment
   9229 Sunset Blvd., Suite 615, Los Angeles, CA 90069
   (310) 772-0008.

For all rights including amateur and stock performances, please contact: Mary Harden
Harden-Curtis Associates (212) 977-8502

PERFORMING THE MONOLOGUES

Rivera's prose demands that the actors bring strong vocal skills: playing the structure, imagery, and sound of the world is imperative. These pieces require an energy that is not naturalistic, but rather one that impels the action forward. In the first two selections, the featured characters are motivated by equal parts world-weariness and hopeful confidence. The actor must find the delicate balance between the characters' seriousness (the one character he/she is playing) and the unexpected moments of transcendent delight, and demonstrate a committed passion for both.

Notice how the energy in Manuelo's speech is cumulative, as he moves from speaking generally about men and women to specifically about his relationship with Flora (and with other women). The actor should look for that build, and magnify the subtle shifts in language to enhance the monologue's structural strengths and reveal the character.

For Cassandra, the performer must embrace and respect the uncertainty of the world of the play. To penetrate the environment in this monologue is to understand how emotional dimension emerges through Cassandra's shifting realities. Notice how even though this is a reflective monologue about the way Cassandra feels, she speaks in words of action—"I think," "I hear," "I try," etc. Truth, poetry, character—the actor must honor all three elements in Rivera's work.

Another Word for Beauty is Rivera's most recent work, a musical about the real life annual beauty pageant at El Buen Pastor women's prison in Bogotá, Colombia. In the play, we meet Isabelle, described as a bombshell and gifted sniper. During this flashback to the jungle, Isabelle lives her inner monologue before successfully defending her country with a clean kill. Isabelle is driven by her strong desire to make her husband proud and to rid her country of the "evil doers." It is important that the actor playing Isabelle have as much confidence as the character. Note how the beginning of the monologue is a series of beliefs and values about the other—it is clear that Isabelle has internalized the propaganda to which she has been exposed. In the final section of her monologue note the use of "I." Using the rhetorical device of repetition, the "I" becomes an effective and persuasive argument that clears her conscience of any guilt.

EXCERPTED FROM

BOLEROS FOR THE DISENCHANTED
José Rivera

Character: Manuelo (male), early twenties.

> *A silver-tongued, handsome bachelor of his place and time (1950s Miraflores, Puerto Rico); during this exchange with his fiancé, Flora, Manuelo confesses his beliefs about fidelity, his expectations for their future, and the nature of relationships.*

Manuelo: God made men and women differently, Flora. That's the first thing you need to know. I didn't make this difference between man and woman, God did—and I have inherited those differences. I cannot control them. A man is, basically, despite language, culture, religion, and the invention of television, a creature of instinct, like a dog. We are controlled by such desperate forces, Flora, such demonic energy . . .I just hope you never experience them yourself. They make a man do crazy things. Things that are repulsive and wrong—but, here's the catch: things that must be done. Yes, Flora. A man must sin. It's in our blood. It's innate and natural and it is a command of our bestial selves. A man must be with a woman. There I said it. And God, in his infinite flexibility, has created certain special women for men like me to be with. These are not the chaste virgins of his acquaintance: his sisters, cousins, *novias*. No, these girls are other men's sisters, cousins and *novias*. They are built with the special purpose of fulfilling nature's special plan for men like me. So we don't dirty women like you. So you can stay pure, closer to God and the Holy Spirit. Flora, come on. Do you ask a tiger not to stalk the antelope? Do you ask the fish not to, to, to do what fish do all day? No. You let nature be. You let the rain fall. You let the flower blossom. And you must let a man be a man, Flora. I have waited a year for you. A man cannot stop being a man for a year. That's sin. And our engagement is for yet another year. Two years in which my flower will not blossom! Is that fair? Because in those two years, you continue to be a woman. You clean for your father, you cook for him, obey him, you learn from his wisdom. You fulfill the strict destiny penned by God for womanhood. You get to be you. So why shouldn't I get to be I? Or me? Whoever Manuelo Ramon Delgado really is? You see, I'm just trying to be fair here. Flora, there is love. And there is sex. And they are two different things. The love I feel for you is inexpressible. It's bigger and deeper than the oceans that encircle this whole earth with their oceanic bigness and deepness. No! That's wrong! That's poorly said, Manuelo! I love you to my dying breath, Flora. I love you in truth, in trust, in holiness, in sin, in pleasure, in family, in wonder, in God's presence, in all my capacity and imagination. I love you like the page loves the pen that writes the eternal words "I love you" on its white, pure skin. Believe me, Flora, please.

HUMAN EMOTIONAL PROCESS

José Rivera

Character: Cassandra (female), eighteen to forty; a woman of child-bearing age.

Rivera's examination of the human experience is set in a land of metempsychosis and radioactive toxic waste. Cassandra and Lorenzo relive the war of the sexes in their incomplete house. When the laws of the land change Cassandra finds herself alone without her one true love.

Cassandra: Lorenzo! Do you hear it? That's the sound of the earth's rotation. That rusty, squeaky spinning sound . . . so hard to hear sometimes. Sounds like crickets? Or rustling leaves? So sad and far away . . . you can only hear it when you're absolutely alone in the world. When all your loved ones are gone or silent. That's me right now. I don't hear you, dear Lorenzo. Not your laughter or that painful little sigh after making love. Not your sarcasm or your evasions and cheap jokes. You've broken free. You've escaped my arms and flown to older dimensions and erased your presence in our biosphere and left me to wander the dumb, unfinished house like a weak wind. I've been trying to hear the echoes of your words, hoping they'd still be bouncing around this tired house like magic rubber balls. Sometimes I think I hear them—your voice still attached to the space. I try to chase them and catch them and stick them in my ear and hope they wander down to my heart and fill it, fill it, fill it with you! But I think I'm only dreaming. But no, in my complete loneliness, all I hear is the rusted spin of the world, monotonous and shrill and just barely within perception . . . they say only dogs and crazy people can hear that . . . I'm afraid that if I listen to it too much, for too long, that I will really lose my mind, dear Lorenzo.

Excerpted From

Another Word for Beauty

José Rivera

Character: Isabelle (female), twenties.

Dressed in military garb and carrying an M16, Isabelle speaks to herself and aims at a distant target.

Isabelle: I know you're a commie piece of shit motherfucker, I know you don't believe in God, and all you want to do is distribute condoms to the peasants and corrupt their morality with your godless socialism and your Marxist bullshit and if you really feel that way, you cowardly little bald motherfucker with your little moustache and probably very little microscopic dick, why don't you take your sick ideology and your pathetic existence and catch the first motherfucking train to Siberia and you can tell your lies to your buddies in the Kremlin and the KGB and stop raping all the pretty peasant girls and giving them social diseases and getting them pregnant with your little Bolshevik monsters, you scum, you dirt, you excrement, you Castro-loving, Che-fucking pitiful excuse for a man, that's right you ugly fuck, I'm talking to you, because you don't know it yet but my whisper is the last human sound you're going to hear on this good earth of ours, the same earth you're trying to pollute with your Ho Chi Minh bullshit and your Maoist motherfucking deceptions, and that's because you have only another few seconds to live, fat-boy, soon as I get a clear shot on your ass, motherfucker, stop moving around prick, just sit for one-point-two-five seconds and you'll be mine, and this jungle will be the last sight your eyes will ever take in, and those birds are the last floating notes of music you'll enjoy and I'm going to make your wife a widow, you cocksucker, and your children are never going to know the warmth of your lap again, and it's a good thing too, you can't molest them with your Das Kapital homosexuality and your women's liberation shit and I, I am a warrior, I am a defender of my country, I am a peace keeper, I am what stands between your godlessness and chaos and my beautiful nation, and I have no mercy, I am a killer, I want one clean shot at you, that's all I'm looking

for, and I'll wait all day if I—yes, yes, sit there, sit there, sit there, sit there, right there, right there, God—
  (She shoots. She Looks. She smiles.)
Ha! Kiss my ass, mutherfucker!

ELAINE ROMERO

ABOUT THE PLAYWRIGHT

"For me, playwriting is an act of excavation," says Elaine Romero. "It can be an excavation of my own psyche, or a political or social dynamic." Romero has led life as a global citizen; a Latina raised in Southern California and a resident of Tucson for many years before moving to Chicago, she has also lived in Paris and Japan and can trace part of her ancestry to the Crypto-Jewish legacy in New Mexico (the subject of her play *Secret Things*).

Complex characters who are as much citizens of the world as they are rooted in a specific time and culture is the hallmark of Romero's drama. Defined by layers of action and reaction, these characters emerge as complex subjects navigating both their specific emotions and circumstances while suggesting the archetypal, universal, and political. "I'm a fan of politics that have been humanized and dramatized," Romero explains. "I think there's a way to write a strong political play without landing in agit-prop land. I delight in the balancing act of that. I want to have as much empathy for my antagonists as my protagonists. I love the quandary of being challenged to love someone I hate."[80]

Ultimately, Romero's plays are driven by the desire to explore our most basic connections to each other. "Elaine has a tremendous sense of human fragility," says one colleague. "She has so much tenderness for the world, and I think that's what makes her very special. There are plenty of writers who are very hard-edged . . . but Elaine is one of the few who's always trying to enlist love into the world." [81] That passion comes from a very intuitive place, explains Romero: "I don't believe in talent. Once you have the interest, you just need to find access to your subconscious and open your heart, and then you can write."[82]

LIST OF PLAYS

Mother of Exiles
A Work of Art
Graveyard of Empires
Wetback

---

80   Adam Szymkowicz, "I Interview Playwrights part 280: Elaine Romero," 10 November 2011. http://aszym.blogspot.com/2010/11/i-interview-playwrights-part-280-elaine.html

81   James Reel, "Playwright of Passage," *Tucson Weekly*, 1 June 2000. http://www.tucsonweekly.com/tucson/playwright-of-passage/Content?oid=1066406

82   Reel, "Playwright of Passage."

Ponzi
The Dalai Lama is Not Welcome Here
Something Rare and Wonderful
Rain of Ruin (short version)
Alicia
Walk into the Sea
A Simple Snow
Like Heaven
The Sniper (with Anthony David)
Catalina de Erauso
Secret Things
Before Death Comes for the Archbishop
Day of Our Dead
Barrio Hollywood
¡Curanderas! Serpents of the Clouds
The Fat-Free Chicana and the Snow Cap Queen
If Susan Smith Could Talk
Walking Home
Living Dolls

PLAYWRIGHT INFORMATION

Website: http://www.elaineromero.com

PERFORMING THE MONOLOGUES

Elaine Romero's *Barrio Hollywood* is a family drama that explores poverty, interracial dating, and family loyalty. Amá is the matriarch of the family but in many ways she is a child. She dreams of winning in poker and running away to the Canary Islands, but she is trapped by her economics and her son's tragedy. The selection below is not a soliloquy: she has a relationship to her interrogators and is responding to their questions. The actor playing Amá might be speaking to several people, but the imagination should be focused on one person at a time. There are also times when Amá is speaking to herself and then to God. These shifts of concentration are imperative to the playing piece. When is Amá seeking connection to her interrogators? When is she lashing out at one person? When is she lashing out at the world? When does Amá get lost in her own world? When does Amá recognize she's been found out and gone too far?

Secret Things was inspired by Romero's encounter with New Mexico State Historian Stanley Hordes, the leading expert on the subject of Crypto-Jews in New Mexico. Abel is powerfully attracted to Delia, a journalist for *Time* magaizine. Speaking to the rabbi, he seeks approval for the flood of feelings Delia has stirred in him. This finely crafted monologue has a clear beginning, middle, and end. Notice Abel's journey: he begins by reflecting on his own behavior and past and continues to his possible future. When Abel verbalizes "wife," he suddenly has a whole new world of possibilities. The actor should physically and vocally open as he dreams of his future with Delia.

Excerpted From

Barrio Hollywood

Elaine Romero

Character: Amá (female), late forties.

Amá has been the round-the-clock caregiver for her son, who has laid comatose in their South Tucson home since a terrible boxing accident. Now she enters in handcuffs, and is having a difficult time responding to interrogation.

Amá: My son. My child is dead. And you blame me? He killed him. Michael took Alex's throat in his hands and he killed him. I saw the whole thing. That horrible man murdered my son. I am a witness! I want that man to go to the electric chair! I want him dead! Let him feel what it feels like to be murdered.

(More upset)

My son was going to be fine. He had a difficult few months, but he was going to be fine.

(Short beat)

I did not sneak off. I went out for some air.

(Short beat)

No, I did not know he was dead when I left. I had no idea until you said it to me. What do you mean—contradicting myself?

(Beat)

You already have ideas in your head. I can see them floating around in there. I can see that!

I didn't go to school. I don't have perfect English like you, but I can see this. This is not right.

(Short beat)

I saw everything. Don't pretend. When you know.

(Breaking down)

The truth. Let me see Graciela. She knows why this happened.

(To herself)

Taking me from my church. From my prayers. When my God comforts me. That's who I love. That's who I listen to. *El siem-*

pre está conmigo. You and your fancy cars. You and your guns. You've never done nothing good for me.

(Short beat; yelling to someone as if he's leaving)

Give me back my suitcase! My son gave me that. *Para mi cumpleaños.* For my birthday trip. He's giving it to me as a gift. When Graciela turns thirty, I turn forty-eight. Only two days apart.

(Getting emotional)

I saw that pretty island on Channel 52. I saw it in *Spanich.* It was a beautiful place with canaries up in the trees. And water—bluer than your eyes. You can see little canaries there like lizards in the desert. Singing all the time. Making everybody happy. And everybody could be happy if some people let God do His job.

(Amá starts crying)

Simple things. That's all I ever wanted.

(Short beat)

I didn't kill Alex with my hands but by wanting so much. And he wanted so much to give me those things. He fought when he was bleeding. When he couldn't see. He fought for money. But I kept wanting more. And you know how God feels about that! You must accept what He gives you. And smile. BECAUSE THAT IS HOW GOD WORKS! He makes the rules. He decides. And you take it. Whatever hand you're dealt. But you gotta keep your poker face on. You gotta look like you're winning or you lose that much more. My grandfather taught me that. He was a poker player from Chihuahua. He knew how to fool people into believing him.

(Quickly)

That's not what I meant.

<small>EXCERPTED FROM</small>

SECRET THINGS LEVELS OF THE HEART
Elaine Romero

Character: Abel Sanchez (male), thirties.

A Chicano from New Mexico, Abel has "returned" to Judaism after discovering his Jewish roots. He is confiding in and seeking advice from his rabbi about a girl who makes him dream about the future and question his past.

Abel: I met this woman.

> She's Jewish. I mean, I did her family history. I mean, she doesn't even know she is, so I guess she's not. I don't know what it means. I've never told you. About my past. I slept with so many women. I honestly don't know how many. And I feel very bad. I hurt a lot of feelings. I feel that was wrong. I feel a little messed up over it, frankly. And I, uh, had this commitment. To myself. When we did the Rite to Return. To not do that anymore. I mean, to let the floodgates open up again. I just don't know what would happen. So, I haven't done anything. I just closed myself off. And I want to find the proper way to be open again and I just can't. I just feel this fear—this block. I don't know. Maybe I want the next woman I make love to to be my wife. Would that be crazy? I mean, me and this woman are nowhere near having sex. I mean, we haven't even kissed. We haven't even held hands. We've barely talked. And she's threatened to never talk to me again. But I think she really likes me, and I most definitely like her, and I, uh, would like to get to know her better. Um, she's really really sharp. Maybe sharper than me. And I really really like that. I mean, I feel so alive. I mean, like when we're talking we're both really thinking hard. And I love that. Because when you're old. When you're really really old—that might be all that's left—is somebody you can think with. Somebody who can share your thoughts. And finish your sentences. And laugh at your stupid jokes. And still find you attractive when you are not remotely attractive at all. Because they've found a way to peer into your soul. And they like it. Am I asking too much?

THE ROYAL MEXICAN PLAYERS:
ALVARO SAAR RIOS AND MICHELLE LOPEZ-RIOS

About the Company

The Royal Mexican Players are living proof that Latino/a theatre is alive and well all across North America, and that one does not have to be permanently based in New York, California, or South Florida to be successful. Based in Milwaukee where both members teach at the University of Wisconsin-Milwaukee, the Royals have been creating theatre together for a decade and conducting workshops at universities and institutions all over the United States.

Alvaro Saar Rios and Michelle Lopez-Rios craft theatrical pieces that draw upon their experience as Mexican-Americans, from sketch comedy to solo performance to two-handers to devised work. Founded in Houston in 2004, the group continues to develop work together while simultaneously maintaining separate creative and teaching careers (Alvaro has written several young audience plays, and Michelle is a well-respected director and vocal coach). Discussing his one-person show *One Hot Texican Summer*, Alvaro sums up what he has learned about writing: "I realize that the closer to the truth you are, the funnier it is."[83]

List of Productions

One Hot Texican Summer (or the Summer I Found Out I Was Mexican)
Bienvendos a Milwaukee/Welcome to Milwaukee
Nuestro Voz, Nuestra Historia (Our Voice, Our Story)
A Trip Through the Mind of a "Crazy" Mexican
The Crazy Mexican Show

Playwright Information

Company website: www.royalmexicans.com
Michelle Lopez-Rios: www.michellelopezrios.com,
www.accenthelp.com

Performing the Monologues

"We believe everyone has a story to tell. Though we often tell it through humor, we always tell it with love and respect."[84] This is Alvaro Saar Rios and Michelle Lopez-Rios's philosophy for

83 Jeannie Kever, "Latino playwright brings his heritage to the forefront," *Houston Chronicle*, 18 April 2006.
84 Interview with Micha Espinosa, 2013.

performing. Alvaro's one man show *One Hot Texican Summer* follows the Houston native with just that mixture. A seven-year-old boy experiences a summer of *Ranchera* music and unforgettable memories. The shifting narrative voice from child to adult and past to present is imperative for finding the humor and ultimately making the piece effective. The voices should be differentiated but not stereotyped. A child-like perspective and change in physicality is enough to make little Jojo pop. If the piece is too long, an alternate beginning is suggested at the line "I brought the blender and set it on the table."

Bienvenidos a Milwaukee /Welcome to Milwaukee is an excellent example of the community-based shows celebrating latinidad, immigration and migration created by "the Players," funded by Milwaukee Repertory Theater's Education Department and United Community Center in conjunction with the "Caras Vemos: Corazones no Sabemos" touring art exhibit. After viewing the performance, students explored through a series of performative workshops how they (or their families) came to Milwaukee. The stories, played by two actors, are a series of male and female monologues told through the eyes of Donny, a college student on a class assignment, who gathers stories about his community but discovers much more about himself. As Nobody reaches the end of her story, she is a different person for having shared it. It is important that the memory hold meaning: is this the first time she's told this story? How difficult is it to retell? How joyful?

293

EXCERPTED FROM

ONE HOT TEXICAN SUMMER
(OR, THE SUMMER I FOUND OUT I WAS MEXICAN)

The Royal Mexican Players
(Alvaro Saar Rios and Michelle Lopez-Rios)

Character: Jojo (male), twenties to thirties.

Little Jojo (age seven) takes cooking lessons from his big brother.

Jojo: "Hey, you like milk shakes?"
That's how my big brother convinced me to zoom towards the kitchen in search of a blender.
But not just any blender. Dad's blender.
(Jojo opens cabinet. Then quickly closes it.)
"Is there a way we can make milk shakes without using dad's favorite blender? He did say we should never touch it."
"Don't worry, lil' bro. Nothing is going to happen."
My big brother had said this to me many many many times before and many times something DID happen. Lots of things. And yet, this time when he said it, I believed him. Maybe because I had milk shake on the brain. Summer was already hot and only getting hotter and there's nothing like a cool milk shake to help you forget that. I brought the blender and set it on the table while my big brother got the rest of the ingredients. Milk, ice, vanilla ice cream, and cinnamon. Then, we threw everything in there with a dash of cinnamon on top. Not too much. My big brother covers it. ZZZZZZZZZZZZZZZZZZ—
"Ummmmm . . .does it look a little green to you?"
"Green? What are you talking about? My milk shakes are never green."
"No. Not GREEN Green. Green-ish."
"You want a milk shake or not?"
(Jojo nods.)
"Get some cups."
I run to the cabinet and pull out my favorite plastic Scooby Doo cup and pick whatever for my big brother. I put them on the table and he pours the milk shakes all the way to the top. It still looks a bit greenish.

"You first," I tell my big brother.

"I'm the chef. I don't have to drink first."

"Together?"

"Together."

One. Two. GLUBGlubGlubBglbubglbu. And there it was. The coolest, coldest, smoothest milk shakes in the world made by none other than The Fluff Brothers. Just the taste of it, made me forget everything else that was going on in my seven year old life.

It's like the time I ate my mom's fidello after three months of basic training . . . or when I learned how to successfully make my dad's homemade lasagna while in undergrad . . . or when I smoked my first Cuban cigar after getting into Graduate School.

And yet, the only difference between those times and this time is that there was a point after drinking that milk shake that my lips started to tingle. No. Not tingle. Burn. Then my tongue. Then my throat.

And it wasn't the kind of tingling burn you get after you drink a Big Red too quickly. It was the kind of burn you get after you drink a whole bottle of Tabasco sauce.

You see, what I failed to mention was that this blender was off limits for a reason. Not because my parents were worried that we were gonna accidentally purée our fingers off. We had insurance. They didn't want us using it because this was the blender my dad used for chopping up jalapeños for his homemade salsa. In the fifteen years he owned it, it was only used for chopping up jalapeños. He barely rinsed it much less washed it. And my dad loved his salsa HOT! How hot? Hot enough to put hair on your chest, man or woman.

It should be no surprise that was the last time I ever had the desire to drink a milk shake. No matter how hot it got outside, you couldn't convince me to drink one. Not even if it was free.

As for things that burn my mouth like jalapeños and salsa . . . to this day . . . I put it on everything I eat.

EXCERPTED FROM

BIENVENIDOS A MILWAUKEE/WELCOME TO MILWAUKEE

The Royal Mexican Players
(Alvaro Saar Rios and Michelle Lopez-Rios)

Character: Nobody (female), early twenties.

*A Mexicana afraid of revealing her identity, she gathers
confidence as she shares her story with Donny.*

Nobody: We left Aguascalientes when I was five or six. Right after
the country had what they called the Peso Crisis. My parents told
me when the crisis happened the price for everything doubled
and tripled. Bread. Milk. Gas. Meat. Cheese. Everything.
It didn't matter if you had a job because you couldn't afford
anything. It got so expensive that my parents couldn't even
keep their house. So, instead of staying and starving, my parents
decided to move in with my grandparents who lived up here.
In Cedarburg, WI.
I wish I could say we moved up here like regular people move
here. Getting on a plane or driving a moving truck loaded with
furniture. But we didn't have permission to come into this country
so if we really wanted to get here we had to do it "carefully."
My dad woke me up in the middle of the night.
*"Ponte los zapatos. Vamos a visitar sus abuelos. Ándale. NoN-
oNo. No juguetes."* We left everything. No suitcases. No boxes.
Nothing. And we got into this van. It had no seats in it so we
had to sit on the cold metal floor. There were other people in
there too. I asked my mom if she knew any of them. She shook
her head. Nobody talked while we were in there. It was so quiet
I fell back asleep.
When I woke up, my mom was carrying me. We weren't in the
van anymore. We were walking. And none of the other people
were there. It was just us.
"Estámos en los Estados Unidos."
We walked for that whole day. It felt like a million miles. I don't
remember how long it actually took us to get to Cedarburg. It
felt like at least a month because of all the times we had to stop
and stay at strange people's houses. And every time we left it
was always in the middle of the night.

I remember right before we got to my grandparents' house, we were in the back of a truck and lights were just zooming by and I see this sign. It's big and colorful. AND. In English. I asked my Dad, what it said.

"Dice . . .uhhhh . . .Bienvenidos a Milwaukee."

We didn't live with my grandparents for too long. We moved to the South Side of Milwaukee. And I hated it. Because it wasn't home. We had no furniture. No TV. We couldn't go outside and play with the other kids because my mom was worried we were going to get caught. We barely had beds and there were times when it was colder in the house than it was outside. How could this be better than staying in Mexico? But we stayed.

It's been hard. Especially when I read about people like me who get treated like slaves because they're afraid of getting sent back. I'm afraid, but in the end it's worth it. College would not be possible for me if we had stayed down there.

And every time I see that big colorful sign—that actually says Miller Brewing Company. My dad knew as much English as I did back then—the first thing that comes to my mind is Welcome to Milwaukee.

EDWIN SANCHEZ

ABOUT THE PLAYWRIGHT

"I've heard people comment on a play by saying, 'I didn't like that moment, it was out of character,'" observes Edwin Sanchez. "I'd say that was probably the best moment, the moment that made that character believable. People have different sides to them, and that's what interests me."[85] Indeed, Sanchez has the ability to register these complexities through a vast matrix of figures driven by the question of their own identity: abusive fathers, religious devotees, precocious children, drag queens, lawyers, movie stars, and street hustlers are all treated with the same detail and respect, with no attempt to hide their considerable problems and contradictions.

A native of Puerto Rico and longtime resident of New York City, Sanchez often sets his plays in circumstances that are both brutal and sublime; no matter how desperate or confused things become, the possibility of redemption and truth always seems within reach. After beginning his career as an actor and growing frustrated with Latino stereotyping, he turned his attention to writing, immediately producing work that one critic noted was full of "tremendous emotional conviction."[86] "I started writing because I didn't see myself on stage and I knew I existed," says Sanchez. "I knew there were gay Hispanic men there, but they were never seen." Regardless of the characters' specific identities, actors and audiences are likely to respond to the musicality of each one's unique voice, which Sanchez suggests is at the root of his creative process: "The most important thing about a character is finding out what song speaks to me about them. Like if they were walking down the street and they heard a song, they would stop and say 'That's my song! That's my song!' And I go, 'Okay, now I know the character.'"[87]

LIST OF PLAYS

Trafficking in Lost Souls
Unmerciful Good Fortune
Clean
Diosa
Floor Show: Dona Sol and Her Trained Dog
Barefoot Boy with Shoes On
Fatty Tissue

---

85   Thomas Connors, "Destiny's disciple," *American Theatre* 13:3 (March 1996): 7.
86   Ben Brantley, "Theater Review: Clean," *New York Times*, 19 April 1995.
87   *Urban Latino* (1999) no. 22; from Contemporary Hispanic Quotations

Icarus
Back Story
La Bella Familia
The Road

PLAYWRIGHT INFORMATION
Contact: edwinplaywright@aol.com

PERFORMING THE MONOLOGUES

The first two selections are from Sanchez' acclaimed drama *Unmerciful Good Fortune*. The play intertwines the lives of good girl lawyer Maritza and her streetwise client Fatima. The intensity of Sanchez' writing requires actors with emotional availability. Maritza is straightforward, earnest, and yet vulnerable. Fatima shifts from compassionate woman to seductress to arrogant murderer. It is important that the complexities of their wants and desires be fully realized and the stakes be kept high. What if Maritza doesn't get a confession from Fatima? What if she recognizes her attraction to Fatima? What would happen to Fatima if Maritza won't hold her hand and she can't use her powers? What if another attorney gets assigned to her or if she never gets the splinter from her heart? By clarifying the stakes, the selections become much stronger.

Clean is Sanchez' black comedy on impossible love. Note the clear structure of this monologue. Norry begins with a confession, logically follows through examining within the problem and concludes with a prayer. Honor this structure. A prayer is different than a wish, or a vow; Norry is in the presence of something bigger than himself. The problem is bigger than he is. How easy is it to confess? Keep the stakes high. Norry admits to the priest that this is a last resort, not knowing that the priest is also struggling with love and intimacy. When Norry says, "I'm happy with myself," is he? Have fun delving into the subtext of this rich and character-driven writing.

EXCERPTED FROM

UNMERCIFUL GOOD FORTUNE

Edwin Sanchez

Character: Maritza Cruz (female), twenty-six.

*Bronx-born, Puerto Rican single mom Maritza is an
assistant district attorney. In a bare interrogation room,
she questions a suspect, Fatima, who has just admitted
to murdering 28 people. Maritza poses a very personal
argument to Fatima, who is reluctant to give her the
whole story.*

Maritza: All knowing, huh? What's your level of education?
It's a very simple question.
I would just like to know what your qualifications are for deciding who lives and dies. I mean, is it an elementary school
drop-out who's making these decisions? Did you take a correspondence course? Who?!
I used to get beat up by girls like you. The tough girls. The gang
around my block was called "Las Hembras." I could count on
their making fun of me every single day. If one of them dropped
a pen they would just say, "pick it up," and I would. With a smile
on my lips. The smile of submission. "Why do you think you're
better than us?" Smack-smack-smack. "Who told you to talk?"
Smack-smack-smack. I took it all. I never snapped. I think about
those girls now, "Las Hembras." Where are they now? Dead.
Welfare mothers. No future. I saw one of them on the subway
and I held her stare. I would not look down until she did.
Smack-smack-smack. She did. Does this mean I won?
She didn't have the guts to find out. Life beat the guts out of
her. I would have preferred running into an old friend. And she
and I would have a lot of catching up to do. We had been good
friends. Life had been sweet. We had shared secrets and good
times. Old school friends. She would ask me to be the godmother
of her child. A girl she would name after me.
So good to see you again. Smack-smack-smack.
Call me. Here's my business card.
Soon.

EXCERPTED FROM

UNMERCIFUL GOOD FORTUNE

Edwin Sanchez

Character: Fatima (female), twenty-eight.

*Fatima, a Puerto Rican clairvoyant from the Bronx,
now in prison, speaks to an attorney assigned to her
case for the first time.*

Fatima: You know how a splinter feels? You know the relief you
feel when you finally get the tweezers just so and you pull the
splinter out? The wound is still there but the hurt has been pulled
out. I have this splinter in my heart. Come on, just let me hold
your hand. Just once. I can't trust you if you won't trust me. If
I can't see into your life what's the big deal?
I'm just gonna hold your hand. Pretend it's your boyfriend.
So, Ms Cruz, as a gesture of good will you were saying you
were going to let me hold your hand.
I didn't want this thing. And I sure as hell never called it a gift.
My mother said my father was scared of me when I was a little
girl. I would stare at people. Like I'm three months old and I'm
staring into people's faces. Everybody in my mother's family
did *la brujería*. But when I got to be thirteen I realized that they
were like grooming me to be the child bride of Satan. Later for
that shit. I ran away. Lived on the streets for three years. That's
when I joined my girl gangs. A girl's gotta have herself some
representation on the street; you know it's the truth. I would
never have chosen you. Anybody but you. You're too close to
call. And now only you can pull this splinter from my heart.
Only you can give me relief.

EXCERPTED FROM

CLEAN

Edwin Sanchez

Character: Norry (male), twenties.

Norry, a worldly drag queen in the Bronx, has fallen in love with a virgin housewife with whom he shares the love of dressing up. He seeks confession and advice from his priest. The deal he's willing to make with God means taking off his wig for good.

Norry: Forgive me Father for I have sinned.
   When you took the vow, you knew you were giving up a whole lot, right? But you did it 'cause you had to. 'Cause the call was so strong you had to. It was like destiny, you know what I'm saying? I thought if anybody would know about denial it would be you. I confess, Father.
   (Pause)
You are my last recourse. Trust me, the words Catholic and comfort don't go hand in hand in my brain. Okay, my sin. For the last three years I have dreamt of this woman. Going against everything I am. Everything I am happy to be.
The problem is she's a she. The problem is I'm going to have to change who I am to love this person. The problem is we're not even the same size. I used to dream of being accepted, so I found a world, a small world, where I could be. Where if I follow the rules I could be accepted. But, I never stopped resenting the rights other people took for granted. The gentle kiss, the hand holding in public, the "Hello, we're a couple, we fuck, and how are you?" that men and women take for granted. Bitter? I left bitter in the dust. I see families, "traditional families," and I get teary-eyed even as I laugh at them. Aren't they just the stupidest thing? Hello? Are you still there? Hello?
Feel free to interrupt me at any time with those pearls of wisdom that are just dying to leave your lips.
I am happy to be who I am. I am proud to be who I am. So why can't I forget her?
   (Pause)
Father, I think you know what I'm talking about. Can you broker a deal with God for me? If your God, the God, any God can take

her away from my heart after these three years I will give them my plumage. Just give me peace . . . and give her happiness. That's it. That's my prayer.

TANYA SARACHO

ABOUT THE PLAYWRIGHT

"Every time we go home, it's all we talk about," says Tanya Saracho about the violence and confusion that surrounds communities living on the border between Mexico and the United States. "Right now, we're held hostage by this thing. It's so complicated that it has no name, but we all know what we're talking about."[88]

Tanya Saracho is a writer, performer, and director whose work reflects her own experience as an immigrant (born in Mexico and raised on both sides of the border with Texas), with particular sensitivity towards issues facing women in immigrant communities. "I want to complicate the image of what a Latina woman is without standing on a soapbox," she explains. "I'm dedicated to telling her stories—to letting us look at life through her eyes."[89]

Saracho manages to craft her characters with humor and honesty, regardless of whether the setting is the American urban landscape (*Enfrascada*, *Our Lady of the Underpass*) or a northern Mexican pecan orchard (*El Nogalar*). "She is a warm, funny and energetic writer," says one critic, "beautifully in tune with the struggles of ordinary people, especially the young. She cuts through cliches, capturing the gulf between perceptions and personal realities."[90]

LIST OF PLAYS

Kita y Fernanda
Surface Play
Our Lady of the Underpass
The House on Mango Street (adaptation)
Enfrascada (A Jarring Comedy of Hoodoo Proportions)
El Nogalar
Mala Hierba
Song for the Disappeared
The Tenth Muse
Quita Mitos

88 Rob Weinert-Kent, "Mexican? American? Call Her Writer," *New York Times*, 22 March 2011.
89 "Kita Y Fernanda Opens Sept. 25," Art Botantas, 12 September 2008. http://artbotanas.blogspot.com/2008/09/kita-y-fernanda-opens-sept-25.html
90 Chris Jones, "El Nogalar at the Goodman Theatre," *Chicago Tribune*, 4 April 2011.

PLAYWRIGHT INFORMATION:

Personal blog: http://tanyasaracho.blogspot.com/

PERFORMING THE MONOLOGUES

Tanya Saracho writes in the language of the contemporary young Latina—some have playfully compared her play *Enfrascada* to the television series "Sex and the City" for the way in which the quick-witted comedy so efficiently and believably represents familiar and sympathetic characters. This approach allows young Latina performers to find their voice, a fresh vehicle that can set the female perspective free.

This means that understanding the humor—whether deliberately offered by the characters or subtle revelations of their own comedic flaws—is critical for anyone (male or female) performing Saracho's work. Sometimes the characters mock each other, sometimes they self-deprecate—what is fun for the actor is the ability to play these nuances. Once you find the humor, however, it is important not to wallow in it—stay focused on your ability to isolate the joke and move on. Don't "sit on" the joke—keep moving forward, as these are characters whose casual humor is best highlighted through their sustained intentions and actions.

The actor approaching Memo's monologue from *El Nogalar* will need to find a flair for transformational playing, as the monologue offers a series of shifts, prompted by a memory that organically weaves pain, pleasure, delight, and frustration. The actor needs to embrace the immediate changes in time and identity that accompany this memory, so that this revelation from the past retains immediacy in the present.

EXCERPTED FROM

EL NOGALAR

Tanya Saracho

Character: Dunia (female), late teens/early twenties.

*Feisty and ambitious, Dunia is the housekeeper for the
Galvan family which has fallen on hard times. Inspired
by Anton Chekhov's* The Cherry Orchard, *the setting is
a pecan grove in Northern Mexico is under threat by the
drug cartel. Dunia, wise beyond her years, gives advice
to displaced Anita. Dialogue in brackets is translated
from the Spanish, and may or may not be included in the
monologue according to the performer's discretion.*

Dunia: Pedro is not so bad idea for now. He is better than the dumb
one I was going out with before, more handsome than this poor
little counter I was going with. Is that how you say contador?
Ah, yes. Accountant. Not counter. *Sí, ese era todo un ñoño.* Who
wants a *ñoño*? How you say *ñoño*?

I need a real man. Who wants a *ñoño* like that? *¿Imagínate?* We
will start getting into kissing and he will faint and have a heart
attack from excitement. *Así que los pusimos de patitas en la
calle.* [So we kicked him to the curb.] Goodbye baby. Men are
easy. There is not one easier animal on the planet than a man.
I'm not being a bad person when I say this. So yes *las feminis-
tas* who like to say progressive things on the morning shows.
They will speak to us about equality and things like this. *Pero
no.* Men are stupid animals. They are smart, but they are stupid
animals. *Esto de lidiar con ellos es fácil.* [Dealing with them
is easy.] But only if you have . . . *moneda con que negociar.*
[*Currency to trade.*]

You have to have . . . something they want. And no I'm not talking about sex. That only lasts three minutes and that's all you got.
You lose them after they're done. No, I'm talking something else.
Like to possess. Men like to know they are masters and owners
of you. And you must let them know that this is so. Even if it is
a lie. Then you will never find happiness with a man.

(quickly and pleased)

Uy, my English has gotten so good since you came this week. No, for pretend. You only must let them think that you are something to be won. You make a face at me, but you profoundly you know it is true. This is what our mothers and grandmothers teach us from always and we stop listening because we say we are modern but they are always correct.

EXCERPTED FROM

EL NOGALAR

Tanya Saracho

Character: Memo (male), twenties.

An entrepreneur and man of his time. Memo used to work on the Galvan family ranch, but now has the opportunity to help the financially strapped Galvan women by using his connections with the cartel. In this monologue, he reveals his childhood experience with the matriarch of the family, Maite.

Memo: My life is written out in the bark of those pecans. That orchard is the first thing I can remember. Me running around with no shoes, carrying those baskets of pecans back to the silos.
(Beat)
Oh, man. Beer and tequila don't mix.
(A queasy moment)
When I was like, I don't know how old, old enough to feel like I was a full-grown man, my father gave me one of those beatings that break off a bit of your soul. The old man was taking out a whole day of frustrations on my back. Going at it hard as he could with that whip when out of nowhere Maite appears and pushes him off me. She gives him one hard slap on his leather face. She curses something at him and then drags me with her to the silos. She says, "don't cry little man." I'm standing there in front of her, bleeding, shaking. And slowly, very slowly she takes off my shirt. Then she starts to hose me down. "Don't cry, little man," she says even when I had stop crying.
(Pause)
Shit, after that, I followed her like a puppy. Too old to be doing that and I know her parents had said something to her. Well, because she was just divorced and with a kid and well, it wasn't proper. But she didn't care and I didn't care. We went every-where together. We . . .
(Beat)
One day, I guess it was when her father found her the new hus-band. That day she took me from cracking pecans, and . . . she

just took me by the river to this little wall the bank makes. She'd been crying. She said, "take off your clothes, little man." Oh, man, I took off my pants so fast. Almost fell in the water. She starts laughing and takes off her dress. I have never . . . I have never seen something more beautiful in my whole life. With that light that day. With the sun on her. And all of her just standing there. And me tangled on the ground with my fucking pants. She says, "stay there, little man. You can look at me, but you can't touch." So I freeze there. Looking. For I don't know how long. Then she pulls up her dress and runs. She ran so fast, so fast that she left her sandals there. When I went up to the house to give them to her the next morning they said she was gone. That she'd gone off to live in Monterrey where she was going to be married. Just like that, they took her away from me.

(Pause)

Me and these trees, we're the only ones who remember. Right by that river there. Not far from the bank. "You can look, but you can't touch."

313

EXCERPTED FROM

ENFRASCADA
(A HOODOO COMEDY OF JARRING PROPORTIONS)
Tanya Saracho

Character: Carolina (female), twenties.

Married and longing for a baby, Carolina belongs to
a group of New York Latinas who use the wisdom of
the ancients: the magic of Santeria, Brujeria, and good
old Hoodoo jarring spells. Her friend Alicia is trying
to use this magic to win back the love of her man. In
this scene, Carolina has had enough of Alicia's bad
breakup spiritualism and gives her the tough love she
desperately needs.

Carolina: Are you listening to yourself? Ali, I think we've officially
gone too far here. ? No, I think that this is getting out of hand.
You're about to desecrate the grave of a . . .
I think Karina was right, Ali. I think you're losing yourself a little
bit. The Alicia I know would understand that she is crossing a
line by putting that jar on the baby's grave. Shoot, the Alicia I
know wouldn't ever be in a cemetery in the first place! I can't
believe I'm about to say this, but I miss the Alicia who didn't
believe in all this. She's reasoned.
It took you, you're gone. And so fast that it's kinda scary, Amiga.
I'm sure it hurts like hell. Jeez, it's your whole life, you know?
Your whole life came crushing down and you had to try to fix
it. I get it. I do. And out of anyone here, I'm the most in support
of your methods to get him back. Come on. You've seen me
do all sorts of craziness with Vic. I get that. What I don't get is
this. What are you doing? This isn't you. The way you've been
handling yourself with Diego. It's not you. It's cheap. You're
sleeping with him while he's still with that girl. How can you
disrespect yourself like that? What is your life about right now,
amiga? You're about nothing but jars. *Te enfrascaste a ti misma*
amiga.
 Ali, a guy shouldn't take over your whole life like that. You
know what? I think I should go.
    (She starts to leave)

Alicia he is not leaving her. He's about to have a baby with this girl and babies, they seal the deal. Trust me. They seal the deal. He doesn't want you and nothing you do is going to make him want you again.

OCTAVIO SOLIS

About the Playwright

After over two decades and more than twenty plays, Octavio Solis has made his mark as a writer who "loves to do the unexpected . . . [he] has blended the visceral and the magical, the emotional and the intellectual in plays about Latinos—and not about Latinos."[91] Solis has drawn comparisons to playwrights like Arthur Miller for his "extraordinary ability to look with compassion into the hearts of his ordinary, flawed characters," with storytelling "so rich in imagery, it is uniquely infused with poetry, sexual desire, childlike wonder and violence all at once."[92]

Born in Texas, Solis admits to being uncomfortable with the label "Latino writer." "I am a Latino," he says, "I am from Texas; I'm Mexican. In the final analysis if we are born or naturalized and raised here, we are all Americans." Still, he is acutely aware of and embraces the complexity of his existence, particularly as it relates to issues of transborder identities, stories, and cultures. "The Latino stuff is just labels, but the border is *real*. My mother and father came across the border. I was conceived there and born here. And the border was like in our backyard, practically. So, I am really, really connected to the border, and everything it means. It is the repository of so many stories, so much lore and myth that I am really connected to the mythology of the river."

Wherever his plays are set, Solis' characters seem to be defined by borders both internal and external, often in a rich, poetic language that requires actors of great sensitivity. "I write for actors," admits Solis. "Having been an actor myself, I think I know how actors want to be challenged . . . I want to write words that actors are going to *love* saying. The challenge is finding actors trained outside the strict parameters of realism, finding actors who have the emotional depth, willing to go the distance."[93]

List Of Plays

Pastures of Heaven
Ghosts of the River
Quixote
La Posada Magica

91   Karen Wada, "Cloudlands: Singing and Tragedy," *Los Angeles Times*, 1 May 2011.
92   John Moore, "Theatre: Lydia," *Denver Post*, 27 January 2008.
93   Teresa Marrero, "Q+A: Octavio Solis," Theater Jones/North Texas Performing Arts News, 21 May 2013. http://www.theaterjones.com/ntx/features/20130521082921/2013-05-21/QA-Octavio-Solis

Santos & Santos
Lydia
June in a Box
Lethe
The 7 Visions of Encarnación
El Paso Blue
El Otro
The Ballad of Pancho and Lucy
Gibraltar
Prospect
Man of the Flesh
Bethlehem
Dreamlandia
Marfa Lights
Cloudlands (with music by Adam Gwon)
Burning Dreams (with Julie Hebert and Gina Leishman)
Shiner (with Erik Ehn)
Se Llama Cristina

PLAYWRIGHT INFORMATION

Website: http://www.octaviosolis.net/

PERFORMING THE MONOLOGUES

Octavio Solis' plays have an emphasis on lyrical language. Solis' mixture of muscular poetry and brutal realism give his work a distinctive voice. The *Dreamlandia* and *Lydia* selections are excellent examples of his beautiful heartfelt writing, and actors rave about being given the opportunity to play his text. Set on the border between the United States and Mexico and based on *La Vida es Sueño* (Life is a Dream) by Pedro Calderon de la Barca, *Dreamlandia* introduces us to ferocious and tender-hearted Lazaro. In *Lydia* we are introduced to Ceci, lying in a near-vegetative state in her El Paso home since an accident right before her 15th birthday; she seeks to be seen, heard, and felt as her family struggles to live the American Dream.

Take your time learning these pieces, really own the language, as there is plenty of depth to be found. Speak, think and feel simultaneously every word of this heightened Spanglish text. Both pieces require actors capable of physical as well as vocal transformation to the raw visceral experience of Solis' unique world.

319

EXCERPTED FROM

DREAMLANDIA

Octavio Solis

Character: Lazaro (male), twenties.

Lazaro is chained on an island in the Rio Grande, where he was raised in captivity. The only culture he knows to draw from is the world of fashion magazines and TV Guide. Alone, he sees a figure and calls out:

Lazaro: *¡Escúchame!*
  (Celestino goes.)
Sombras. Shadows. Gassy dreamfuckers. As if *que sí*. As if *que no*. You know what rise they come from? Your cuts and punctures. Ghosts slip out the seams and walk. Cry for the homeblood. The wound is mouth. The mouth has voice. Voice has blood. Blood is home. Home bleeds Lazaro. And all the time the voices are saying only no. *Cada vez que no.* Every ever no. Never to be home. Never to see. Never to feel. It makes *el pinche* heart a gash. *Ay!*
  (He violently yanks at his chain.)
Cadena. You one big motherfucking piece of jewelry. Hang on me, sister. Hang your shimmer on, your metal *luz*, your clink and your clank and the weight of that sound, hang your *pinche* links on me and let me show the world I may be screwed *pero*, honey, I know how to accessorize!
O God, come to where the flavor is!
Gimme one day's good glossy full page dream *de* liberty!
Let me stand in the ad *de mi* own manhood long enough to feel *suave, y si no suave*, then *con puro* attitude! How can you leave me like this, in my own rags, with my body reeking me up *y mis* glossy girls smiling in my face! How can you let them treat me *como un animal*? I have seen Italian leather!
Es el mero skin of God.
Black me out, *ese!* Just black me out! I got no place but this, I got no recall, no friend, *nomas el* Sugar Man *con los* cc's of T-rex *y mi* Happy Meal! I got no hope to hang on. Just fucking black me out, just—
  (Blanca rises out of the water like a vision. He hides.)

Whoa. *Ruquita.* Wass your game? What you play *en mi* sandbar?
The dreamfuck sends me a cover girl. As if *que sí.* Oh, *mira.*
Her skin, not white but tinted-glass, full-page lips, the scent of
Obsession in the *Vanity Fair*, issue 46, *página* 29, I be so good
at these delusions.

EXCERPTED FROM

LYDIA

Octavio Solis

Character: Ceci (female), late teens.

Struggling to be heard, yearning to be heard—Ceci transforms for the audience into the hormonal beautiful articulate girl she was once.

Ceci: She touched me and I flew. Touched my fault-line. And I flew. With her hand, laid holy water on my scar. And I flew on wings of glass. My body *como una* bird racing with the moon on a breath of air. Flying out of range of pain, purpose, this thing we call *Vida,* soaring into the blueness of memory, closing my eyes for the thud to come.
I wake to this. Life inside my life. No wings, no glass, no moon. Only *Loteria* which means Bingo which means chance which means play. So I play the cards into view.
A card with me printed, *La Vida Cecilia,* rag doll thumbing the stitching in her head, forming the words in her vegetable tongue, what happened to me, *porque no puedo* remember, I must remember.
There. A card called El Short-Order Cook. Broken man drowning in old rancheras and TV. I hear *voces antiguas* calling his name, Claudio, my poor Papi Claudio in your personal winter, drowning out the will of Mami saying come with me across the *río,* give up that lie you thought was you and live mine, live American with me. So the dish ran away with the greasy spoon and a girl jumped over the moon but you don't spikka the English, only the word No, which in Spanish means No, No at work in bed in your dreams in your *cantos perdidos.*
Aquí, the Mami Rosa card, dressmaker of flying girls, sewing up my unfinished seams; a beautiful woman losing beauty by the day, see it gathered at her feet like old panty hose, ay Ama! You were Rosie Flores, clerk for the County, making your life here, Anglo words like lazy moths tumbling out your mouth, you were toda proud, but now. You're Rosa Reborn holy-rolling me to sleep with the prayers of your new church. Your prayers

for us to be family which hasn't really been family since they stopped putting cork in soda bottle caps.

Ayy. My wild card, *El Carnal Mayor*, Rene, my elder volcano, bustin' noses just by looking at 'em, both hands fulla middle fingers for the whole world, checking every day for hate mail, but always *nada.* Cars go by and honk *Puto-Puto-Rene-Puto!* but cowards, my brother is invincible.

The army recruiter don't want you, huh, not like those other flag-draped Chicanos on our block, even those that come back alive look like they gave up the ghost, that's kinda what you want, that damned ghost taken out of you. 'Cause you're all messed up with some hard-core macho shit nobody gets.

Ándale, plant a kiss on my head like that saint in church with the chipped nose—dry-kiss and move away. Simón, *carnal*, Before the disgust starts to show.

Misha? *¿Eres tú?* Card with the inscription Little Shit. *Carnalito* Misha bringing to my *nariz* fragrances of the street the school his body, yes, the musk of you coming of age, coming into yourself, coming all over yourself. I hear your little secrets like crystals of salt in the pockets of your eyes, sad-boy Misha, sad for me, for us, the things that darken the day, King and Kennedy, the killings of students, the killings of Nam—

Mi familia. All sad and wounded cause of somethin'. Somethin' that broke. I gotta read my scar for the story, it's in there, I know it! *¡Aguas!* I see her. The girl that touched me . . . her face in a mirror looking back . . . showing me her own sccc—ggghn mmm her- own—ssccrrmmgfmhm . . .

CARIDAD SVICH

About the Playwright

On her website, Caridad Svich describes herself as a "playwright, songwriter, editor and translator living between many cultures, including inherited ones." Born in the United States, Svich can trace her roots to Argentina, Cuba, Spain, and Croatia; like the playwright, her plays seem to inhabit an "in-between" creative space. Most of her plays feature original songs and music, multimedia projections and fragments of popular culture that offer a familiar but disquieting landscape that can be equal parts chaos and poetry.

Regardless of the setting of the plays or the ethnic origin of the characters within them, Svich infuses each element of her work with the idea of crossing, transcending or erasing the borders between cultures, people, and planes of existence. As the introduction to a recently published collection of her plays puts it, "Her characters live and love and fight and breathe in an unremitting present filled with ghosts from their individual and collective pasts, with whom they conspire to reveal the cracks in the cozy world that wants to separate death from life, myth from history, and culture from consciousness."[94]

List of Plays

Full-length plays:
Alchemy of Desire/Dead-Man's Blues (a play with songs)
A Little Betrayal Among Friends
Any Place But Here
The Booth Variations
Brazo Gitano (text with songs)
Fugitive Pieces (a play with songs)
The House of the Spirits/La Casa de los Espiritus
In the Time of the Butterflies/En el tiempo de las mariposas
Instructions for Breathing
Iphigenia Crash Land Falls on the Neon Shell That was Once Her Heart (a rave fable)
The Labyrinth of Desire
Luna Park
Magnificent Waste
Thrush (a play with slaughter songs)

---

94 Tamara Underiner, "Cruel Mercies and Tender Ecstasies: An Introduction to the Work of Caridad Svich," *Instructions for Breathing and Other Plays* (Chicago: Seagull Press, 2014).

The Tropic of X
Twelve Ophelias (a play with broken songs)
Prodigal Kiss (text with songs)
Wreckage
The Way of Water
Spark
Gupta
Archipelago
Carthage/Cartagena

Short Plays:
Antigone Arkhe (part of the Antigone Project)
Gleaning/Rebusca
but there are fires
Finding Life
Torch
Scar
Self-Made (a border crossing)
A Short Time After
Turn the Dark Up, Bow Down, This is a Hymn
Nightwood
Transient Animations (formerly titled *Begging the Eclipse*)
Come Burning (after T.S. Eliot and Vivienne)
Torn Limb
A Clear, Blue Thing
Carnival [one-act]

PLAYWRIGHT INFORMATION:

Website: http://caridadsvich.com/

PERFORMING THE MONOLOGUES

One of Caridad Svich's strengths as a playwright is her skillful use of heightened language, and her monologues offer actors a compelling framework for both embodying a story and representing a range of emotions through the use of language and physicality. Be sure to pay particular attention to her use of evocative images, which offer both literal descriptions and sensorial clues. Allow the words of the characters to suggest images and take the time to "breathe" those images into your performance.

You will also notice how Svich's use of simile and a musical cadence give her work the quality of poetry. Honor the rhythm of the dialogue as it is written, noting the use of parallel sentence structure and repetition (as in the consecutive lines that begin "You wish" or "I wish" in the selection from *Luna Park)*; alliteration ("I have done my father's doing," from *Iphigenia*); and the contrast between harsh and soft images ("In the heat and grime / I send my thoughts through the air and hope they reach you," from *The House of the Spirits*).

It also might benefit the performer to study these monologues as a reflection or reinterpretation of other texts: knowing the stories of Iphegenia will give the actress performing this monologue increased depth and nuance. Similarly, the monologue by Esteban Trueba must be understood in the context of who Esteban becomes as an embittered older patriarch as *The House of the Spirits* unfolds, and a reading of Isabel Allende's original novel is likely to provide the actor with a rich backdrop. Finally, *Luna Park* makes both implicit and explicit reference to the music of the alternative 1980s rock band The Smiths, with the lyrics of singer Morrissey providing a strong and powerful counterpoint to the lived existence of the play's characters.

EXCERPTED FROM

*IPHIGENIA CRASH LAND FALLS ON THE NEON SHELL
THAT WAS ONCE HER HEART (A RAVE FABLE)*

Caridad Svich

Character: Iphigenia (female), late teens/early twenties.

The play is a reinterpretation of the Greek play Iphigenia in Aulis, *by Euripides. In Svich's play, Iphigenia, the
daughter of Adolfo the General and narcotized Camila,
is a mix of naive schoolgirl and young woman fighting
for her survival. She's hung up on rock star Achilles
and seeks to escape her destiny. In an unnamed Latin
American country during a time of unrest, her journey
begins with her flight from the city.*

Iphigenia: Iphigenia was born centuries upon centuries ago.
I watched her grow up, only to see her die over and over, story
upon story.
I have lived inside her skin
Which has been rearranged
So that she will always remain a young girl
With delicate wrists and tender breasts.
And I have kept silent.

I have done my father's doing,
I have honored my mother's way.
I have let myself be adored by the far-away gaze
Of a crowd who want to get a look at the girl,
A good look at the girl,
Whom fortune has blessed.
Now on this day of saints,
All I want is to be free of Iphigenia,
To be free of her certain fate.

I'm going to the northernmost point of the city.
I'm going to shake loose the bad luck piñata
That has rained down on my head black birds and black wings.
I'm going to dance in the safe of an aircraft hangar that's been
turned into a ballroom.

329

And I'm going to let my body reign over the ragged people
with their pale gleam.
I'm going to ooh, and aah. I'm going to let my body be.
And stop, stop being the general's daughter
Who lives in a walled- up garden by the light of the police.
Iphigenia is spun out onto a dark street.

Dear gods, let me be anyone but Iphigenia. Erase my memory,
escape my death.
Only let me spin, oh god's, let me spin, for what I seek is an
angel's rest.

EXCERPTED FROM

THE HOUSE OF SPIRITS (A PLAY WITH SONGS),

LA CASA DE LOS ESPIRITUS (UN OBRA CON CANSIONES)

Caridad Svich

Based on the novel by Isabel Allende

Character: Esteban Trueba (male), twenties to forties.

Svich's play spans the 1920s to the1970s. In this monologue, it is sometime in the 1920s, and Esteban, the patriarch of the family, is young and desperately in love with Rosa the Beautiful. In order to gain fortune and her hand in marriage, Esteban works compulsively, determined to succeed. He writes Rosa a letter from the mines. The play was commissioned and produced in the author's Spanish-language version by Repertorio Español/*Spanish Repertory, New York. Both versions are provided and could be artistically combined.*

Esteban Trueba: I barely have time, Rosa.
  The work is long and hard here in the mines.
  And the only hours I have to myself are Sunday evenings
  When all is quiet
  And I can put down on paper
  What I've been thinking about all week.
  I speak to you, Rosa
  In my mind while I work.
  In the heat and grime
  I send my thoughts through the air and hope they reach you.
  The other miners look at me. Perhaps they think me strange.
  But all I can do is think of you
  And of how rich we'll be when we're together –
  Each day I hold your image in my mind
  And pray that you've not forgotten me.
  How many days 'til I see you again?
  How many days 'til we're married?
  I won't rest, Rosa, until you're mine.

Esteban Trueba: *(Spanish)*

> Apenas el tiempo tengo, Rosa.
> El trabajo es largo y duro aquí en las minas.
> Las únicas horas que tengo para mí mismo son los domingos
> por la noche
> Cuando todo está callado
> Y puedo poner en el papel
> Lo que he estado pensando toda la semana.
> Hablo contigo, Rosa
> En mi mente cuando estoy trabajando
> En el calor y la grima
> Mando mis pensamientos por el aire y espero que te lleguen
> Los otros mineros me miran. Tal vez me encuentran extraño.
> Pero sólo puedo pensar en ti
> Y los ricos que vamos hacer cuando estemos juntos –
> ¿Cuántos días hasta que te vea otra vez?
> ¿Cuántos días hasta que nos casemos?
> No voy a descansar, Rosa, hasta que seas mía.

EXCERPTED FROM

LUNA PARK

Caridad Svich

Character: Daniel (male), early twenties.

> *This play is a comic drama about a group of twenty-somethings whose lives are forever changed after a magical day and an unexpected tragedy in Luna Park. The day has just begun; Daniel, a Brazilian who has experienced life and is not afraid of love, has just met Leslie, and there is an instant attraction. He shares his past and his wishes.*

Daniel: I've had friends die. Just like that.
People I saw practically every day, people I hung out with, spent time . . . routine, right? Nothing you'd think about. And then one day—gone. Wiped out. No reason.
Except hatred. There's lots of that. And that's what I've lived with most of my life.
People all around hating cause that's what they know,
That's how they've been raised.
"Hate that one, he's brown, he talks different."
"Hate the other, he's white, he talks different. Or he believes in a different God."
It's hate all the same. Just a fact. No tears. Cause well . . . what good are they?
I understand that. Not wanting to cry. Not having to.
Cause you're spent and can't anymore. So, you bury things. Deep down.
You push everything into a little corner in your brain and just forget
cause it feels good to forget everything;
To play *fútbol*. Soccer, like you say.
Be in the moment.
Live for the now, and just get on with things.
 . . . But wishing?
It's always there, kicking about in your system, in the metaphysics of it all . . .
Cause wishing is elemental. Like breathing almost.

333

You wish for someone to love you.
You wish for someone to be found.
You wish for silly things, stupid things . . .
Gadgets, games, music,

and then there's
what you wish for
that's totally else . . .
less tangible things,
impossible things
that you think just by wishing
can be possible.

Like I wish I didn't feel pain. Ever. Impossible, right?
I wish there was a feeling of happiness that could last more
than a minute.
I wish everything wasn't such a big deal,
and that we could just talk to each other
without tensing up
and thinking about things we don't want to think about.
Bad memories. Yeah. They flood me. I shrug them off.
That's what I've learnt to do, but it's not what I want.
What I want is
that they would go away
and never come back.
I wish my thoughts wouldn't stray all over the place.
I wish people believed in something and really believed in it
And not just said they did
because it looks good in a newspaper headline.

I wish this park was inside me so I could take it with me wher-
ever I go,
So I could take you with me . . .
I wish I could go home,
and knew what that meant.
I wish that pool over there smelt of violets instead of chlorine
So we could dip into it and feel the breath of the ancients:
they could give us their wisdom; we could give them our youth.
I wish I could look at you without thinking about my whole
life . . .

Teatro Luna

ABOUT THE COMPANY

Founded in 2000, Teatro Luna is a Chicago-based company that devises and develops theatre that honors Latina lives and the work of Latina artists. They have created over two dozen original pieces and helped jump-start the career of Latina writers, actors, designers, directors, and producers who represent the next generation of theatre professionals. The company describes their mission on their website:

> We decided to approach our work as theater artists from the perspective that stories matter, that our histories matter, and that our stories represent experiences beyond our individual lives that are not often heard. We use an ensemble approach to create performance based on autobiographical experiences and true-life stories. Whether we are building shows as a collective, incubating single author plays, or developing solo performance, we begin by talking to each other about our lives, about our own experiences with the themes of the play or workshop, and use our varied experiences as the starting point to create performances that speak to diverse Latina lives.

Teatro Luna often devises their projects in conjunction with other educational and theatrical institutions, weaving teaching and mentoring into their process. Because each project and each voice is so distinctive, it is impossible to generalize about what makes Teatro Luna's work so powerful and unique. What is inarguable is the way in which Teatro Luna's work has made an impact on the lives of both the people involved in the creative process as well as their audience. Hard-hitting, entertaining, and brutally honest, they are voices that demand to be heard, offering stories that demand to be told in the boldest and most brilliant of ways.

LIST OF PLAYS

Generic Latina
Dejame Contarte
Piece of Ass
Maria Chronicles
S-e-x-OH!
Lunatic(a)s

336

Machos!
S-e-x-OH! The Remix
Lunatic(a)s Redux
GL 2010 - Not Your Generic Latina
Crossed
A Very Luna Christmas
Luna Unlaced
Generation Sex

> *In addition to the above plays, Teatro Luna has pre-sented a number of shorter works, monologues, and theatrical pieces in a variety of festival and workshop presentations, as well as several world premieres of single-authored work; more information is available on their website.*

COMPANY INFORMATION

> Official Website: http://teatroluna.org/
> Facebook: facebook.com/teatrolunachicago
> Twitter: @teatroluna

PERFORMING THE MONOLOGUES

Teatro Luna's shows are monologue-driven and created by writing teams determined to make a dent in the canon with the exploration of Latina-specific themes. The über-talented Luna ladies have a highly successful devising method for generating new material from within the company and with workshop participants. The three monologues below are stand-alone pieces from different shows, but were all used during their 2013 road show *Luna Unlaced*, a performance salon of music, dance, storytelling, burlesque, poetry and everything in between.

Giffords was written by the Luna company member Kristiana Rae Colón, whose work has unconventional formatting. Note the lack of capitalization and the limited punctuation. The Lunas offer these notes for performing the text:

> *The formatting intends to honor the linguistic particulars of dialects of marginalized people and communities of color. This is a feature of Colón's work as a playwright. It began as an homage to her literary predecessors, Ntozake*

Shange and bell hooks, and has evolved into a personal style that privileges the natural patterns of speech, breath, and phrasing over the often arbitrary conventions of grammar and punctuation. Rarely are working class people of color believed to have nuanced, thoughtful responses to national tragedies like the mass shooting at a supermarket in Arizona that wounded Representative Gabrielle Giffords, and perhaps it is because we are afraid of how incisive an unapologetic response to America's internal injustices might be.[95]

Take your time, honor the writing, and don't allow your portrayal to move into caricature. Researching the timeline of the event and the response from the Arizona community would be helpful to create a nuanced performance. Decide whether the character is in a public space or a private space.

The second selection *Paletas* (Popsicles) was based on an interview that Teatro Luna conducted with a man which was then later adapted for a female actor. Teatro Luna philosophically embraces the opportunity to normalize same-gender relationships without making the sexuality of the character a rule of the narrative, thus the monologue can be performed by a male or a female. The Lunas describe this selection as "an anthem to all who are proud of who they are and where they come from, regardless of their ethnicity or national origin."[96] The actor performing the piece should utilize direct address to the audience. He or she is most likely speaking to his or her best friend. Even though the script does not specify a location, it is up to the actor to penetrate the environment. The more specific the actor is with their possible choices, the more clarity he or she brings to the story.

In the final selection, we are introduced to Liliana, whose one desire is to have a happy life at home. *A Very Luna Christmas* was developed and devised using the real holiday stories of the Teatro Luna company members. It is important to respect these characters. Do not view Liliana as a religious zealot. See her as a three-dimensional teenager who has led a sheltered life, who is confused, and who is searching for meaning. Don't let the contemporary language lead you into stereotype. Make strong active choices and pursue her objective of happiness.

---

95   E-mail from Abigail Vega and Alex Meda to Micha Espinosa.
96   E-mail from Vega and Meda.

EXCERPTED FROM

CROSSED, OR HOW GOING SOUTH FLIPPED OUR SCRIPT GIFFORDS

Kristiana Rae Colón
Created by Teatro Luna
Developed by Miranda Gonzalez
and Alexandra Meda

Writing Team: Liza Ann Acosta, Kristiana Rae Colón, Melissa DuPrey, Gaby Ortiz Flores, Christina Igaraividez, Dr. Yolanda Nieves, Elizabeth Nungaray, Karla Estela Rivera.

Character: Female, twenties to thirties.

Female: when the news broke   i was selling jewelry at the oasis
on interstate ten   flatscreens blaring in between vendors
& merchants   you ever notice how you can tell
something really bad happened by the font they used?   like if
the BREAKING NEWS marquee is in all red but with a white
glow around the letters
maybe a truck flipped over   maybe there was a car chase
      but if there's like lightning bolts or crosshairs going
through the B & the N   probably some towers fell
      or someone brought a gun to school
      & shot his principal and all the bullies or
someone brought a gun to the supermarket & shot
a congresswoman
      & a nine year old girl   & a grandmother   and—

i'm there trying to sell ceramic olmec pendants to gringos &
all of a sudden the toshiba in between the mcdonald's & the
starbucks is overwhelmed by frantic pundits trying
to piece it all together   & i wish i could tell you that my
first thought was a prayer that no one died   but the truth is
my first thought was *dios mio por* favor please
      please don't let the shooter be latino
      or an arab that looks latino
my god by now i don't know which would be worse
      tengo hermanos en arizona   and cousins
some of us have papers and some of us don't

already the minute men are sicking their german shephards on
half naked river crossers before the southwestern heat has a
chance to even dry their hair   & arizona state police are
itching to tattoo serial numbers on the forearms of every brown
person they catch in a traffic stop   can you imagine what it
would be like if a mexican shot an
american politician?   a blonde white congresswoman?   it would be southern
reconstruction all over again   guatemalans hondurans
mexicans chained together
and dragged through the desert by patriots in pick up trucks
     as if america needs another reason to imagine every brown
person here
     is a latent terrorist

so when i saw the name Joséph zamudio on the screen
     i thought   well   time to pack my samsonite
& start driving to canada before they set up road blocks and
start sending all latinos to concentration camps   b u t
then
que eso? a hero?

it turns out the shooter   like most of the shooters who like
to roll up in public places guns blazing   was a white
man   & one of the men that disarmed him   preventing more carnage   was latino   legally carrying a weapon
and didn't use fatal force to subdue the suspect   respect for
human life even when a lunatic is waving a semi-automatic

yet if zamudio stepped out of his car with a snickers bar
     or a pack of skittles in his hand
arizona police
would light him up like a christmas tree
before he even got a chance to show them his papers

EXCERPTED FROM

CROSSED, OR HOW GOING SOUTH FLIPPED OUR SCRIPT

PALETAS (POPSICLES)

Miranda Gonzalez
Created by Teatro Luna
Developed By: Miranda Gonzalez
and Alexandra Meda

Writing Team: Liza Ann Acosta, Kristiana Rae Colón, Melissa DuPrey, Gaby Ortiz Flores, Christina Igaraividez, Dr. Yolanda Nieves, Elizabeth Nungaray, Karla Estela Rivera.

Character: Male or female, twenties to thirties.

Character: I gotta say, cherry flavored frozen popsicles are the best flavor. Its old school. And I have to get the skinny ones, the fat ones, that are in the bigger plastic container, just don't feel right in my hand, ya know. It feels foreign. *(takes a bite)* I read somewhere taste buds change over time, like when human beings are young they like certain tastes or flavors, but it all changes when they become an adult. *(takes a bigger bite)* Well that sure as hell isn't true. I could eat a whole damn box, I'M FEDERALY, *TOMA (makes a hand gesture used in Mexico that is equivalent of the middle finger)*. My fiancé hates it when I buy these, makes my son want some too, he's two, and of course he read somewhere or saw on Dr. Oz, that the sugar content is high and they use too much dye *y algo de* fructose corn syrup, to which I respond,

"Ahhh man, come on all those damn writers, bloggers whatever, *que se van a la verga*, look at me I came out juuuust fine!"

He hates it when I say those things, says I sound "so Mexican", says it like he hates it "you sound so Mexican." "*Pos que la chingada, Soy, Cabron!* And you love this Mexican."

He's South American, so you know how they are *(gives a look)*, think they're better than everyone else.

"Just because you came here on a plane doesn't mean you're better than me."

Man, I caught his family up in a lie one day. They thought that this Mexican didn't know anyone else who was Peruvian, so one day we are sitting at a 4th of July Picnic and I hear my fiancé say,

"My family came on a plane, from Lima."

and his mother is shaking her head oh so proud, like *(shakes his head saying yes)* so I interject and say,

"You know I have this friend Joey that works with me, he's Peruvian, and he says that a lot a people lie about being from Lima and that the majority of the people are from the small towns that are hours away, he says that they are just trying to act like they are a higher class."

And my fiancé is all like, "Well, we are from Lima" and I'm like, "How do you know?" and he's like, "Cause I know" and I'm like "How, you've never even been there, you don't even talk to your family over there" so he's all mad and he turns to his mother and is like,

"Mami, ¿somos de Lima verdad?"

And his mother gets all flushed and red because people are listening to all of this, and she starts making these sounds like *(imitates the sound of someone at a loss for words)* eh, eh eh, and my fiancé is ON her like *(gives a stare, like a come on and talk)* and she finally says,

"Bueno, I grew up in a town called Paracas, only 20 minutes from Lima."

   (beat)

Lie. THAT WAS A LIE! Because I looked it up, I google mapped that shit and its three hours from the big city! Needless to say my fiancé was SALTY! He was mad, more so because I was right! For about a week he didn't argue with me about anything, until we come to the frozen popsicle aisle in the grocery store and I go to grab a box, and he finally snaps,

"Why do you like those so much, I don't get it, they're not good for you and you know what happens when the baby sees you . . ."

And he is going on and on about how I don't listen and I'm not on his side and I just don't get it, and I just couldn't take it anymore, so finally I snap back.

"You know why, because they remind me of when my family came here, they remind me of what it took, they remind me that my dad slaved for five years picking fruit in Arizona to get me, my mom, and my brother here, they remind me of the fence that the coyote drew up so I could crawl through it when I was 8, the first time my dad put a quarter in my hand to buy one of these, and the day he saw me graduate college, So if I feel like giving my son a cherry popsicle every damn day till he is 50, just to remind me of all that it took for me to get here then so be it, and I don't give a fuck what Dr. Oz has to say about that!!!"

As you can imagine, I won that argument. *(Long beat)*

Man, I'm proud that I'm from a small town, I'm proud that I was poor, and I am proud that I am SO MEXICAN." Maybe it is true. *(beat)* Maybe your taste buds do change. *(long beat)* All I know is I love these, my God do I love these.

EXCERPTED FROM

A VERY LUNA CHRISTMAS: AN AMERICAN HOLIDAY STORY

LILIANA

Abigail Vega
Created by Teatro Luna

Developed By: Paula Ramirez & Abigail Vega
With contributions from: Sindy Castro, Jazmin
Corona, Amanda de la Guardia, Alexandra Meda,
Alyssa Vera Ramos, Angelica Roque

Character: Liliana (female), fifteen to twenty.

*Monika, Liliana's aunt's partner, is driving the car.
Liliana sits in the passenger seat. "Lord, I Lift Your
Name on High" is playing on the radio. Liliana turns
it down,*

Liliana: First, of all, I really want to say that I am so glad you are
here with my aunt. She is totally important to me, and I really
love getting to meet her friends. And I want you to know that I
am a Christian, but I totally DO NOT JUDGE you for your life
choices. I'm not one of those Christians.
I mean, I can totally relate to you. I mean, I'm not . . .gay, but
I'm a sinner, too. I was a sinner, like big time, but I've turned
my life totally around. I was not a good person, Monika. I know
you're probably thinking, oh, this girl's like, what? Twenty-one?
What could she have possibly done in that short period of time?
She's so innocent. And to that I would say, first of all, I'm really
eighteen, but thanks for thinking I look older, and second, I'm
not as innocent as you might think. If I hadn't met Jesus at the
exact time I did, I don't know where my life would be now!
Alcohol, drugs, marijuana. I was offered a cigarette at a slumber
party in the eighth grade once. I almost smoked it. I mean, it
ended up being a candy cigarette, but I didn't know that in that
second, but whatever. The thought was there. And you know
what? God knew that. He totally knew that.
So all I can be is overwhelmingly grateful that I accepted
Christ into my heart when I did. My friend Becky invited me
to her church, and honestly, I only went because they served

this really good, like stuff crust everything pizza at their youth group on Wednesday nights, and Mom was on this health food kick, and I was dying inside, I was like, GIVE ME PIZZA and OH MY GOD. Wait. I just realized something. God was using Mom's health food craze to get to me. Those diet foods were like my Noah's ark. Wow. I will never look at Jenny Craig the same way again.

But anyway, so I went to church with Becky, and I was all, okay, this is fine, whatever, but then they started singing, and all of a sudden, I feel this tug. Like on my heart. Like, we were two songs in, and I started crying. Sobbing, on the floor, making a fool of myself. And I'm thinking, okay, what was in that pizza? But then I looked up, and Becky and her brother Chuck were just looking at me and smiling. And in that moment, I totally got it. Everyone in this room was just so in sync you know, like they were so different, they led such different lives, but for this moment, they were so together in their love. And there was love in that room. And I guess that made me really sad, I don't know, because I don't really ever remember being that loved. Or feeling that kind of love. Definitely not since my dad left. But probably not before that either. Not really, anyway. These people all had a common goal and that was praising the Most High, the Creator of All Things. And, at the end of the day, what's wrong with that?

So, I'm pretty sure I accepted Jesus into my heart, like, three seconds later, and listen, I am a totally different person now. Completely different. I mean, you didn't know me before, so your point of reference isn't really there, but I am. I am just so incredibly happy with where I am in my life. I just wish my family had that same happiness.

Monika? Have you accepted Jesus as your personal Lord and Savior?

CÁNDIDO TIRADO

ABOUT THE PLAYWRIGHT

"As a Latino writer it's tough," says Cándido Tirado about playwriting. "I want to move an audience and get them upset about the realistic issues we deal with as a society."[97] In a career that has lasted nearly three decades, Tirado's subjects have ranged from baseball (*Clemente: Five for Five*), music (*Celia: The Life and Music of Celia Cruz*, co-written with his wife Carmen Rivera), street life (*Momma's Boyz*), and the cutthroat world of amateur speed-chess (*Fish Men*—Tirado is himself a ranked chess master). Tirado's passion for social justice anchors his work and underscores the importance of his voice, often explored through characters in harsh circumstances whose personal values and integrity are put to the test. Tirado "injects such verbal zest and ingenuity into each of his characters that their downward spiral becomes as sad as it is inevitable," wrote one reviewer of *Momma's Boyz*. That is not to say that Tirado's plays are obsessively tragic or depressing, as each character is as much defined by their cherished connections to each other and their noblest aspirations as they are to their circumstances, and his work "provides a first-rate example of precisely how this childlike, yet intensely honed element of play can work, even when it is put in the service of a deadly serious subject."[98]

Though his plays resonate with Latino communities and often specifically reflect Tirado's Puerto Rican heritage, his characters come from all walks of life, and are rendered as such so that they would be powerful to audiences and actors of all backgrounds. "I'm a Latino playwright in this country. But . . . I like to do more symbolic characters, I like to do metaphorical characters. In *Momma's Boyz*, there are three young drug dealers. . . . but they don't have to be Latino actors to play them. They could be Italian or Irish or African American; as long as their culture is that of the street, impoverished, where drugs or crime seem like a way out. I had a friend from Italy who saw the play and said, "Wow, that seems like me and my two friends.""[99]

97 Madeline Rodriguez, "Interview: Cándido Tirado, Puerto Rican Playwright," *gozamos.com*, 26 June 2012. http://gozamos.com/2012/06/interview-candidotirado-puerto-rican-playwright/
98 Hedy Weiss, "Momma's Boyz a vivid portrait of kids in a troubled, violent world," *Chicago Sun-Times*, 31 October 2011.
99 Lesley Gibson, "A Conversation with Cándido Tirado," *OnStage Magazine*. Retrieved from http://www.goodmantheatre.org/articles/a-conversation-with-Candido-tirado/ 30 December 2013.

LIST OF PLAYS

Full-length plays:
Fish Men
Momma's Boyz
First Class
King Without a Castle
Moribundo
The Barber Shop
Some People Have All the Luck
When Nature Calls
Salsa Nights
Celia: The Life and Music of Celia Cruz (co-written with Carmen
    Rivera)
Abuelo
Two Diamonds
Hey There Black Cat
The Kid Next Door
La Cancion
The Missing Colors of the Rainbow
Hindsight is . . .
And the Pursuit of Happiness
House of Souls (co-written with Carmen Rivera)
Palladium (co-written with Carmen Rivera)

One-acts:
The Border Game
Clemente: Five for Five
The Bullet Test
Declaration of Love
Like Human Beings
Ilka: The Dream
Hands of Stone
X and Y Stories (monologues)
The Night I was King of the Copa (monologue)
From Dating to Death in Five Easy Steps
The Art Class
Heart Stopping Sex
Swallowed by the Sea
The Cat
Don't Whisper

The Veil
The Medea Project
Annie and Alvaro (co-written with Carmen Rivera)
The Bust Stops Here
The Dog Ate My Homework
Detention
Wait a Minute
From Here to There
In the Name of Love
Who's Next?
The Class Room
MC: Orange Juice
Gotta Do What You Gotta Do
The Applicants
The Film Makers Group
Laughter and Tears
The Discovery
Puta Bitch
Porto Rican—That's Right—Porto Rican
Mad Dog
A Dinner Affair
Ghost Plant

Playwright Information

Website: http://www.candidotirado.com/

Performing the Monologues

Momma's Boyz was praised as "A triumph of the urban theatre genre, it is bold without being brash. It is emotional without being maudlin. It uses conventions like reverse chronology and magical realism without making one think of 'Pulp Fiction'."[100]

The play opens with Mimic's monologue. This character requires an actor with great verbal and emotional facility. It is important to remember that Mimic is at heart a very young man—still able and eager to play. Mimic has extra sensory perception, the gift of

---

[100] Scotty Zacher, "Review: Momma's Boyz (Teatro Vista)," *Chicago Theater Beat,* 29 October 2011. http://chicagotheaterbeat.com/2011/10/29/review-mommas-boyz-teatro-vista/

premonitions. It is important that that gift be a truth for him. Mimic has a pulse, and the actor must think and feel it in that pulse: when it breaks, so does the character's thinking and/or heart. A good example is when Mimic doubts himself towards the middle of the monologue. It is important to honor that change in impulse before moving on to the good news about the movie.

Tirado, besides being an accomplished and national playwright, is also known as co-founder of Educational Plays Production, which tours New York public schools presenting plays with social issues concerning youth. Tirado generously offered one of these poignant and hilarious gems. *Wait a Minute* comically explores teen pregnancy and the responsibilities of taking care of a baby. Britney is over-the-top fun. It is important that the actor playing Britney create the imaginary environment around her including penetrating the eyes of each of her children. Find a vocal build at the end of the selection in order to cap the final moment.

EXCERPTED FROM

MOMMA'S BOYZ

Cándido Tirado

Character: Mimic (male), late teens.

Mimic has fallen into the ghetto life but has much bigger dreams. He sneaks into the funeral parlor to say his goodbyes to his best friend since grade school, Shine. He reluctantly heads for the casket. Mimic deeply mourns and reflects on his/their choices.

Mimic: Remember when we used to played cops and robbers in the stairwell in the projects? Those were the days. We'd shoot one another and get right back up. Thug always wanted to be the criminal and get away with the crime. We used to execute him a lot . . . You don't shoot your peeps. You know what I'm saying? You don't do that shit. If you got beef with someone, you deal with it. You just don't pull the trigger first. I had a feeling selling drugs wasn't a good idea. Gotta learn to listen to my feelings more. I shoulda said no when you and Thug was trying to talk me into it. It wasn't like I really wanted to do it. I could've worked at the video store for cash. Just wanted to be with my peeps. Yo! Oh shit! Oh shit! Déjà vu, son! I saw myself standing here talking to you and you was in that same casket. That shit was mad real, kid. And I had this feeling like something freaky was going to happen. That's freaky right? I hate this gift I got. That's what my moms calls it ever since I told her one day that a kid wearing a red baseball cap was going to get hit by a car, and a kid got hit by car and guess what he was wearing? Guess! A red baseball cap! If only there had been a sign of how things would turn out like the Bat signal calling Batman. Maybe there was, but the money sign in our eyes blinded us and shit. Things didn't turn out too good, did they? You're in a dead store. Thug's in jail and me . . . I'm getting the fuck out of the projects, yo. I'm moving downtown with Rain. Taking acting serious. She's been there for me through all of this . . . This is so fucked up, man. Things will never be the same without you around. This is so unfair, yo. I mean, everybody deserves a second chance, right? I'm gonna have mines. Thug will some day have his, but you . . . You ain't having one six feet under. I guess it doesn't matter 'cause if we'd do it all over again, we might end up doing the same thing. Right? I don't know, maybe not. Some shit been bugging me. I don't understand why didn't you leave. Why did you have to get in Thug's face when you knew he had a gun? Thug says you knew. Why didn't you tell me he had a gun? I don't understand that shit either? I'm not blaming you, but if you knew you could've left and you'd still be here hanging with me. I had things under control, didn't I? Didn't I? Fuck, man . . .

Oh, oh! I didn't tell you, but I just got a part in a movie with Robert DeNiro. Word! Serious. Guess what I'm playing. Guess. Your friendly neighborhood drug dealer. I already got experience. Check it, I only got one line, but at least I get to speak you know? I say, "Yo, wha ju wan?" I already got it memorized and shit. I'm going to dedicate my performance to you because when I was auditioning I was shitting bricks and I felt you there rooting for me. And when I win the Oscar I'm going to dedicate it to you, too. Remember I used to say I'd take you to the Oscars when I got nominated. We was going to turn that mother out.

(Acts as if he's holding the Oscar statue in his hand while giving an acceptance speech.)

EXCERPTED FROM

WAIT A MINUTE

Cándido Tirado

Character: Britney (female), nineteen.

Britney makes light of motherhood to her friend Teresa while her children are running wild at the park because misery loves company:

Britney: It's nothing more beautiful than having a baby. That's why I got seven. Lucky seven, but got another one on the way. Lucky eight. Babies give you unconditional love. The way they gaze into your eyes, but by the time they become two years old, they get in your nerves. You don't know! All they say is no, no, no. I can't stand them after that. If the baby I'm carrying is a boy I'm going to call him Usher Rodriguez. If it's a girl I'm going to name her Angelina Jolie Rodriguez. Nice right? You like the names? I like to name my kids after celebrities ... I feel like that they can be celebrities, too. Their fathers don't care. They never come around. They're a bunch of lowlifes. But the father of the baby I'm carrying. He's so cool. And he promised me he'll never leave me . . . Yea, yeah, the others promised the same thing too, but this one is different. And he said that he'll take care of all my kids. You know him. Your boyfriend's best friend. Deandre! Yeah Deandre! He's the best! I like the way he talks with his deep manly voice.
(Talks to one of her kids.)
What's the matter Paris Hilton? Stop whining. So stop crying. So he hit you again? That boy is getting in my last nerve. Michael Jackson Rodriguez get over here. I said get over here. Don't make me say it again if you don't want your foot up your . . . let me tell you something you thug wannabe. If you put your hands on Paris again, I'ma get the belt. Now get out of my face. Cristina Aguilera Rodriguez, weren't you supposed to be taking care of little Snoop Dog Rodriguez? Yes, your brother! Where did you leave him. In the park? You better go get him girl. Yes now! It's getting dark out there. You better don't give me attitude. Cristina I said go get him. And you better not slam that

door. Did she slam the door. I tell that girl came out just like her father. Teresa, look at my baby Justin Timberlake Rodriguez. Isn't he cute? He can dance, too. Show Aunt Teresa some steps. Why not? Oh, yeah? Excuse me a minute, Teresa. Will Smith Rodriguez give Justin Timberlake his toy guitar back. Do you hear me? Will Smith don't give me no lip. Remember what happened to you last time? Go with your daddy. If you can find him! He's hiding out from the marshals because he owes me child support. But they'll get him and I'll get my money if that's the last thing I do. Teresa, Children are so wonderful. Wait a minute. Snoop Dog why are you crying? Cristina hit you? Cristina Aguilera Rodriguez now you got me angry. Michael Jackson Rodriguez stop grabbing your crotch boy. I shoulda never let him watch Michael Jackson videos. These kids don't know how to behave. I want all of you sitting on your behinds right there quiet! Cristina, don't! I want your mouth closed. Y'all have no manners. We have company! Now I'm going to talk to your aunt Teresa . . . Will Smith Rodriguez I know she's not your real aunt but if you want to keep getting toys for Christmas from her . . . Yes from Santa Snoopy Dog. You, Will Smith, you better call her auntie. Now it is mommy time. So I'm going to talk to Teresa for a few minutes. Teresa, I think Deandre lost his cell phone 'cause he don't answer the phone. Or maybe he forgot my phone number because he stopped calling me. It's only been two weeks but I'm worried about him. When you see him could you tell him to call me? Girl I can't wait until you have a baby. You're going to be so happy!

LUIS VALDEZ

ABOUT THE PLAYWRIGHT

"No other individual has made as important an impact on Chicano theater as Luis Valdez," writes noted director and scholar Jorge Huerta. "From street theatre to melodrama-within-a-play, to a vision of the past and the future, Luis Valdez takes us on theatrical explorations that offer no easy solutions."[101]

Indeed, Valdez' impact cannot be underestimated. A migrant laborer in his youth, his experience in activist politics on behalf of workers like himself led him to found the company El Teatro Campesino in Delano, California in 1965. Drawing on street traditions from around the world in order to educate and advocate for farm laborers, the group's work helped bring the traditions of Latino performance into the Age of Aquarius. A decade later, Valdez' groundbreaking play *Zoot Suit* blended Broadway-style visuals with a critical examination of the so-called "gang" problems in post-war Los Angeles. Valdez later wrote and directed the film *La Bamba*, about Latino rock idol Richie Valens.

Valdez' plays both borrow from and challenge conventional styles and genres. As much as any playwright, Valdez is able to create theatrical experiences that are both seductive and provocative: in one moment, he can draw you in with richly drawn characters and profoundly intense emotional conflicts, and in the next make you question your own relationship with the world outside the theatre. "What Valdez hopes for is your visceral response to his plays," writes Huerta. "His Truth does not come solely from books. Luis Valdez understands the dance, invites us to join in that dance and, hopefully, we can."[102]

LIST OF PLAYS

Valley of the Heart
Corridos Remix
Earthquake Sun
Mummified Deer
Bandido!
I Don't Have to Show You No Stinking Badges
Los Corridos
Zoot Suit
Mundo Mata

---

101   Jorge Huerta, introduction to *Zoot Suit* by Luis Valdez (Houston: Arté Publico, 1992): vii, xx.

102   Jorge Huerta, "El mundo de Luis Valdez." *Mummified Deer and Other Plays* by Luis Valdez (Houston: Arte Publico, 2002): xii.

Bernabe
Dark Root of a Scream
Actos
The Shrunken Head of Pancho Villa

PLAYWRIGHT INFORMATION
Website: http://www.elteatrocampesino.com/

PERFORMING THE MONOLOGUES

I Don't Have to Show You No Stinking Badges is a multi–layered view of cultural stereotypes, the Latino experience in Hollywood, and the toll of the American dream on a family. It is important to note that the set is designed to look like a television studio setting of a home that one might see on a typical American sitcom, including lights and cameras, even though it represents the home of a real family. Thus, there is always an implied "live studio audience" which heightens the reality of these selections. In order to fully and truthfully portray the character of Sonny, the actor should research the many injustices that Chicanos have suffered in the United States. Valdez' own work is an excellent place to start, as he frequently dives into rich characterizations while also excavating the Mexican-American experience. In order to be able to commit to the humor and richness of being a "Lech Walesa," it is important to investigate the life of Walesa, the first democratically elected president of Poland, Lech Walesa—a trade-union organizer, human rights activist, and Nobel prize winner. In the second Sonny selection, it is advised not to hold or mime a gun. The actor can keep the stakes high without actually using the prop or referring to it.

Mummified Deer was inspired by a 1984 newspaper article describing an 86-year-old woman in Juarez, Mexico, who was found to be carrying a 60-year-old mummified fetus in her womb. Valdez uses the metaphor to allude to the Indio heritage that many Chicanos share but have little knowledge of. In Armida's opening address, the aim is to clearly and precisely set the stage, without losing her sense of urgency (she is on her way to Mama Chu, dying in a hospital). Note that the monologue quickens in pace on the last line. It is imperative that the last line be a springboard into the next scene, even if taken out of context for audition purposes. I suggest finding a different rhythm or voice for the "just a couple of bucks 'til payday, compadre" line.

EXCERPTED FROM

I DON'T HAVE TO SHOW YOU NO STINKING BADGES

Luis Valdez

Character: Sonny (male), seventeen.

> *The Reagan years. After withdrawing from his pre-law studies at Harvard to become an actor, Sonny, a second generation Mexican-American, returns unannounced to his middle-class suburban home on the outskirts of Hollywood, California. Confident his parents are not home, he extracts a portable cassette recorder, presses PLAY, and draws an anxious breath before he speaks.*

Sonny: Greater East Los Angeles. February 20th. 6:30 p.m. Home away from home away from home. Concept for possible "Twilight Zone." i.e. —"Sonny, the Harvard Homeboy Comes Home." So what's on your mind, homes?

Sonny's mind is on my mind, homes. Little Son, *mamacita's* little *m'ijo,* daddy's little chicken. Chicken Little. The sky is falling!

(Paces, growing agitated.)

Fuck. The whole inside of your refried skull is falling, Sonny boy! Raining cats and dogs. A veritable *chubasco* of cranial slime, drowning your brain in your own biological soup, the primordial chicken broth of your own egg, your *huevo,* one egg instead of two. With two *huevos* you might have been born a human. Add a polish sausage and you might have been born a man. A Lech Walesa in solidarity with your Polish balls!

What are you doing here, Sonny? Your *mamá* and *papá* have great expectations. Are you real or are you Memorex? Reach out, Reach out and touch someone, asshole!

EXCERPTED FROM

I DON'T HAVE TO SHOW YOU NO STINKIN' BADGES
Luis Valdez

Character: Sonny (male), seventeen.

At his breaking point, holding a gun, the house sur-
rounded by police, Sonny confronts his parents and
reveals why he left Harvard.

Sonny: You still don't get it, do you? What it's like being a Chicano at Harvard? The sense of isolation and guilt. Do you know how many times I've denied you? Lucy used to do it all the time. Do you think she gave a damn? I'm talking about SHAME! HUMILIATION!—all those scum-sucking roles you've played in the movies all these years! DRUNKS and WHORES and ASSLICKING GREASERS! And for what? So Lucy and I could make something of ourselves? Well, we have, Dad! We've become SOMEBODY ELSE! Anybody else but your CHILDREN!— ACTORS faking our roles to fit into the GREAT AMERICAN SUCCESS STORY: go away, move away, change your name and deny your origins, change your SEX if need be, but become NEUTER, like everybody else! You see, in order to ACT TRULY AMERICAN, you have to kill your parents: no fatherland, no motherland, no MEXICAN, Japanese, African, Jewish, Puertorrican, Philipino, Armenian, Latvian, Chinese, Indian, Arabian, Norwegian, old-country SHIT! Well, I damn near succeeded . . . Thanks to good old Anglo-Saxon Protestant, MONROE JAMES!
My roommate at Harvard . . . He was everything I ever wanted to be. Tall, rich, blonde, but he wasn't much company, so I preferred to do my homework in the library. One night I was working on a paper—writing with all my conscious skill to make the syntax of my English sentences as perfect as they could be. I couldn't tolerate the thought of being anything less than brilliant, you see. If you're not white, you have to be brilliant, just to be considered acceptable. Well, I got stuck . . . on one paragraph . . . First, I restructured the sentences, hoping to eliminate a certain kind of circular logic in the paragraph. I hate being REDUNDANT . . . Then the linear order of the words

began to bother me. MY ENGLISH WAS BREAKING DOWN! Then I couldn't tolerate the space between the words. Finally, I got stuck on a hyphen, a lousy hyphen, so I scratched it out. And the HOLE between the two words became an unbridgeable GAP, and I FELL! . . . into a sea of nothingness.

So ran, I ran like my life depended on it all the way back to the dorm. Then . . . when I opened the door to our room, I spotted Monroe, holding a gun to his head. Neither of us said anything. He just smiled, and pulled the trigger. My fucking role model! He blew his brains out!

Mummified Deer

Luis Valdez

Character: Armida (female), forties to fifties.

*It is 1999. Armida is a Chicana of Yaqui Indian an-
cestry attending Berkeley as a graduate student in
anthropology. In a direct address, she takes us back
to 1969, as she begins to delve into the secrets of her
family history.*

Armida: If it hadn't been for Carlos Casteñeda. I never would have
known what deep secrets Mama Chu was hiding. In the Spring
of 1969, *The Yaqui Way of Knowledge* was a bestseller . . . in
Berkeley . . . With tales of indio sorcerors, power spots and
peyote hallucinations, Casteñeda opened the doors of perception
to parallel universes and blew the minds of my hippy generation
. . . But for me, *The Yaqui Way* led back home . . . to reality.
I was four when my mother died, so I was raised by my
grandmother in San Diego. I remember whenever the radio,
always tuned to the Mexican station in Tijuana, played "Señora
Querida," Mama Chu would dance to the music as if it was the
anthem of her soul.
She ran a boarding house for immigrant workers. Her "moja-
ditios" as she called them. For over thirty years, she kept our
large, transient family going—chronically broke and out of gas,
always looking for the quick fix, a small loan, "just a couple of
bucks 'til payday, compadre" as if poverty was our addiction .
. . but it was Mama Chu we were hooked on . . .
Whenever she got angry, she'd say: ¡*No Hagan que se me suba lo
Yaqui*! As if getting-her-Yaqui-indian-blood up was like tempt-
ing God. I had to tempt God just to go to high school. Years
later, when I told her I was going away to graduate school, she
said it would break her heart. She left me no choice . . .

KAREN ZACARÍAS

ABOUT THE PLAYWRIGHT

"I always think of writing as an exploration, not a forgone conclusion," says Karen Zacarías. "I have to learn to trust my characters—let them breathe, be vulnerable, funny, ruthless and contradictory. More often than not, my characters lead me to a plot or story, not the other way around."[103] Whether in dramatic explorations of family secrets (*Mariela in the Desert*); the role of women in the field of science (*Legacy of Light*); the interpersonal dynamics of a suburban book club (*The Book Club Play*); the life and work of a trailblazing 17th Century nun and poet (*The Sins of Sor Juana*); or the absurdist rendering of a family held hostage by an escaped convict on Thanksgiving (*The Bare-Chested Man*); Zacarías' characters emerge from wildly diverse times and cultures with a brutally honest passion.

A native Mexican, Zacarías has found an artistic home in Washington, D.C., where she has become one of the region's "most successful and prolific playwrights."[104] She is the founder of the D.C.-based Young Playwrights' Theater and has written a number of plays for younger audiences. She says that the experience has helped her become a better playwright: "My strongest playwriting lessons have come in trying to create stories that will resonate with young people." More importantly, working with young people reminds her of the power and impact of developing diverse theatrical voices: "These students will hopefully grow to become future audiences of theatre, and demand work that is new and reflects the diverse and universal reality of living in the USA. As artists, especially artists of color, we can't just ask for change from others; we have the responsibility of making change happen ourselves."[105]

LIST OF WORKS

Plays:
Mariela in the Desert / Mariela en el Desierto
The Sins of Sor Juana / Los Pecados de Sor Juana
Legacy of Light
The Book Club Play
The Age of Innocence
    (adapted from the novel by Edith Wharton)

---

103 Caridad Svich, "Karen Zacarías: A Writer's Tightrope." *American Theatre* 23:1, 54-59.

104 Ellen McCarthy, "Karan Zacarías," *Washington Post*, 8 May 2009.

105 Svich, "Karen Zacarias."

How the Garcia Girls Lost Their Accent
  (adapted from the novel by Julia Alvarez)
Just Like Us
  (adapted from the memoir by Helen Thorpe)
Romeo and Julieta (bilingual translation)
The Bare-Chested Man
The Invisible City
The Other River

Theater For Young Audiences—Musical
  (music by Deborah Wicks la Puma)
Jane of the Jungle
Ferdinand the Bull
Cinderella Eats Rice and Beans
Chasing George Washington: A White House Musical
Oliver de Brasil
Looking for Roberto Clemente
The Magical Piñata
Frida Libre
Einstein is a Dummy
Ella Enchanted

LIBRETTO:
  The Sun Also Rises (Washington Ballet)

PLAYWRIGHT INFORMATION

  Contact: KZacarias@aol.com
  Agent:Earl Graham, Graham Agency:
  Grahamacynyc@aol.com
  Company website: http://www.yptdc.org.
  Young Playwright's Theater of DC

PERFORMING THE MONOLOGUES

Mariela in the Desert is the winner of several awards including the Francesca Primus Prize and the National Latino Playwrights' Award. Zacarías' play unlocks the story of a family's wounds. Blanca is the daughter to the artists Mariela and José, once the golden couple of Mexico City artists. She returns to her desert home and begins to unravel the betrayal that has left her parents grieving and isolated from the world. Zacarías' characters have a distinct way of viewing the world informed by the place and time in which they live. Research into artists of the Mexican Renaissance, including Diego Rivera, Frida Kahlo, José Clemente Orozco, David Alfaro Siqueiros and Rufino Tamayo is imperative to being able to envision, and ultimately embody the emotional life of these characters. The physical setting and time for this play not only define imaginary places in which the events took place, but mean very different things to each of the characters. In this desert, dreams do not come true, artistic inspiration dies, and tragedy unfolds.

A Spanish translation of the play was produced at *Repertorio Español*; the monologues are provided in both English and Spanish.

EXCERPTED FROM

MARIELA IN THE DESERT

Karen Zacarías

Character: Blanca (female), twenty-one.

Mexico, 1951, on a rustic ranch in the Northern Mexican desert region. Blanca, a talented and vulnerable artist, returns home and confronts her mother about their family secret.

Blanca: You should have painted him. I painted it, but it doesn't feel like me. My whole new life, does not feel like mine. There's this girl, in Mexico City, that laughs, and loves, and paints and I watch her and realize I have no idea who she is. Where she came from. I'm so lost, I can't MOVE, I can't breathe. I can't paint! I sit at the blank canvas and stare.
(Beat)
How did Papi do it? Every time I put a brush on canvas . . . I think of *The Blue Barn* . . . of that green boy. Of that orange bird. And nothing—nothing—I've ever done comes close to being so beautiful and so . . . so . . . TRUE. How did Papi paint *The Blue Barn*? How did he find that inside of him? After so many years? How did he see I was an orange bird? How did he see that Carlos was green? How did he know to smear the paint with such force . . .to create such texture that the paint feels like the thick plaster of a cast? How did he know to paint a red flame in the midst of it all? How did Papi break away from a lifetime of seeing the world from the outside . . . and see the world from the inside?
(Pause)
Oh God.
(Beat)
Papi didn't paint *The Blue Barn*, did he?
(Pause)
That painting is our family.
(Beat)
You're painting me right now, aren't you? Look at me! Please look at me!

When *I* was twelve years old, I lived in the bottom of a well in the desert with a little brother that cried all day, a father who cried all night, and a mother who never cried at all. Tonight I return to a home where my brother has long burned away, my father is sick and dying, and my mother . . . my mother . . .

(Mariela looks at Blanca.)

. . . is buried alive

It was a terrible accident. When I look at that painting, Carlos isn't gone. I look at *The Blue Barn*, and I know exactly where my brother is. And I know who I am too.

(Pause)

Mami, did you paint *The Blue Barn*?

Blanca: *(Spanish)* Lo pinté yo, pero no lo siento así. Nada de mi nueva vida la siento mía. Veo esta chica en la ciudad, que ríe, ama y pinta y me doy cuenta que no tengo idea de quién es. Estoy tan perdida que no puedo ni moverme. No puedo respirar. No puedo pintar. Solo puedo sentarme ante el lienzo vacío y quedarme mirándolo.

(Pausa) ¿Cómo pudo Papi . . . ? Cada vez que rozo la tela con un pincel . . . pienso en el Granero Azul. En el niño verde. En el pájaro naranja. Y nada-nada que yo haya hecho siquiera se acerca a algo tan bello y tan . . . tan verdadero. ¿Cómo fue que Papi pintó el Granero Azul? ¿Cómo lo encontró dentro de sí . . . después de tantos años?

¿Cómo pudo ver que yo era un pájaro naranja? ¿Cómo pudo ver que Carlos era un niño verde?

¿Cómo supo embarrar la pintura con tal fuerza? ¿Cómo supo crear esa textura de yeso y arcilla?

¿Cómo supo pintar esa llamarada en el centro?

¿Cómo pudo Papi escapar de toda una vida de ver el mundo desde afuera . . . y aprender a ver el mundo desde adentro?

Dios mío . . . . Papi no pinto el Granero Azul ¿verdad?

Esa pintura es esta familia. Tú me estás pintando en este momento ¿no es así?!

¡Mírame, Mami! ¡Por favor!

Cuando yo tenía doce años, vivía en el fondo de un pozo en el desierto, con un hermano que lloraba de día, un padre que lloraba de noche y una madre que nunca lloraba. Esta noche regreso a una casa donde mi hermano es solo cenizas; mi padre se está muriendo y mi madre . . . mi madre.

. . . está enterrada viva.
Fue un accidente terrible.
Cuando miro a esa pintura, Carlos no está muerto. Miro El Granero Azul y sé exactamente dónde está mi hermano. Y también sé por fin quién soy.

(Pausa) ¿Mami, tu pintaste El Granero Azul?

Excerpted From

Mariela in the Desert

Karen Zacarías

Character: José (male), fifties.

Mexico, 1951, a rustic ranch in the Northern Mexican desert region. José, a famous artist whose time is fading, confronts his wife, who is also a painter.

José: I never told you how they applauded. Diego! Frida! Siqueros! All of them! How they got on their feet and applauded for me? And *then* they unveiled the Presidential Prize. *(Pause)* So blue. So raw. And I stood up there, stared, and could say . . . nothing. NOTHING! So the president shook my hand and babbled about inspiration and perspiration and thanked me for my fucking talent. *(Pause)* A dozen artists each with a dozen paintings. All hanging in a great grand gallery. I only had eleven. You sent twelve. And out of the hundreds of paintings on the wall, the Academy chose one: one painting to humiliate me.
You painted *The Blue Barn* and then you sent it! Why did you send them your painting?
I am a man! A man with the ability to paint . . . but with no vision. And then I have the folly to live my life with a woman who has a gift; a talent that festers in her head—
Do you know what I would have done if I had your talent?!! I would have led an artistic revolution. I would have changed the course of Mexican art!! There would be books, not chapters written about me!!! God gives you a gift and what do you do, Mariela? You waste yourself on a sickly boy, a decaying house, and keep that talent safe inside your head.
The desert did not fail us! *The Blue Barn* is a masterpiece!! Your masterpiece!
Don't you see, my love? Your painting did not kill Carlos. No!
    (beat)
Your mothering killed our son.
I cannot paint. My son is gone. The only masterpiece of my career, is yours. And now my fiercely talented daughter, a gifted artist like her mother, knows her father is a fraud. I am dead.

José: *(Spanish)* Nunca te dije cómo aplaudieron. Diego. Frida. Siqueiros. Todos. Cómo se pusieron de pie y me aplaudieron. Y presentaron el cuadro que ganó el Premio Nacional. *(Pausa)* Tan azul. Tan elemental. Y yo me quedé paralizado, sin decir nada. ¡Nada! El presidente me dio la mano diciendo no sé qué babosadas sobre el arte y la inspiración y me felicitó por mi talento de mierda. *(Pausa)* Una docena de artistas . . . cada uno con una docena de cuadros. Todos en una gran galería. Yo pinté once; tú mandaste doce. Y de todas las pinturas en esas paredes, el jurado escogió UNA pintura . . . para humillarme.

¡Tu pintaste El Granero Azul! ¿Por qué lo enviaste?

Soy un hombre. Un hombre con la destreza para pintar pero sin visión. Y tengo la mala fortuna de vivir mi vida con una mujer con ese gran don: un talento enconado en su cabeza.

¿Sabes lo que yo hubiera hecho si hubiera tenido tu talento? ¡Hubiera sido el líder de una revolución artística! ¡Hubiera cambiado el curso del arte en México! ¡Habría libros, no capítulos acerca de mí! Dios te da un don y ¿qué es lo que haces, Mariela? Te desgastas atendiendo a un niño enfermizo y a una casa que se derrumba y aprisionas ese talento – y lo pones a salvo en tu cabeza.

¡El desierto no nos falló! ¡El Granero Azul es una obra maestra! ¡Tu obra maestra!

¿Y por qué murió, Mariela? ¿Por qué? ¿No lo ves, mi amor? ¡Tu hijo no murió por tu pintura! ¡A Carlos lo mató tu amor de madre!

No puedo pintar. Mi hijo está muerto. La única obra de valor en mi carrera es tuya. Y ahora mi hija, que heredó el talento de su madre, sabe que su padre es un fraude y un fracaso. Yo ya estoy muerto.

SOURCES, ACKNOWLEDGEMENTS AND PERMISSIONS

NILO CRUZ: From *Capricho* by Nilo Cruz. Published in *Two Sisters and a Piano and Other Plays*, Copyright ©2007 by Nilo Cruz. Published by Theatre Communications Group. Used by permission of Theatre Communications Group.
From *The Color of Desire* by Nilo Cruz. Published in *The Color of Desire / Hurricane*, Copyright ©2011 by Nilo Cruz. Published by Theatre Communications Group. Used by permission of Theatre Communications Group.

VIRGINIA GRISE: From *blu* by Virginia Grise, Copyright © 2011 by Virginia Grise. Published by Yale University Press. Used by permission of Yale University Press.
From *The Panza Monologue*s by Virginia Grise and Irma Mayorga, Copyright © 2014 by Virginia Grise and Irma Mayorga. Published by The University of Texas Press. Used by permission of The University of Texas.

QUIARA ALEGRÍA HUDES: From *Water by the Spoonful* by Quiara Alegría Hudes. Copyright ©2012 by Quiara Alegría Hudes. Published by Theatre Communications Group. Used by permission of Theatre Communications Group.

JOSÉ RIVERA: From *Boleros for the Disenchanted* by José Rivera. Published in *Boleros for the Disenchanted and Other Plays*, Copyright ©2012 by José Rivera. Published by Theatre Communications Group. Used by permission of Theatre Communications Group.

About the Editor

MICHA ESPINOSA is an Arizona-based artist, activist, teacher, and vocal coach. She has performed, lectured, and taught voice around the world since 1992. A member of SAG/AFTRA (and a local Arizona board member), Espinosa has performed in film, television, and regional theatre. She is a master teacher of Fitzmaurice Voicework and a trainer for the Fitzmaurice Teacher Certification, as well as a certified yoga instructor. Currently, Espinosa serves as Assistant Associate Professor of Voice and Acting at Arizona State University's School of Film, Dance, and Theatre, and is affiliate faculty with ASU's School of Transborder Studies. Her research and scholarship examines and contextualizes the current climate with the training of actors of non-dominant groups. She is passionate about social justice in actor training, global perspectives, and the cultural voice. michaespinosa.com.

About the Biographer

JASON DAVIDS SCOTT teaches film and theatre history at the School of Film, Dance, and Theatre at Arizona State University, and has previously taught at Stephen F. Austin State University and the University of California Santa Barbara. After earning his BFA in Cinema Studies from New York University's Tisch School of the Arts, Dr. Scott worked in the entertainment industry for over a decade in public relations and feature film development. He earned his MA and Ph.D. from UCSB and has published articles about film history, popular culture, and the history of actors and acting. He currently serves on the board of the Mid-Atlantic Popular & American Culture Association and is editor of their annual journal, the Mid-Atlantic Almanack.